More Praise for *Women of The Street*

"Meredith Jones has given Wall Street a new compliment: 'Invest like a girl'. Her book shares insights and stories that illustrate the strength, talent, character, and return-generating prowess of women. Institutional investors, both male and female, should take a close look and not be surprised when they find better investment outcomes."

—Jim Dunn, CEO, Verger Capital Management, LLC

"*Women of The Street* offers critical insights into what creates superior market performance. The fact that it happens to be a woman writing about women adds to its veracity and import. Fear of missing out should strike those who think they can skip it. It's too well-written and researched to do so."

—Denise Shull, author of *Market Mind Games*

"Diversification is one of the cornerstones of investing. However, we have yet to apply the concept to create diversity among those who manage money—either professionally or personally. How does gender affect investment behavior? Why aren't there more women investors and why should there be more? Meredith Jones tackles these critical questions and more with data and a dose of humor—a winning combination. Beautifully written, this book is a must read for women and men alike."

—Suzanne Duncan, Senior Vice President, Global Head of Research State Street Corporation, Center for Applied Research

"In stressed markets, when judgment matters most, women tend to be more rational and less emotional. They manage money with strong conviction, but not to the point of arrogance, admit mistakes more readily, and are less compelled to follow the herd. These characteristics support Jones's conclusion that women can invariably achieve superior performance as asset managers."

—Thomas W. Strauss, Chairman, Ramius LLC

Women of The Street

Why Female Money Managers Generate Higher Returns (and How You Can Too)

Meredith A. Jones

palgrave
macmillan

WOMEN OF THE STREET
Copyright © Meredith A. Jones, 2015.

All rights reserved.

First published in 2015 by
PALGRAVE MACMILLAN®
in the United States—a division of St. Martin's Press LLC,
175 Fifth Avenue, New York, NY 10010.

Where this book is distributed in the UK, Europe and the rest of the world,
this is by Palgrave Macmillan, a division of Macmillan Publishers Limited,
registered in England, company number 785998, of Houndmills,
Basingstoke, Hampshire RG21 6XS.

Palgrave Macmillan is the global academic imprint of the above companies
and has companies and representatives throughout the world.

Palgrave® and Macmillan® are registered trademarks in the United States,
the United Kingdom, Europe and other countries.

ISBN: 978–1–137–46289–3

Library of Congress Cataloging-in-Publication Data

Jones, Meredith A.
    Women of the street : why female money managers generate higher
returns (and how you can too) / Meredith A. Jones.
        pages cm
        ISBN 978–1–137–46289–3 (hardback)—
        ISBN 1–137–46289–2 (alk. paper)
        1. Women stockbrokers—United States—Biography. 2. Wall Street
(New York, N.Y.) I. Title.

HG4621.J66 2015
332.6082—dc23   2014041238

A catalogue record of the book is available from the British Library.

Design by Newgen Knowledge Works (P) Ltd., Chennai, India.

First edition: April 2015

10 9 8 7 6 5 4 3 2 1

Printed in the United States of America.

"The rooster may crow but the hen delivers the goods."

—Proverb

Contents

Acknowledgments

There are a great many people who made this book possible, most of whom I've tried to thank early and often. Unfortunately, Felix Frankfurter was correct when he said, "Gratitude is the least articulate of the emotions, especially when it is deep." I am therefore afraid my copious "thank yous" have not been particularly eloquent or complete, so I'm giving it another go here.

First, the biggest "thank you" goes to all of the women who graciously and selflessly gave the time to be interviewed for this book. Without your support, *Women of The Street* would never have been written. A simple "thank you" hardly seems adequate.

I would also like to express my deep appreciation to my literary agent, Leah Spiro, and to my Palgrave editor, Laurie Harting. Y'all took a chance on a book about women and finance, and for that I'm sure you'll get stars in your crowns.

There were a number of other people who supported me on my publishing journey to whom I can't express enough thanks. Tim Weaver provided his keen eye and sharp tongue as an early reader, and also provided his invaluable research skills when I did my first diversity-investing piece at Barclays Capital. Daniel Crosby, who has to be one of the kindest souls I've met on this planet, kept my spirits up through the difficult process of writing a book. Brian Portnoy introduced me to my agent and encouraged me to write *Women of The Street* in the first place. Joe Schlater and his lovely bride, Elizabeth Havens, were wonderful sounding boards, and were eager to suggest interview candidates. Greg Dyra was also quick to comb his Rolodex at the slightest hint. Lauren Widelitz and Susan Mc Guire helped me crunch numbers for the "Women in Alternatives" white papers at Rothstein Kass. Catherine Sellman, Michelle Gass, Kristina Koutrakos, Richard

Wayner, Kerry Jordan, Somer Washington, John McColskey, Holly Singer, and Sarah Bumpers encouraged me to take that research further. Denise Shull was a godsend as I navigated the publishing waters, and always reminded me to breathe. Donna Holmes was a constant advocate for the book, and also a great friend and fellow cat lady. Steve Menna and Doug Halijan helped sort through contractual issues, which wasn't glamorous, but they did it with style.

I am blessed to have a small but supportive group of friends who are still talking to me after this project. Sheldon Griffin, you deserve a medal of some sort for going through this process with me. Margaret and Greg Kyser kept me fed through a month of Sundays (literally) during my most furious scribbling. My college roommate, Jennifer Laughlin Reed, has always believed I have superpowers. Lauren Augustine and Jen St. Clair dragged me to the Redneck Riviera a mere ten days before my deadline. Erin Hussey and Caryn Klein made sure I stepped away from my computer for figure skating and workouts—without them I may have finished the book, but I would not have still fit in my pants. And Lisa Sergi and Steve Cuneo were like verbal Prozac when the going got tough.

And finally, my mom and sister, Linda Jones and Megan Jones, were subjected to all my highs and lows while I was conceiving of, shopping, and writing this book. They were early readers, staunch supporters, and occasional ass-kickers, depending on the needs of the time. My aunt Sandra Downs and my late grandmother, Annette Robinson, are equally guilty of making me the crazily independent woman I am today. And, really, I wouldn't be here at all without my mom or my dad, Buddy Jones, so I guess *Women of The Street* really starts with them. Let me know if you need their email addresses for compliments or complaints.

PART I

The Research

Introduction: "The Women"

In 2007, I traveled to Evanston, Illinois, to meet what had up to then been for me an urban legend of the alternative investment industry—women portfolio managers. Sure, I knew that women portfolio managers existed. I had tracked several women-owned or managed funds in various hedge fund databases for a few of my nine prior years in the industry. This was, however, my first in-person sighting.

Constance (Connie) Teska and Kelly Chesney of Pluscios Capital Management run a fund of hedge funds based in Illinois. I spent all afternoon with them, exchanging ideas, talking markets, and comparing investment philosophy. They gave me their history in the investment industry, and I shared mine. We didn't braid one another's hair or exchange recipes, but aside from that, it was as deep a bonding experience as I have had in my professional life.

I left that meeting and did what any Southern woman does with good news to share: I called my mom.

Even though my mother is not in the investment industry, she listened intently to my re-cap of the day. From then on, she never missed an opportunity to ask about Connie and Kelly.

"How are The Women?" she would ask.
On another day: "What do you hear from The Women?
After the market crash in 2008: "Are The Women okay?"

When I look back on her use of that generic terminology, I realize that I am in many ways to blame for her language. My mom, like most people, had only a passing familiarity with the hedge fund industry. She had never heard me, or anyone else for that matter, tell stories about the market exploits of a non-male investment wizard. George, John, Warren, and Julian were familiar names to her. Connie, Kelly, Leah, Nancy, Catherine, Renee, and other female monikers were completely foreign.

My mom is not alone in believing the hedge fund industry specifically, and the money management industry in general, is a man's world. At the writing of this book, I estimate that there are fewer than 125 female-owned or managed hedge funds out of roughly 10,000 or more funds worldwide. John Coates, senior researcher in neuroscience and finance at Cambridge University, has said that "[e]ven with massive diversity pushes I don't think there is more than 5 percent women taking risk in the financial world, starting from the trading floors to the asset managers."[1] Certainly, there is a wealth of female participants in the hedge fund and investment industries. You'll often find women marketers, investor relations staff, operations and compliance personnel, or financial officers. Rarely do you find a woman in the driver's seat as the decision-maker who decides what to buy and sell and when.

As a result, those few intrepid female portfolio managers have had to look pretty far afield to find mentors and role models. One portfolio manager I interviewed as background for this book described her investing idol to me in detail. Nicknamed the "Witch of Wall Street," this manager's mentor developed a tried-and-true methodology for growing and protecting wealth:

- invest conservatively
- keep substantial cash reserves
- don't let emotion rule your investments

This investment philosophy served the Witch of Wall Street well, creating a vast pool of wealth estimated to be $2 billion.[2] Unfortunately, this portfolio manager has not been able to meet her mentor and learn her market wisdom directly.

Why didn't they chat? Because the Witch of Wall Street, otherwise known as Hetty Green, died in 1916.

This female portfolio manager, faced with a dearth of investors who thought and traded like she did, researched a woman who had been dead for nearly a century to use as a role model. Hence, one of the many reasons I decided to write this book.

When people ask why I feel a project like *Women of The Street* is so important, I can now practically anticipate the questions and objections.

- If there are so few women in the industry, why bother?
- Why doesn't anyone ever talk about men who perform well?
- Isn't the sample too small to draw any real conclusions?
- Are you a sexist?

These questions come up so frequently that I now answer them almost by rote.

It has been proven, in my research and that of others, that women invest differently than men, upon whom a wealth of investment research has been conducted. Collectively, women's approach, which is in many ways similar to Green's tenets above, has proven profitable and reliable, and it outperforms the industry at large. More women portfolio managers in the investment industry would be good for investors. Being able to choose an investment manager whose approach more closely mirrors your own is also a positive. Diversification of investments, be it by strategy, asset class, or gender, is good for all investors. Deploying some of the techniques that women instinctually use can be beneficial to investors, male and female. The fact that I'm researching women's unique and potentially valuable investing skill set does not mean I'm a sexist. It simply proves I'm a capitalist.

Finally, providing women with role models who did not own Civil War bonds is crucial to attracting more female portfolio managers. They need to know there is a place for them in an industry that tends to celebrate only big and splashy wins, such as George Soros' $10 billion bet against the British pound and John Paulson's $3.7 billion subprime mortgage win.

The investment industry is one in which both the tortoise and the hare exist. Not surprisingly, we hear stories only about the hares who make a big killing on a few risky deals. Even more intriguingly, we all know that at the end of the fable, the tortoise wins. And, as Margaret Thatcher famously quipped, "The cock may crow, but it's the hen that lays the eggs."[3]

This book celebrates the steady and consistent execution of an investment strategy that results in long-term outperformance. The portfolio managers interviewed exemplify the best traits that women investors tend to exhibit. Their example will help encourage the next generation of women portfolio managers, and their wisdom can inform your investment decisions, no matter what your gender. At the end of the day, I hope you learn from them and that this book makes you invest "like a girl."

CHAPTER 1

The Feminine Investing Mystique

Why should an investor care whether a money manager wears Louboutins or loafers?

Because money—how to keep it and how to make more of it—is on everyone's mind. That's why it pays to invest in the "broad" market. The research in this chapter is clear: women investors think about investing differently than men. They have a set of innate skills that can translate into higher returns on investments. These skills can foster not only better profits for investors but also more diversification within investment portfolios. If you want to be a better investor, or if you want better returns, you should try investing "like a girl."

Why Women Money Managers?

In the past five years, the number of institutional investors (corporate and public pensions, endowments, and foundations) with mandates expressly for women-owned or managed funds has increased. Illinois, New York, Maryland, and Pennsylvania, among others, now have specific investment directives for "emerging managers," defined as firms owned by women, minorities, disabled persons, or veterans.

In some cases, institutional investors in these states and others want to more closely match the investment style of their portfolio with their constituent base. The investment methodology of women is simply different from their male counterparts'. This divergent approach, coupled with the excess returns it can bring, is increasingly attracting investors. In the first quarter of 2014 alone, public funds in Connecticut and New York collectively allocated more than $1.3 billion to diversity mandates, including, but not limited to, women-owned and managed funds.

Many people ask me why gender does and should matter in investing. Let's assume an investor represents a retirement plan for teachers. According to the National Center for Education Statistics, there were 3.7 million full-time equivalent elementary and secondary school teachers (as of fall 2012), 76 percent of whom were female.[1] Roughly 7 percent were non-Hispanic black and 4 percent were Hispanic.[2] Yet their money has historically been managed by the one group under-represented in those statistics: white males.

For the general public, the story is much the same. According to a Family Wealth Advisors Council study, 95 percent of women will be the primary financial decision-maker for their families at some point in their lives, and women currently control 51.3 percent of personal wealth.[3] In a post on "Understanding the Increasing Affluence of Women," author Judith Nichols asserted that "American women by themselves are, in effect, the largest national economy on earth, larger than the entire Japaense economy."[4] By 2030, women will control roughly two-thirds of the wealth in the United States,[5] and yet only 30 percent of Registered Investment Advisors are women,[6] a figure that has been relatively stable for the last decade.[7]

In short, people are, and should be, thinking about who manages their money. According to the Investment Company Institute, most investors do not own individual stocks. In 2002, 52.7 million US households owned equities, primarily through stock mutual funds in their retirement plan, and only 17 percent had exposure to invididual equities.[8] Not only was this percentage low to begin with, but the amount of money being invested directly into equities has been steadily declining, with net capital outflows every year from 2002 to 2012.[9]

In comparison, the amount of household assets invested with registered investment companies (RICs) has increased dramatically. In 1980, only 3 percent of household assets were managed through RICs. By 2012, that number had increased to 23 percent.[10] As a result, most individual investors spend more time picking investment funds than individual stocks. Until recently, the behavioral component of money managers (mutual funds, hedge funds, and other investment advisors) was not much of a consideration for most investors. However, with the advancement of neurofinance and continuing research into the behavioral factors that influence how we invest, the behavioral characteristics of our money managers are gaining importance.

The simple fact is, as much as we don't want to admit it, most investors, including professional money managers, do not always act rationally. Every investor has certain prejudices, from loss aversion to overconfidence bias, that impact investment decisions. It is impossible to find an investor without these individual predispositions. While a computer model eschews personal emotions, even artificial intelligence remains subject to macroeconomic behavioral biases. The January effect (in which stock prices tend to increase in the first month of the year) is an example of a macrobehavioral bias, as is just about every investment bubble in history.

Because you can't escape the impact of behavior on investments, it probably makes sense to at least think about the cognitive and behavioral style of the money managers you hire, whether you invest with mutual funds, hedge funds, or your local investment advisor/ wealth manager. Your goal should be to choose money managers who maximize the profitable traits (cognitive alpha) that you have, while mitigating your less profitable investment biases.

The Outperformance of Female Investors

Of course, behavior isn't everything. The managers to whom we entrust our funds must also generate returns consistent with our risk/ reward goals. Frankly, many investors (institutional and individual) remain in crisis. You may have heard, either in the news or directly from your own pension or retirement plan, that the US pension system is dangerously underfunded. The assets required to fund current and future retirement obligations are not available. This puts a pension fund in the unenviable position of either having to reduce benefits for current and future retirees or, worse yet, defaulting on its obligations to its plan participants.

According to a November 2013 Loop Capital Markets[11] study of 247 of the largest state pensions and 77 local pensions, only 14 states had funded ratios of 80 percent or higher at the end of FY2012. And the problems are not limited to public pensions. The 2013 Milliman Public Pension Funding Study[12] examined the fiscal health of 100 corporate pensions in the United States. The study showed that the plans generally have enough assets to fund 100 percent of the accrued liability for current retirees and inactive members. However, these same plans have only 27 percent of the assets required to cover the accrued liability for active, nonretired plan members.

Like institutions, most individuals in the United States do not have the assets to retire. An October 2013 Wells Fargo study[13] found that 37 percent of Americans believe they will never be able to retire, while another 34 percent of the middle class believes they will have to work until at least their eightieth birthday.

As I said before, money—how to keep it and how to make more of it—is on everyone's mind. Which is where women money managers come into play.

A number of studies have demonstrated that women investors outperform men. The first of these was published in 2001 by Brad Barber and Terrance Odean, both then professors at University of California, Davis (Odean has since joined the faculty at Haas School of Business at University of California, Berkeley). In their study "Boys Will Be Boys: Gender, Overconfidence, and Common Stock Investment," Barber and Odean examined account data for 35,000 household accounts held at a large discount brokerage. They found that women tended to outperform men by a margin of roughly 1 percent per year.[14]

While 1 percent might not seem like a huge margin, over time it can be meaningful. If an investor invests $10,000 and makes 5 percent per year for ten years, he or she ends up with approximately $16,289. If that investor adds just 1 additional percent per year, he or she nets an additional $1,620.

Women also proved to be better investors in a 2009 study by Vanguard. In the 2007–2008 period, which included the mortgage debacle, the Lehman Brothers collapse and the Bear Stearns fire sale and that was marked by sharp market declines and high volatility, the account values for women fell by 13 percent, compared to 16 percent for men.[15] During that same period, 38 percent of female retirement investors either held their account balances steady or actually made money, compared with 34 percent of male investors.[16]

There appears to be a similar pattern of outperformance among professional money managers. An article in *The Finance Professional's Post* reported that the female-run hedge funds in the AsiaHedge Composite Index posted a total return of 153.26 percent for the period January 2000 to December 2007, compared with an overall benchmark return of 88.82 percent for the same period.[17] Likewise, Hedge Fund Research, Inc. (HFR) found that women-owned hedge funds gained 9.06 percent for the period January 2000 to May 2009, compared with 5.82 percent for the composite hedge fund index.[18] Furthermore, a review of six academic papers on gender and performance by Rania Azmi from the University of Portsmouth revealed that four of her reviewed studies found a relationship between gender and fund performance, while one uncovered a correlation between gender and returns.[19] Only one paper that Azmi reviewed found no evidence of gender as a determinant of fund performance.

Additional research has continued to bolster these results. In 2012, I constructed the first large hedge fund benchmark for women-owned or managed funds. The index was constructed from the average monthly performance of funds that reported performance to either HFR or HedgeFund.net (HFN), and that were also reasonably believed to be women owned or managed.[20]

In my 2013 study, "Women in Alternative Investments: *A Marathon, Not a Sprint*," the Rothstein Kass Women in Alternative Investments Hedge Fund Index (RK WAIHF Index) showed a clear pattern of significant outperformance by women-led funds.[21] Figure 1.1 shows the performance of the RK WAIHF Index from January 2007 through June 2012. During this period the average female-led hedge fund gained 6 percent versus a decline of –1.1 percent for the HFRX Global Hedge Fund Index, which is a widely used proxy for overall hedge fund performance. The RK WAIHF Index also outperformed the HFRX Global Hedge Fund Index over the prior one-, three-, and five-year periods.

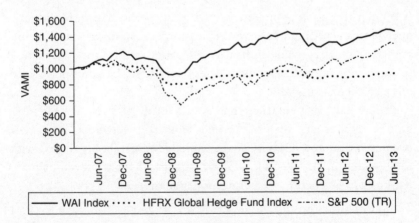

Figure 1.1 Women-Owned and Managed Funds Outperform.

Source: Rothstein Kass (acquired by KPMG in July 2014). Reprinted with permission of KPMG, LLP.

Not only did the women-led index provide a higher rate of return, but it also had a higher percentage of positive performance months than its hedge fund benchmark.[22] The Index also outperformed the Standard & Poor's (S&P) 500 over the period, based on straightforward returns and loss measures.[23]

In addition to outperforming collectively, the constituents of the RK WAIHF Index individually performed well. During the period measured, there is no year in which the HFRX Global Hedge Fund Index ranks in the top 50 percent of the women-owned or managed funds, and in four of the six and a half years measured, the Index generally performed worse than all but the bottom 30 percent of the women managers studied.

On a risk-adjusted basis, the women-led fund constituents of the RK WAIHF Index easily outperformed the HFRX Global Hedge Fund Index, which appeared in the bottom quartile, or 25 percent, of women-owned or managed funds during all but the last 12 months.

Indeed, there is a small but growing dataset on the performance of female investors, be they individuals or women-owned or managed funds. It certainly appears that women can and do outperform, in some cases meaningfully. For institutional and individual investors, that excess return is not only welcome but needed if funding gaps, retirement, and other financial goals are to be met.

Cognitive and Behavioral Alpha: Why Chromosomes Matter in the Market

It is one thing to demonstrate historical outperformance, but as anyone who has ever read an investment prospectus knows, "past performance is not necessarily indicative of future results." It is important to know not only that women money managers have outperformed but also the reasons why.

Perhaps surprisingly, there has been a lot of research on this topic despite a shortage of professional women investment managers. A compilation and analysis of the available research, combined with the research in *Women of The Street*, suggest there are seven primary reasons why women make better money managers:

1. less overconfidence
2. differentiated approach to risk
3. better trading behavior

4. hormonal factors
5. "out of the box" thinking
6. the ability to admit mistakes
7. a more consistent execution of strategy

My Portfolio Is Bigger Than Your Portfolio

Overconfidence has been studied in behavioral psychology for decades. The "overconfidence effect" occurs when an individual's confidence in his judgment exceeds his objective accuracy. Overconfidence exists in any number of professions. Doctors, engineers, lawyers, nurses, psychologists, weather forecasters, and managers have all been studied for the impact of overconfidence on their professional outcomes.

For example, a 2013 Baylor University study of 118 doctors demonstrated that, on easy cases, doctors had a confidence level of 7.2 out of 10 and[24] fifty-five percent of those doctors correctly diagnosed the patient. Interestingly, on difficult cases, the doctors still rated their confidence level highly, at 6.4, while only 5 percent pulled a Dr. Gregory House and gave the correct diagnosis.[25]

Clearly, the more difficult the task or the more unpredictable the outcome, the more overconfidence plays a role in poor decision-making. And few would argue that the markets have been anything but predictable post-2008. To illustrate the issues related to overconfidence, in a 2010 study titled "Expert Judgments: Financial Analysts vs. Weather Forecasters," Tadeusz Tyszka and Piotr Zielonka asked two groups of experts to predict the value of the Stock Exchange Index and the average temperature, respectively, for the next month. Despite a rather comical reputation for inaccuracy, approximately two-thirds of the weather forecasters were successful in their predictions compared with only one-third of the financial analysts.[26]

If no one can accurately predict market behavior, does it matter whether you are a man or a woman? Yes. Simply put, men tend to exhibit more overconfidence than women. In a 2013 study, Sabine Hügelschäfer and Anja Achtziger studied the confidence levels of men and women at different stages of the decision-making process. They examined overconfidence as study participants both considered a decision (for example, buying a car) and implemented that decision (actually buying a car). They reported that the actual performance of the women tended to more closely match their anticipated performance when they implemented a decision. When they were

anticipating (deliberating) an action, they tended to be underconfi-
dent. Men, on the other hand, were overconfident when deliberating
and even more overconfident when implementing a decision. As a
result, the women were more prone to choose less risky but potentially less profitable actions.[27]

When it comes to overconfidence and finance, there are clear
divides between men and women. In a Prudential study of more than
2,000 investors, 37 percent of the men polled felt they were very well
prepared in financial decision-making, compared with 22 percent of
women respondents. While 45 percent of male breadwinners felt very
well prepared to make wise financial decisions, only 20 percent of
female breadwinners felt similarly.[28] In the Barber and Odean study,
"[o]n average, both men and women expected their own portfolios to
outperform the market. However, men expected to outperform by a
greater margin (2.8 percent) than did women (2.1 percent). The difference in the average anticipated outperformance of men and women
is statistically significant ($t = 3.3$)."[29]

Overconfidence can cause any number of problems for money
managers. Too much conviction can inspire overconcentration into a
single position, holding a stock too long, or not taking profits off the
table, among other things, all of which can immediately or eventually have a negative impact on fund performance. During my time as
director of research at an investment firm, I watched as a male money
manager piled 80 percent of a portfolio into a single stock, rode his
conviction from high-dollar equity to penny trade, and STILL uttered
the words "it will come back to me." Overconfidence, or hubris, can
kill returns faster than market volatility or violent sell-offs.

Perhaps John Coates, a senior research fellow at Cambridge
University, best summed up the dangers of overconfidence in the
markets: "Every blow-up in a bank of $1 billion or more occurs at
the hands of a trader at the end of a multi-year winning streak. You
become euphoric, delusional and overconfident. You take way too
much risk and there are terrible risk-reward trade-offs."[30]

Risky Business

Speaking of risk, one of the more backhanded ways by which people
dismiss the superior long-term returns of female portfolio managers
is to point to gender-specific risk aversion. Women take less risk,
they say, and therefore generate lower, but steadier, returns. Truly

outstanding returns are not possible with women managers because of an ingrained aversion to riskier, high-reward investments, according to some industry "experts."

There have been a number of studies that examine gender and risk aversion. One example can be found in the study "Gender Difference in Financial Risk Aversion and Career Choices are Affected by Testosterone," by Paola Sapienza, Luigi Zingales, and Dario Maestripieri. They found that men exhibited significantly less risk aversion than women when presented with a 50/50 lottery that returned either winnings of $200 or $0.[31] Other studies, many of which were not focused on financial risk-taking specifically, found similar results.

However, while it does seem that women do approach risk differently than men, it does not appear that they eschew it altogether. In a 2001 study, Robert A. Olsen and Constance M. Cox found that "women investors weight risk attributes, such as probability of loss and ambiguity, more heavily than their male colleagues. In addition, women tend to emphasize risk reduction more than men in portfolio construction."[32] For the record, a focus on "downside protection" and "risk aversion" are in no way synonymous.

Further research from Helga Ferh-Duda, Manuele de Gennaro, and Renate Schubert found that probability weighting, rather than risk aversion, is gender dependent. While the researchers discovered that women's and men's valuations of financial outcomes are relatively similar, "relative risk premiums demonstrate that gender differences, if they do exist, systematically depend on the size of the probabilities of the gambles' larger outcomes. Furthermore, we unequivocally show that women weight probabilities differently than do men. On average, female probability weighting schemes are flatter than the males' and, in the gain domain, more depressed. Women appear to be more pessimistic about medium and large probabilities of a gain."[33] This approach can help boost returns and defend against losses on an individual or fund level, and it can also help safeguard the overall markets as well. In a February 2015 study in the *American Economic Review*, Catherine Eckel and Sascha Fulbrunn determined that all-female markets created smaller "bubbles" in asset prices than all male markets, and that "mixed" male/female markets also resulted in smaller bubbles.[34] This was in part due to differences in price forecasting where men tended to forecast significantly higher prices than women.[35]

Which brings us back to overconfidence. Men are more optimistic about probabilities, while women are more pessimistic, which impacts risk decisions, but also doesn't equate to true risk aversion.

Trader Joes (Steves, Johns, Davids . . .)

Another effect of overconfidence is increased trading. In Barber and Odean's 2001 study on trading, overconfidence, and gender, their review of 35,000 household accounts from a large discount broker- age revealed that "greater overconfidence leads to greater trading and to lower expected utility."[36] As a result of overconfidence, Barber and Odean concluded, the men in the study traded 45 percent more than the women investors. Scarier still, the single men studied traded 67 percent more than their single female counterparts. Accordingly, male money managers in the study earned on average 1.4 percentage points less annually than the women. Single men sacrificed gains of 2.3 percentage points per year to the urge to trade.

Nobel Laureate Daniel Kahneman explored this phenomenon fur- ther in *Thinking, Fast and Slow*. He considered Barber and Odean's conclusion that most of the (predominantly male) traders truly believed the stocks they bought would go up, and the stocks they sold would go down. Kahneman concluded that "on average, the most active traders had the poorest results, while those that traded the least earned the highest returns" and that "men act on their useless ideas significantly more than women do, and that as a result, women achieve better investment results than men."[37]

Low T(estosterone)

We have already established that overconfidence is not conducive to portfolio management mastery, but why do males generally exhibit so much more hubris? The answer may lie in their biological makeup.

When I was researching *Women of The Street* in early 2014, I went to see *The Wolf of Wall Street*. While I wasn't incredibly bothered by the 506 F-bombs, the nudity, the debauchery, or the drug use, I was disturbed by the almost complete lack of female professionals in the movie, those representing "the oldest profession" notwithstanding. Ultimately, the movie showcased only one female broker. This lack of trading floor estrogen certainly wasn't unheard of in the 1980s and early 1990s, but it did beg one question: would Stratton Oakmont, the company profiled in the movie, have been as lupine if more women were included at the helm? Some research clearly answers "No."

John Coates, while researching his book *The Hour between Dog and Wolf: Risk Taking, Gut Feelings and the Biology of Boom and Bust*,[38] took saliva samples from 17 male traders on eight consecutive days, morning and afternoon. When analyzing the hormones present in the samples, Coates discovered that testosterone levels were significantly higher on the days that a trader made more than his one-month daily average. When high testosterone was present in the mornings, profits for the day were also greater.

Coates suggests that traders become addicted to the feeling of euphoria, or the "winner's effect," that is pure biology at work. It is so elemental, in fact, that we see the same behavior in animals, such as bucks, when they fight in the wild. Winning a fight makes them more apt to fight, and to win. Until they inevitably stop winning. When under the influence of testosterone, male investors, particularly younger males whose testosterone levels are at their peak, may become less rational and more dogmatic, and not execute their strategy faithfully. In fact, recent research from trading profiling firm Financial Skills found in a study of more than 700 summer trading interns that women were far less likely to "transgress specified trading limits" than men.[39]

Coates also studied the impact of cortisol on risk aversion. While he found no statistically significant gender differences in risk aversion during periods of heightened stress (such as a market meltdown), he did determine that men's probability weighting skills became more distorted under stress.[40] When looking at probabilities, people tend to overweight small probabilities and underweight large ones. Probability changes under 45 percent are assigned much higher significance than changes in probability above 45 percent. As a result, if you increase a probability of success from 15 percent to 20 percent, people will consider that increase more significant than a jump of 60 percent to 65 percent, even though the probability actually increased by the same amount.

We already know from Ferh-Duda, de Gennaro, and Schubert that men and women weigh probabilities differently, but Coates also found a "significant sex interaction under conditions of chronically elevated cortisol, with the weighting of probabilities changing significantly in men, but not in women. Specifically, relative to women, male subjects exhibited greater sensitivity to small probabilities and less to large ones."[41] It may therefore be that during periods of elevated stress, men are more likely to misjudge the probability of an investment's success or failure, further compromising their performance at the exact moment it is most detrimental.

Mara Mather (University of Southern California) and Nichole R. Lighthall (Duke University) further demonstrated how cortisol may influence behavior. In a paper entitled "Both Risk and Reward Are Processed Differently in Decisions Made Under Stress," they showed that "stress amplifies gender differences in strategies during risky decisions, with males taking more risk and females less risk under stress."[42] In one study, healthy men and women were asked to play a game in which they inflated a balloon on a computer screen. Every time participants inflated the balloon, it became more valuable, but the risk of its bursting increased. The subjects could choose when to stop inflating the balloon and take their "profits." Males experiencing stress (in this case, holding their hands in 35-degree water), were more likely to continue pumping the balloon in exchange for higher profit, where females were more likely to cash out early. In this particular study, men "earned" more than women due to this risk-taking behavior. However, this was not the case in a similar task involving cards. When under stress, men were more likely to choose cards from a "risky" deck that offered higher reward but higher risk, resulting in lower "earnings" overall.[43]

Certainly it seems logical that testosterone impacts behavior since even the physical brain structure of men and women is different due to sex hormones. We know, for example, that the amygdala, which is a small area of the brain (often described as almond shaped) that perceives threats and aggression, is larger in men than in women. In his paper "Sex Differences in the Responses of the Human Amygdala," Stephan Hamann notes that "the brain regions that differ in size between men and women tend also to be the same regions that contain high concentrations of sex hormone receptors, suggesting that male and female hormones play a role in determining the size of specific brain regions."[44]

Indeed, there can be little doubt that hormones impact cognition and behavior. In their study titled "Gender Difference in Financial Risk Aversion and Career Choices Are Affected by Testosterone," authors Paola Sapienza, Luigi Zingales, and Dario Maestripieri assert that "higher levels of testosterone in males can result in gender differences in behavior and cognition through the organizational or the activational effects of this hormone. The former refers to permanent modification of brain structure and function during prenatal and early postnatal life due to exposure to testosterone, whereas the latter refers to the transient effects of circulating testosterone on the brain during postnatal life, and especially after puberty."[45]

So why could a part of the brain that sounds like a Star Wars character make a difference in trading? Research suggests that the structure of the brain plays a role in how we process information, in this case, fear and emotion. Men tend to activate their left amygdala when presented with negative thoughts or emotions, while women's right amygdala is the more energetic.[46] Larry Cahill of the University of California, Irvine, hypothesized that the area of the amygdala stimulated accounted for women's reacting to stress internally, with feelings, while men tend to react more with the external world.[47] These responses certainly fit well with theories that men have an increased tendency to both overtrade and sell (react) during periods of market stress.

In addition to the amygdala, the nucleus accumbens, the brain's "pleasure center," may also play a role in financial risk taking, particularly when confronted with, well, sex. One study found that "when young Stanford men were shown pictures of partially clothed men and women kissing...that region of their brains was activated. And when they were then given financial tests, the men became more likely to 'make high-risk gambles.'"[48]

Further research by Raquel and Ruben Gur shows that brain connectivity is also different between the two genders. The Gurs examined diffusion tensor imaging (DTI) on 428 men and 521 women aged 8 to 22 and found that men had better connectivity between the hemispheres of the upper and lower brain, as well as strong connections within subregions of the brain.[49] These connections translate roughly to better spatial relations and better perception in motor skill interactions.[50] In women, however, stronger left-to-right brain connectivity and connection across smaller brain "modules" led the researchers to conclude that women perhaps had better skills in the areas of reasoning, intuition, and multitasking.[51]

However, while society has accepted biological and cognition differences in many ways (we've all heard people say that women are sensitive, men are assertive, for example), they have yet to be fully appreciated or leveraged in trading and finance. Perhaps this is because it is unclear what one should do with this information, particularly in a male-dominated industry.

To be clear, no one is suggesting the administration of estrogen-enhancing or testosterone-dampening drugs to control biologically based trading behaviors, although this may or may not have happened at least once in the industry. In his lawsuit against SAC Capital, Andrew Tong alleged that his former boss, Ping Jiang, came to him shortly after he joined the firm and explained that "he had a trading method in which his traders must not be too aggressive; that traders must be more effeminate and to do so, he directed Tong to begin taking female hormones."[52] It is unclear, however, whether Jiang was motivated by profitability or hazing.

Instead, one might consider cognitive diversification. It is widely accepted in investing that diversification is a good thing. We diversify across managers, sectors, geographies, stock and bonds, and time frames, among other things. Wouldn't it make sense to diversify behaviors and hormonal profiles as well?

Avoiding the Herd: Homogenous Thinking and Portfolios

We are all familiar with the herd mentality in investing. The dot-com bubble, market crashes with frenzied selling, and even the January effect are all examples of herd investing. In a 2013 interview with Douglas Clement, Richard H. Thaler explained how herd mentality can trip up even the titans of investing. "If you ask the LTCM [Long Term Capital Management] guys what their biggest mistake was," he says, "they will all tell you the same thing. It was in not appreciating the fact that their bets were more correlated than they realized. Simply the fact that they were interested in these two particular bets meant they were correlated because they're not the only smart guys in the world . . . It's not the same thing as groupthink because they're not talking to each other, but they have the same way of thinking."[53]

The herd mentality in investing is evident from high-net-worth investors to sophisticated money managers such as hedge funds. Recently, a number of firms have begun to analyze 13-F stock filings from large asset managers each quarter. For example, the Holdings Channel reviewed 3,692 13-Fs for the period ending March 2014 and discovered that no fewer than 15 hedge fund "titans" had positions in American International Group (AIG).[54] An article in *Forbes* in August of 2014 highlighted large hedge fund positions in Apple, including well-known funds like Omega, Greenlight, and Icahn.[55]

Of course, if the markets or stocks are trending up, herd mentality can be a good thing. A rising tide lifts all ships, after all. However, when a stock market bubble bursts, or even when a single, widely held position disappoints, the rush for the exits can be crushing.

In speaking with the women money managers for *Women of The Street*, one thing quickly became abundantly clear. At least in this sample, female money managers don't often follow the herd. They tend to look for less crowded markets and underfavored positions. This is not to say all women investors are contrarians, but it does appear that women prefer different universes of investments than their more homogenized male-run fund counterparts. This may account at least in part for the differentiated return pattern exhibited by female money managers.

It's Not You, It's Me: Admitting Investment Mistakes...

As everyone who has ever taken health in fifth grade is aware, women have less testosterone than men. In most cases, women sport only 10 percent of the testosterone of their male counterparts. Lower testosterone minimizes the "winner's effect," which may include reckless behavior and overconfidence. As a result, women investors may be better at admitting mistakes than men. Exiting a position while it is still just a mistake rather than a disaster can help minimize drawdowns. In roughly 16 years in the investment industry, I have never heard a female utter the words "it's too late to sell."

... While Maintaining Conviction

Conversely, women can't be *too* fast on the draw when it comes to admitting mistakes. Since women trade less frequently than men, they do not generally race out of positions at the first hint of trouble. In fact, just the opposite may be true. While women seem more apt to admit mistakes, they may also be better equipped to consistently execute a portfolio strategy. A Vanguard study of 2.7 million IRA investors showed that men were 10 percent more likely than women to abandon stocks between January 2007 and October 2009.[56] Sticking to a long-term investment strategy can help filter out market noise, resulting in more consistent returns and outperformance, as evidenced by the down market outperformance referenced earlier, also from Vanguard.

Practical Application

The research on gender differences in investing is quite compelling, especially for a nerd like me. However, translating theories into practical money management strategies can be tricky. To demonstrate how the innate traits of women translate into long-term profits, I have conducted the 11 interviews in *Women of The Street* with top-performing female money managers who invest in a variety of markets and with various investment strategies. Through these interviews, you can clearly see how theory translates into successful investment strategy.

This research is not just about being a top *female* portfolio manager; rather, it is about how to successfully manage money over the long term. The following chapters provide valuable knowledge about the markets and investment strategy, as well as concrete investment and risk management techniques. My goal is to show both men and women how to apply the innate skills of females to select better fund managers and/or more profitably to manage their own money. If you've ever thought investing "isn't for me" because of the high-flying investment win big/lose big stories in the media, I believe these insights will prove invaluable.

There is a different way to win in investing, and these women have found it.

PART II

From Theory to Practice: Public Equity Investing

CHAPTER 2

Aim Small, Miss Small: Targeting International Small-Cap Stocks

Leah Zell, Founder and Principal,
Lizard Investors

I f you go target shooting with an instructor, one of the more useful pieces of advice you may get is "aim small, miss small." The thinking is that if you point at a target, say, a mugger on the street, and miss, you could be in big trouble. Hello, angry mugger; good-bye, wallet. But if you aim for something small on that same mugger, like his or her heart, you may still miss, but you will have vastly improved your chances of actually hitting your target.

Leah Zell aims small. She has laser focus, both in money management and in her favorite pastime, dual slalom skiing, in which success rests on picking a course through the fall line and executing with precision. At her company, Lizard Investors, she exercises what she calls "ruthless elimination" of stocks to create a top-performing portfolio of international small-cap stocks. Zell embodies keen concentration and determination.

If you saw her on the street, you would think Zell was a typical suburban Chicago mom. On the day of our interview she greeted me at the elevator wearing a bright pink sweater and a pair of black pants. She was also sporting a large cast on her left wrist.

She had been hiking the month before and taken a tumble. Turns out, her arm had hurt for the better part of three weeks. She ignored it and went about her life. Finally, she decided it was time to go to the doctor. After x-rays, the doctor came into the exam room and said, "Leah, I have good news and bad news. The good news is your arm is healing well. The bad news is it's actually broken, so we should probably put it in a cast."

Zell smiles and holds up her cast when she tells me this story, quipping, "I got better information, so I changed course." Indeed, this simple phrase could be the story of Zell's investing life.

Originally, Zell studied European history at Harvard, where she earned her PhD. Then she discovered a love for getting more immediate feedback and doing entrepreneurial research, so she changed careers and took a job on Wall Street. Her famous sibling, Sam Zell, helped her make the decision. Sam is known in the business community as the "grave dancer," and was described in an October 2013 article in *Forbes* as a "72-year-old man with a penchant for both gold chains and profanity, as a corporate barbarian who callously ransacked great journalistic institutions in a greedy pursuit of short-term profit."[1] In contrast, *Forbes* dubbed Leah "the queen of small caps" in 2000.[2] Despite these different depictions, in many ways Sam and Leah are seeking the same thing: great entrepreneurs and companies they can buy at a discount and see grow over the long term.

Zell uses her academic background to deeply research international small cap stocks. After leaving the investment banking world of Lehman Brothers in 1984, she joined the staff of money manager Ralph Wanger. From 1992 to 2003, Zell served as lead portfolio manager for Wanger Asset Management's Acorn International Fund, and through 2005 as lead manager for Wanger Smaller European Companies Fund. Zell spent five years in the top 10 percent of her asset management peers during her tenure as the manager for Acorn International before Zell and Wanger sold the firm in 2003. It is now a subsidiary of Ameriprise Financial under the Columbia brand.

Zell is recognized as a pioneer in international small-cap investing, and in 2008, she set up her own shop. As founder and principal of Lizard Investors and the portfolio manager of Lizard International Fund, Zell and her team gather enormous amounts of information. They analyze stocks fundamentally, from the "bottom up" in industry terms, looking for stocks that have more than one potentially profitable outcome. Then they buy and hold the stocks, often for years at a time. Despite her average two- to three-year holding period, Zell is not at all dogmatic or overconfident about her portfolio companies.

She remains vigilant for potential spoilers, always looking "down the hill" for information that could make her adjust her positioning. As a result, Zell estimates that no position in Lizard's five-year operating history has cost the portfolio more than 2 percent in value. Since inception of Lizard, the fund has generated a 14.53 percent net return through October 2013, compared with the average hedge fund's return of 3.62 percent.[3]

After more than two decades of managing international small cap stock portfolios, the hallmarks of Zell's strategy remain consistent:

- focus on sustainable businesses, not fads
- invest in strong balance sheets
- make sure management is aligned
- insist on good corporate governance
- seek optionality, or situations with more than one potential profitable outcome
- and don't overpay

Sam Zell's "Baby" Sister?

MJ: I believe how you're raised really shapes how you view money and the markets. You grew up the third child of immigrants who made it big in Chicago—what was your childhood like?

LZ: I often joke that all three of us were mistakes, but that there's no question about me. I have a brother who's 8 years older than me, and a sister who is 12 years older than me. My parents were both in their 40s when I was born, although my mother lied about her age. I thought she had been 39 for the longest time.

And I'm not sure if my parents made it so big. My parents were both born in Europe, and they came to the United States as refugees in their 30s. My parents did extremely well, certainly relative to what they might have expected. They were very proud of what they accomplished.

I grew up in a European capsule. You crossed the threshold of our house and everything was *mitteleuropaeisch*.[4] My parents were so ingrained in who they were and where they came from that I don't think they quite appreciated how different they really were.

MJ: Do you think that there were lessons that you learned from watching your parents about work, about life and success?

LZ: I learned that anything was possible, and the most improbable outcomes were not framed as improbable. You set goals, and you went after your goals, and you didn't worry too much about what other people thought. They thought very independently because they didn't know how to do it any other way. Consequently, they taught me to think for myself.

MJ: Did your two older siblings play a role in shaping your worldview as well?

LZ: I grew up both having two older siblings and as an only child, because my sister left for college before I have a memory. My brother was also significantly older than me, so I spent a lot of time as a child by myself. I didn't really have siblings as playmates. I would also say that it is characteristic of the youngest child to always want to stand on the table and shout, "I'm here. Look at me," because by the time you hit your second decade, your parents are already in their third or fourth decade of raising kids and they just can't be bothered. I think birth order is destiny.

MJ: Obviously, one of your siblings has a name that's quite well recognized. You mentioned to me before that in one of your first appearances on CNBC you were introduced on the air as Sam Zell's little sister.

LZ: In my mid-60s.

MJ: Does that motivate you, or does it just kind of piss you off?

LZ: I laugh at this point. It's not a big deal for me anymore.

MJ: I know you got a PhD in European social and economic history from Harvard. How did you decide to make the leap from academia to Wall Street?

LZ: Well, it would be interesting to do a study of what percentage of people actually follow a career that relates to their academic background. As I got closer and closer to becoming an academic as a profession, I began to explore other options.

Being an academic is perhaps much like being a writer. It's a very isolating kind of activity. Most of the work that's important, you do by yourself. As I was doing my PhD research in the archives in Germany, I got locked into one archive by myself for hours, and I said, "Is this really how I want to spend my life?"

MJ: That would probably put me off as well.

LZ: Being an academic is the classic long-distance runner kind of activity. You start something and maybe 10 years later you have a book, and then maybe 10 to 20 years later after that, you get to find out whether your book is considered to be good. The nice thing about managing money is that you find out at the end of the day whether your effort panned out.

Also, in history you know how things end up, and you come up with a storyline as to how we got there. In doing equity research, you know where things start, and what you're really doing is pulling, synthesizing a lot of information to come up with a hypothesis as to where it should go. For me, the two activities really were very analogous to one another.

In addition, I liked that there was a very objective standard of achievement, the performance numbers were the numbers.

Remember, when I moved from academia to Wall Street, Wall Street was very much out of favor. In the late '70s, Wall Street had just gone through a terrible bear market. Many firms had gone under. In my generation, it was distinctly uncool.

The Lehman Years

MJ: But you made the decision to do it anyway.

LZ: Yeah, because there were jobs and they were interesting jobs. Also, by the time I finished my doctorate, I was doing business history. I had one advisor in the economics department and one advisor at the business school, and no advisor in the history department. So I went over to the business school and I got the names of the recruiters for the Wall Street investment banks. They were private partnerships at that juncture, most of them. I wrote, like, a dozen letters and I got three job offers. I ended up taking a job at Lehman Brothers, and I was paid about the same salary as my full professor, which I didn't think about at the time, but when I thought about it afterward, I said, "Well, this is really okay."

It was clear there was an opportunity on Wall Street, and I came from a very business-oriented family. I had been moving throughout my academic career, coming closer and closer to becoming a practitioner. I said to myself, "I'll go down to Wall Street, I'll work for a couple years, learn more about the insides of business, and that will make me a much better business historian." Except that I never went back. I was hooked.

MJ: You said it wasn't considered cool to take the job. What was atmosphere like at Lehman?

LZ: I came from an elite university, and I probably had an attitude. I thought that it would be a piece of cake. The first lesson I learned was that the people that I went to work with were elite and competitive and extremely good at what they did, and that I had no clue.

MJ: Did that motivate you or . . .

LZ: That terrified me. But if one thinks about who was working at Lehman Brothers when I joined, they're people who have since become quite legendary. [Peter G.] Peterson was running the firm. Steve Schwarzman was a newly made partner. Eric Gleacher ran the mergers and acquisitions department. The whole firm was extremely small because it fit into One William Street, which is a tiny building. I don't remember how many partners there were, but I knew them all. They hired five people in my year.

MJ: Did that make it any more collegial?

LZ: I think it was cutthroat, competitive, and hard. It was extremely competitive. It was a private partnership, and every partner's capital was on the line. They only made partners of people who they were convinced would work extremely hard and create value. I have very strong memories of leaving between midnight and three in the morning and taking a cab home across 66th Street. There was a Korean grocer that was open 24/7 where I could buy food. I worked so hard and that was just standard.

MJ: How did you get to your next step from Lehman?

LZ: I was clearly very strong at research, and I was very good at writing. I wasn't so great at the transactional side of investment banking. It was Lehman Brothers that suggested to me that I think about equity research. I think they figured it out before I did.

MJ: Did you take it as a positive at that time that Lehman was suggesting a different direction?

LZ: I think when you're at that point in your career, you're not that discerning. Developing a career is tentatively taking a risk and then seeing whether you get rewarded for taking that risk— or whether you get shut down. I was being given signals that I looked like someone who would do well in equity research, or on the asset management side, as opposed to the investment banking side. I ended up moving to Harris Associates, but I give Lehman credit. They were right.

When I left Lehman Brothers they did one of the classiest things I ever saw. I left before the bonus season, and several months afterward, they sent me a check for my bonus for the year.

MJ: Good Lord!

LZ: It was totally unexpected and I'll never forget it.

MJ: When you left Lehman, you made not just a transition between firms but also in the type of work you were performing. What was that like?

LZ: I loved asset management from the absolute beginning. I thought I was really good at that and I really had some kind of an imaginative gene that allowed me to understand what made a business special. The word *history* has the word *story* in it, and a lot of what we do in equity research and asset management is being able to understand the story. That's for sure my skill set.

MJ: What was it like at Harris, then, with this new position in comparison to being at Lehman? Were you still up until midnight and 3:00 a.m., looking for a Korean grocer?

LZ: No. It was much more cerebral, but it was a lot of fun. I remember that the first company I worked on, somebody said to me, "Why don't you find something about payment processing? It's a new cutting-edge industry." I worked on a small company called First Data Resources, which of course eventually became the biggest credit card processing company in the United States. That was the very first buy recommendation that I wrote.

Harris Associates in those days had two businesses. They had an investment counseling business, and we had the mutual fund business, the Acorn business, which focused on small caps. Those of us who worked as analysts worked on both sides of the business. I did First Data Resources for Acorn, but I did Nestlé, which was the first foreign stock that Harris ever considered, for the investment counseling side.

"Don't Bitch, Switch"

MJ: So you got exposure to what would eventually become both of your loves while you were there.

LZ: Yes. I joined in1984. The mid-'80s were the all-time peak of the dollar. US manufacturing was getting badly hurt because the dollar was so strong. We used to say—it became like a joke—"don't bitch, switch." Instead of complaining about not being able to buy US companies, why don't you look at some of the foreign companies that were benefiting from having a more favorable currency valuation?

In addition, international investing really only became possible in large part in the '80s because previously there had been capital controls. Think about investing in China today. You need to qualify as an institutional investor. You need to get a certificate and so on. Before the mid-'80s it wasn't easy to invest anywhere internationally. I went to Lehman Brothers, and since I had done all my academic work on Europe, I came with the expectation that I would work on European companies. I found out at Lehman Brothers that there was only one partner who had a book of business outside the United States, and it wasn't big enough to warrant a full-time associate.

I was fortunate enough to start doing foreign equities and international equities just as it became possible to invest outside the United States. It was a new thing.

Marvelous Mentors

MJ: Did you have mentors?

LZ: I've been fortunate to have many mentors. You asked about the decision to leave academia, and my brother played, without question, the role of mentor there. I would meet him for breakfast in New York with some regularity, and every time I met him, he would say, "So when are you going to leave academia and join the business world?"

He banged on me, and anybody who knows my brother knows that he bangs very effectively. Even though I talked about the opportunity to go to Wall Street presenting itself, I also had someone who is close to me who said to me, "You can do this and you will be good at it."

I don't know if that's mentoring, but that vote of confidence was important. I also had a professor at Harvard, David Landes. He had an insatiable curiosity about businesses, about families, about entrepreneurship, and about how economies grow. He took me under his wing when I was a graduate student. Without David, I'm sure I would never have finished.

A lot of how I think about companies derives from those years. Mentoring is less somebody consciously teaching you things as it is being in their wake. You learn less by what people tell you than by what they do, and patterning yourself against them. So Sam was a mentor. David Landes was a mentor. Then once I joined Harris Associates, Ralph Wanger was a mentor. Of course, Ralph was the dean of small caps. He had learned it from a man by the name of Irving Harris.

Irving Harris is a legend in the Chicago community, and it was actually Irving who introduced me to Ralph, which is how I got the job at Harris Associates. Irving believed in entrepreneurs. All of these people I mentioned were, be it Sam, be it Irving, be it Ralph, be it David, they were all fascinated with entrepreneurs. Sam actually philanthropically funded the entrepreneurship program at the University of Michigan, and he's also funded one in Israel. So I think somehow that I was meant to do this because my mentors were all people who were in their own way mavericks.

MJ: Do you think that any of their personality traits also inspired you to become who you are?

LZ: I'm a junkie for intellectual stimulation. I like to be challenged. I like people who make me think about things in new ways, and they generally don't tend to be easy people or conventional people.

Inflection Points

MJ: So you learn the small cap and international equity research side of the business at Harris, and then you took the reins at Acorn. At the time, you had two relatively small children. What was that decision process like for you?

LZ: Careers have inflection points that are generally obvious only in retrospect. That was, without doubt, a major inflection point in my life and in my career. I had two small children. I had asked to reduce my hours because my children are only 26 months apart. Let's say I was busy. But then I found that I was in the mommy track and that I was no longer being considered for promotions. I was no longer in the bonus pool. I found this to be very demoralizing, so the decision that I faced was either to retire or to go back full-time and grab the brass ring.

I was in my early 40s. It was very clear to me that I either was going to make a career for myself or not. From an age perspective, I had my children fairly late. I didn't have the luxury of waiting until they were both in school full-time to go back because I would have been too old. So I just took a deep breath and made the decision to go back to work full-time and to make it work.

MJ: Because the alternative was just not acceptable?

LZ: Let me give you another sort of anecdote: after we sold the business—I'm fast-forwarding here—but I had an employment contract and noncompete contract. There was a small window before I started Lizard Investors, and both of my children came to me after about a year and said, "Mommy, will you please go back to work? You are driving all of us crazy." Work makes me happy, and I maybe knew that at that first juncture that if I didn't make the decision to go full-time, it would have long-term consequences that I would not be able to undo.

MJ: What were your days like once you made the decision to go back full-time, take the reins at Acorn, and you had a two- and a four-year-old at home?

LZ: I was blessed, because at that point I was a partner of the business, and that meant that I had a certain degree of freedom. There's a big difference between investment banking and asset management: whether you control your time or not. Anne-Marie Slaughter addressed this when she wrote her article for *Atlantic Monthly* ["Why Women Still Can't Have It All"]. I had more control over my time and could organize it, and I was also in a position that gave me flexibility, and that's really critical.

I've always been an investor, and certainly at Acorn we had a 24/7 trading desk, so the trading was done by the people who stayed up all night, and thankfully, it wasn't me, except when I got really crazy. I worked a lot after my kids went to bed. I'm a night owl, so it would not be unusual for me to work until the European market opened.

I also did a lot of traveling, but I would try very hard to take the last flight out on Sunday night so I could put my kids to bed. I would always try to be back by Friday afternoon. I knew every single flight schedule to Europe by heart. I knew exactly where I could fly to get the last flight out from Chicago.

MJ: So you had the work-life balance part of the equation handled. What about the investing side? How did that evolve?

LZ: When we started the Acorn International Fund, we were, I think, the third or fourth international small-cap fund in the United States. The total number of international funds was probably 1/20 the number of US-focused funds. The assets they had under management were also fractional. When we started the fund, we only had US and international; then it became US, international, and emerging. Now it's US, international, emerging, and frontier. What's now emerging used to be frontier.

At Harris, I worked for a mutual fund complex that was known for doing small-cap stocks. It was a natural product extension to go from US small-cap stocks to international small-cap stocks. Europe was my background, my comparative advantage. Finally, as an emerging area, it was a favorable area for me to pursue as a woman.

If you go into a crowded area, you have to have sharp elbows. If you go into an area where nobody else really is that interested in playing, you can take risk without taking *as much* risk. You can make it up as you go along.

MJ: So the opportunity to be a big fish in a small pond was attractive?

LZ: Yes, yes. We're going to talk about ski racing as a metaphor, maybe once or twice. If you ever do a dual slalom ski race...

MJ: I think we can almost guarantee I won't, but okay...

LZ: In a dual slalom, the kiss of death is if you're listening for the skis of your competitor. You don't want to hear whether he or she is behind you or ahead of you. I think that's what's characterized my career. Instinctually I like to operate as if I'm in a vacuum, even if it's very competitive.

MJ: What else makes it appealing to you?

What we do is, we go around looking for gems and opportunities with flashlights. Certainly, early on in my career, that was very much the case. I remember going to a German small-cap conference in Bad Homburg, which is outside of Frankfurt, which was given by a small-cap specialty firm that no longer exists. This was June 1989, and a company presented that had just gone public six months earlier. It was a software company called SAP. It had about a billion-dollar market cap, which was at the top end of the market cap for this conference.

I thought their presentation was absolutely fabulous. We did a lot of work on it when I got back. Actually, on the plane back from this conference, I wrote a memo suggesting that we start a separate international small-cap mutual fund, which ultimately became the Acorn International Fund.

This conference really got my juices flowing. We did some due diligence. We checked with some of the accounting firms that were recommending and installing the software over the summer of 1989. The Acorn Fund became the largest United States-based shareholder of SAP at that time. We hadn't started the international fund yet.

I covered that stock from the late '80s to the mid- to late '90s. I remember going to see SAP at their headquarters near Heidelberg. There would be a sign that said, "Welcome, Leah Zell."

MJ: There were no skis behind you.

LZ: There were no skis behind me, that is exactly right.

The Outlook for Small Cap Investing

MJ: Do you continue to think small cap investing is a good space?

LZ: Yes, because there are always new companies. We spend a lot of time talking about disruptive technologies. In my 2013 third-quarter letter to clients, I wrote an essay about the half-life of technology companies. I went back and took a look at what were the ten biggest technology companies by market cap going back to the '60s in the United States. There's only one name that has remained on the list over the period of time, and that's IBM because it totally reinvented itself.

MJ: It sounds like evolution is somewhat of a constant for you.

LZ: What's constant is that I tend to have a longer-term time horizon, particularly as the profession has become ever more short-term oriented. That is directly related to my early training as a historian. I was trained to think in decades; now I think in years. I think that the pressure is to think in ever-shorter time periods, which is also evident in increasingly short holding periods.

With computers, everything has become shorter term. As communication has become better, the entire environment has encouraged shorter-term thinking. I can't do that. That's a constant in how I think about investing. I'm by nature an impatient person, so I have been practicing patience my whole life, and I hope I'm getting better at it.

Technology and communication have changed since I started making trips to SAP. The space has, in fact, become much more crowded. You have to work harder to find opportunities. There are fewer stones that have been unturned. That means that being able to extract yourself from the noise is all the more important, because the noise has gotten louder.

I grew up in the business where there was more room for me to make mistakes. I grew up in what I would call more of a vacuum; now the oxygen has been sucked out of the room.

MJ: You think that's because information is so much more instantaneous?

LZ: There is an illusion that you have an information edge. Your edge is really how you frame things and how you think about things and how well you understand the complete picture. That requires you to have patience. There are four words I've always used about this profession: focus, endurance, discipline, and patience. Those are evergreens; they'll never change.

If you read Benjamin Graham's [author of *Security Analysis* and the father of value investing] writings, you realize that there are these constants about investing. The styles come in and out; one day it's pink shirts, and the next day it's tie-dyed blue jeans. You have to able to adapt to the investment environment. But in the end, a company either creates value or it doesn't create value. You either buy it at a discount to its intrinsic value, or you buy it at a premium to its intrinsic value. Your ability to be successful in this business relies on how well you can make those judgments.

A Holistic Approach

MJ: Do you feel that those are some of the reasons your approach is different from your peers'? You take a more holistic view of companies?

LZ: I love that word *holistic*. If we go back to the information overload, I've always thought of doing equity research as a process of sauce reduction. You pull in all these ingredients and you boil it down. What you want to get right are the finite drivers of the business. It's really about figuring out what is important; it sounds simple but it's extraordinarily hard.

Once you've figured out what is important, you must stay focused on what's important and not get distracted by a temporary blip or some kind of new story that will get you off track. Imagine you're skiing down a course. What you're doing is, you're going around what are called gates, which are really like poles. You'd think I'm a really good ski racer...

MJ: I'm actually in awe of your skiing abilities.

LZ: I did it for a number of years as an amateur. The first thing that I learned was to turn early, because if you don't turn early, you get what's known as low in the gates. To get the smoothest, most beautiful lines through the gates, you would set yourself up for your turn before you actually got to the gate. Then you were able to ski more smoothly because you didn't have to make the sharp hairpin turns.

Always look down the course. Don't look at the next gate. Look down two to three gates toward the finish line, and chart your course so you waste the least amount of time and get more directly to where you're going. It's a great metaphor for managing money. Be early, look down the course, have a long-term perspective. Know where you think things should go, and if you're not going there, change directions.

MJ: Do you think that other people in your business have a similar approach?

LZ: Everyone I admire does. There are all sorts of ways to manage money. We all have defined, authentic voices. There are certain technical things we can learn, but then you have to marry those technical lessons with your personality and your inclination.

MJ: International small caps comprise a large and diverse group of markets, companies, and economies. How do you sift through all of that information? What are you looking for?

LZ: We look for five things. We look for sustainable businesses. Is it a fad or is there a reason why this business should exist, and will it be around in ten years? Ten years is a long time for a business to be around. Second of all, is the balance sheet strong enough so they can self-fund if the financing window closes? That was the question that killed a lot of companies in 2008, because they never actually thought the financing window would close. One of the advantages of investing outside the US is that a lot of the countries and companies that we deal with have seen the window open and close before. It's more typical for balance sheets outside the United States. not always, but certainly in certain situations, to be stronger than in the United States precisely because there's this element of conservatism that's baked into the process.

Third, we look for management teams that understand the concept of cost of capital and that are aligned with us. Oftentimes, if you're buying small-cap stocks outside the United States, or even larger companies outside the United States, they'll have a controlling shareholder. Understand who that person is and what their motivations are, and make sure that the person treats noncontrolling shareholders fairly.

Fourth, depending on the market, you want good corporate governance, which is more of an issue in Asia than it is, for example, in Europe or Canada. The fifth factor is compelling valuation. Can we model out what the business is worth such that we can see a return? We must have downside protection. We may temporarily be underwater, but we need to feel that the value of the business and the margin of safety are such that, if we get our analysis right, we won't lose money. There needs to be an asymmetric risk-reward such that we can meet our return hurdles, which are in excess of 20 percent compounded per annum.

The last factor, which overrides all of the others, is when you're investing on the long side, you want optionality. You want to be able to see a couple of ways in which you can win, and not just focus all of your analysis on one possible outcome.

MJ: How is managing your hedge fund different from managing a mutual fund?

LZ: When I was managing the mutual fund, you were managing it against the benchmark. In retrospect, I describe that as more of a "paint by numbers" exercise. If Japan had X weight in the index, you would overweight it or underweight it, but it would be a very radical decision to not be invested. Somebody else I know in the business has described it as a Noah's Ark approach, where you need two of everything. In order to do that, you need a very large team and you need to delegate. You find that your team operates more in silos, where your South Asian guy doesn't really spend a lot of time talking to your Northern European guy.

What I do today is quite different. What I'm doing today is that I look for exceptional opportunities. I don't think about it in relative terms but in absolute terms. We happen to have investments in Japan, but it would not bother me to have nothing there, if I couldn't find an opportunity that I thought fit the return profile that we're looking for.

I call it ruthless elimination. That means that 90 percent of the ideas we look at, the question is how fast can we get them off our desk. We spend most of our time looking at outliers.

Maintaining Optionality

MJ: **What would you say your typical holding period is?**

LZ: Statistically, it's two to three years, but it's really more of a barbell, because sometimes you find out you made a mistake and you want to move quickly.

MJ: **Exercise your optionality.**

LZ: Exercise your optionality, that's exactly right. The best ideas, you really want to hold for a long time.

MJ: **You mentioned SAP as being a stock you discovered early on. Are there other trades that stand out in your memory?**

LZ: I remember buying Hennes & Mauritz, now known as H&M, when it was predominantly a Swedish department store company. They were making their first forays out of Sweden and trying to figure out whether they could internationalize the business, which, by the way, is the same issue SAP faced when we bought it. When we bought SAP, it was predominantly a German business. The thesis was that the software was good enough that they would be able to export it outside of Germany and sell it specifically into the United States.

I remember a stock in Hong Kong that we bought called Li & Fung; we bought that in the early '90s. It's had quite a storied history—largest outsourcing company in Asia. One of the great advantages of having worked for Acorn is that the great names stayed in the portfolio for extended periods of time. I think it's probably unheard of today.

We are always looking to find the exceptional small-cap stock that has the ability to grow into a mid-cap (medium-size company) and a large-cap (large company) stock. That's really what the game is about. In the end, there aren't that many, so you hit a lot of singles and doubles.

MJ: If you're unable to find enough exceptional names to be fully invested, do you compromise or stay in cash?

LZ: No compromises.

MJ: Any examples of stocks that didn't work out as you hoped?

LZ: We've made some mistakes, but we've been fortunate enough that, when we've made them, we've been able to exit them without too much damage. That's the optionality at work.

MJ: You haven't had anything blow up on you, so to speak?

LZ: I wouldn't say I've never had anything blow up on me. There haven't been any major blowups since we started Lizard. One of the reasons is because we're so, so picky about what we do. Ultimately, I suppose that the biggest risk in this business is fraud. A name we owned for three weeks rang a bell to an earlier company I knew about that turned out to be a fraud. We figured out that the CEO had been involved in the prior situation. We sold the company, and it subsequently turned out to be a fraud.

I think we got out flat or made a little bit of money. Luckily, there have been mistakes but not disasters in the current portfolio.

MJ: Are you quicker to exit a position than you are to put one on?

LZ: I'm personally very sensitive to issues of integrity. If I learn something, for example, about a management team that makes me question their integrity, I will pull the emergency cord and get out.

This is a batting average game. Sometimes you get out of things and you should have stayed in them, and sometimes you get out of things and it's exactly the right thing. In every single trade, there's somebody on the other side who has an opposite point of view. It's all about risk mitigation.

MJ: Is hedging an effective and practical part of your strategy at this point?

LZ: On the currency side, I definitely hedge because I see currency risk as something that I can take off the table at essentially no cost.

Fundamentally, I think there are not as many great short ideas as there are great long ideas. We have decided philosophically that we will not run a dedicated short book. We won't put shorts on simply to offset our long positions, so we will not target a net long percentage.

I think shorts are in so many ways the inverse of longs. I think with longs, you want all that optionality. With shorts you want much less optionality. You want actually to have a greater degree of conviction—you want to really eliminate all of the possible good outcomes and be fairly confident that the business is unsustainable. Shorts are intellectually very challenging.

The Perfect Storm

MJ: How do you keep from being overconfident?

LZ: This is a business where you're always making decisions on insufficient information. You have to be realistic about the fact that at any juncture you could be wrong. There's this very fine line. Conviction and hubris—they're really on the same spectrum. You need to have enough conviction based on the work you've done, but not so much conviction that you're not willing to change your mind when there's contrary information. Sometimes you don't know why you're wrong, you just know you're wrong.

We all make errors. When you catch a mistake in this case, you deal with it when it's a small mistake. You don't let it become a big mistake.

MJ: There was a period in 2000, I believe, where you went from being in the top 10 percent of money managers for five years to the bottom quartile.

LZ: That was a particular perfect storm for me. Obviously, the markets imploded, but we also sold our business in 2000. I lost my team. About half the people who worked for me cashed their checks and left. I spent particularly 2001 and 2002 completely rebuilding the business, hiring a new team, and training people from scratch. I was really at some level the proverbial boy with his finger in the dike.

Even though performance in that short time frame took a hit, by the time the team was reconstructed and by the time I left Acorn International, performance had not only come back, but it has been outstanding ever since.

MJ: Do you see the difficult markets as a challenge or an opportunity?

LZ: I think these have been good years for Lizard because we are really fundamental stock pickers. What's been difficult about these environments have been the macroeconomic and market dynamics. If you try to trade the macros or the markets, you've gotten whipsawed. On the other hand, if you've focused at the level of the individual investment opportunity and bought it with the intention of holding it for three to five years . . . I'm sure you've heard the idea—I think it's a Warren Buffett idea—that you should buy every stock as if the market's going to be closed.

MJ: Do you think that's part of your edge? Do you think that the fact that you take such a long-term view is part of your advantage?

LZ: To the extent that I have a bit of an outsider's mind-set, I don't pick up on what's going on in the market—the short-term stuff—as much as other people. That leaves me room in my head to think about what I own. If we own things that I can explain to my grandmother, then I don't worry too much.

I worry about the companies we own, but I don't worry about the market. Worrying about the market is worrying about something you can't control, you can't predict, and it's not productive.

MJ: If a company of yours took a hit during a day because the entire market sold off, is that just noise to you?

LZ: I may feel bad about it . . . [laughs] I may feel good about it because I can buy more. The really great thing about what

I call ruthless elimination or investment by exception is that we have only a small number of positions. We have only 30 names. If you don't turn them over very much and you keep on reading about them and reading about them, you get to know them pretty well. The better you know what you own, the less you're likely to be shaken out of it for reasons that are extraneous to the intrinsic investment case.

Lessons from Lizard

MJ: Finally, what advice do you wish you had been given at the start of your career?

LZ: I think being your own person is really, really important in this profession. This is not a profession where you follow the crowd. In order to do that, you have to have confidence in yourself and can't let others dictate your self-worth. I would say the same thing about anyone who wants to be an entrepreneur.

Having confidence in yourself and believing in yourself is mandatory. That doesn't mean that you don't have down periods, and it doesn't mean that you don't have times when you question yourself, but you have to be your own mirror; that is the first thing I would say.

The second thing I would say is that no career follows a straight path. There are always going to be ups and downs. You have to ride it, learn from it, and adapt. Turn early and look down the course. Know where you want to go, but then get there with flexibility, integrity, intellectual honesty, and authenticity.

I've also been privileged to have known many, many successful people. The ones I admire the most are the ones who are still challenging themselves and still learning. Another way of saying it is, you need your own internal concept of excellence. You need to pursue excellence, and probably part and parcel with that you need a very good BS meter.

CHAPTER 3

Quite Contrary: Going Long in Mid-Cap Stocks

Thyra Zerhusen, Founder, Fairpointe Capital

The phrase "against the grain" first came into use in 1607 when William Shakespeare included it in the play *Coriolanus*. Although it is generally accepted that the phrase derives from attempting to plane wood against the grain, causing it to fray rather than lie flat, there is actually no concrete origin story for the expression. Google "against the grain" today and you are just as likely to get barraged with gluten-free diatribes as to discover the source of this contrarian catchphrase.

I met Thyra (pronounced "Tu-ra") Zerhusen while she was battling a bad cold and, despite watery eyes, coughing, and a budding case of laryngitis, she described a career and investing philosophy that epitomizes being, in Shakespeare's words, "guided/By your own true affections."[1] Let's face it: it's not for nothing that most of the articles written about Zerhusen mention that she was once fired for insubordination. But where most people associate insubordination with misconduct, what you actually find with Zerhusen is quiet confidence that her investment decisions are sound, regardless of short-term market, investor or, at the time of her dismissal for insubordination, employer noise. She's often buying when others are selling. In short, she is guided by her own inner voice.

Educated in Germany and Switzerland, Zerhusen's original loves were engineering, life sciences, and economics. After obtaining her Master's degree in economics from the University of Illinois, Chicago, she knew she wanted to work in the field, but wasn't exactly sure where she fit in. Her resume circulated around the HR department of Harris Bank before the director of equity research expressed an interest in meeting her. "I didn't even know what equity research was," she quips. So she called a friend, who recommended two books on the topic. She quickly read Eugene Fama's tome on the investing and aced her interview.

Six years later, after a successful run at Harris, Zerhusen accepted a job at Sears managing its pension funds. She was there more than a decade before Sears opted to outsource its money management functions. From Sears, Zerhusen went to the Burridge Group, and then to Talon Asset Management. Along the way, she honed her mid-cap investment specialty and took the reins at the struggling Allegheny/Chicago Trust Talon Fund (CHTTX), which she still manages today under the same ticker but updated name: The Aston/Fairpointe Mid-Cap Fund.

During her tenure at the fund, she's seen assets grow from $20 million ("going on $18 million," she jokes) to just under $6 billion. She's seen a host of market environments, including two of the greatest bull markets in history (1982–1987 and 1987–2000), the Tech Wreck, the Great Recession, and the subsequent 2009–2014 market run-up. Over the last ten years, her mutual fund has produced a compound annual return of 11.4 percent, beating both the S&P 400 (10.5%) and the Russell Mid-Cap (8.7%) indices. It also has a five-star rating from Morningstar over the last one-, three-, and five-year periods, and a four-star rating over the last ten years, leading *Smart Money* magazine to include Zerhusen twice on their annual list of the "World's Greatest Investors."

The road has not always been smooth, however. In 2008, due to the overall market sell-off, Aston/Fairpointe dropped more than 40 percent. Zerhusen, however, ignored calls from her investors to sell, as well as pleas to move into relatively "safer" large cap stocks. In fact, she bought when others were selling, and, as a result, the fund gained over 66 percent in 2009.

Having such a long and successful run in the markets is no accident. In fact, Zerhusen's tenets for investing are the same as they were when she first took over her fund:

- Always use the valuations as your guide.
- Start with a small positions and increase your holding on dips in the price.

- Know your companies and always ask yourself what could go wrong with the company, their products, or the market.
- Trust yourself and take emotion out of your investment decisions.
- You don't profit from doing what everyone else does. Don't be afraid to be contrary.

Refrigerator Moments

MJ: Equity research at Harris Bank was your first job in finance. Was it love at first sight?

TZ: Yes. And, believe it or not, every month you got a report card on how your recommendations turned out, the ones you made six months before. You had 15 or 17 analysts all ranked, so you knew who could pick stocks and who could not. It was a very analyst-driven environment. You could write approval memos, but you had to go through top management and defend the approval memo in front of the investment committee. There was a very high standard because our research was sold to other banks around the country. It was almost like being on the sell side, writing research reports, but you were never pushed to recommend anything like Wall Street sometimes is. The bank was on the same side as the clients.

MJ: So how were your report cards? Worthy of being displayed on the refrigerator?

TZ: My report cards were really good. We also had an industry diversification fund. You could, within your industry, say, "Okay, I want to put this stock in the fund," or "I don't want to include anything from my industry because everything is overvalued." The research director knew whether you usually were right or not. So when I went to him and said I want to buy this or sell this, he just wrote the ticket and said. "Take it to trading."

MJ: I imagine that was a good validation for having gone the equity analyst route.

TZ: It was a fantastic route for me.

MJ: I believe you were raising a son while you were at Harris. How did manage your work-life balance?

TZ: He was very young then, and we usually had au pair girls staying with us. They were from France and Switzerland, and we still have good contact with some of them. Overall, I think I was quite lucky, and my husband was supportive and it worked out very well.

I asked my son once whether my working negatively affected him. But I think he was quite proud of me. He came back one time, years ago, and there was this *Barron's* article that I was in. My picture was on the front of it. I had a party at the time for an international women's group, and an old girlfriend of my son's from high school was there. She had asked him, "How's your mother?" and he whipped out the *Barron's* and showed it to her. She told that story in front of everybody.

MJ: Another refrigerator moment. So after Harris you managed money for a pension?

TZ: I went to the Sears pension fund, and there I became more of a generalist. I followed totally different industries and had to work myself into it. I was at Sears over ten years before Sears decided to outsource investment management. I became a partner at a small-mid-cap management firm.

Based on the results that I had there, I was hired to manage the fund that we still manage here today. It still has the same ticker symbol, CHTTX [The Aston/Fairpointe Mid-Cap Fund]. In 1999, there was only $20 million in the fund. I worked for the subadvisor, and my assignment was to make it into a mid-cap product. Up to that time, the fund could invest in anything. I made it into a mid-cap fund, which was my expertise.

The Two-Star Investment

MJ: And the fund was not performing particularly well at the time?

TZ: They were about to shut it down. They didn't do it only because the performance improved quite a bit. I remember when

I joined them I had my Sears retirement and profit-sharing money that I took to Schwab. I said, "I want to put this money into this fund [CHTTX]." Schwab looked the fund up and said, "Oh no! You don't want that fund. It only has two stars. It's down 7 percent!" Then I said, "I will be the co-manager there." They became all quiet and they put the money in the fund. It was funny.

MJ: You left Talon in what year?

TZ: Late 2003. At that time, I was managing maybe $220 million in the fund, plus some other accounts. All the accounts came with me.

MJ: The fund was doing well. What prompted you to leave Talon?

TZ: I think I needed more support, marketing support. The fund was a little marginalized. The fund was small, and it was not important to Talon. So I joined another firm. I joined with around $200 million and that firm [Optimum] had probably $500 million. The fund grew in leaps and bounds. But again, there were no real synergies there, and so we left. I wanted to be in charge of my own destiny. I founded Fairpointe when we were about $4 billion, and now we're touching $8 billion. In just three years.

MJ: Clearly that turned out to be a good decision.

TZ: Support is very important because everybody has different designs on the future. Now I can just focus on managing the money. We had to jump through a lot of hurdles and compliance and prove we could have our own firm. I could always prove that I could manage the money, but whether I could manage a separate firm was a different question.

MJ: Even though you had a successful background in money management, people still questioned the business aspect of running your own firm?

TZ: Administration and running a firm, and all that stuff. We had to prove that we could, and we were able to do it.

MJ: Why mid-caps?

TZ: There are a lot of advantages in mid-cap stocks. For instance, we run a relatively large, concentrated portfolio. In mid-cap, one really important thing is that you meet the management. With large caps like IBM or Google or whoever, it's difficult to get 40 minutes with the CEO. In mid-cap we can have a lot of contact with the CEO of the firm. They come to our office repeatedly when they are in Chicago.

We use that contact to understand the companies better, to find out what makes them tick, what's their thought process, where do they see worldwide, best opportunities. You learn a lot by spending an hour with management. We had the founder of Nvidia in our office a year and a half ago. Nvidia makes chips for video games, but also for super computers and other applications. Basically they are competitive with Intel.

Originally in their space, Intel tried to eliminate them. We asked the founder if he would ever sell out to another company, and he said that was the last resort. You see all his money is in the stock. His children's money is in the stock. We got to know the human being who runs the firm. That is invaluable. And now they are getting huge royalties from Intel.

MJ: You can spend time with the management of small cap companies, too. So what really sets apart mid-cap stocks for you?

TZ: We would have to have so many more stocks in the portfolio if we did small caps. Also in mid-cap you still have liquidity, and in small caps you don't. We have to be cautious with liquidity, given our size. In addition, the management of mid-cap companies is already more experienced.

Some of our mid-cap stocks are on their way to becoming large caps. They are still growing, and are still less mature than large caps. But they already made it through the hurdles of being a small cap company.

MJ: How many positions do you have in the portfolio at any given time?

TZ: We have about 50. We tend to know them really well. Also some of the stocks in the portfolio we've had for ten years.

Long-Term Investing

MJ: You have stocks right now that you've had for ten years?

TZ: They may be very small positions, and some we've owned twice because we sold them due to changing valuations and bought them back, but yes. For example, FMC we bought in 2001 before they split. FTI was part of FMC. The companies split in 2001. We bought it right before the split, and it went from $19 per share to $13 per share, a big drop. We went to see them, and we were really impressed with management. Now that the companies had separated, they were focused only on their business. I remember thinking to myself, "This is the company I should have, rather than the FMC chemical part."

FTI is involved in subsea technology. At the bottom of the sea they can centrifugally separate the water and the sand out, and just get the oil up. Nobody else could do that for the longest time. That gave them a huge advantage. Then they got a big contract.

We bought more at $13 per share. We knew the management really well. Normally, when something like this happens and the valuation becomes super attractive, we know the company well enough that we know we can add to our position. Knowing the company, that they have a good balance sheet, that debt-to-capital ratio is not bad, we knew they could make it through a slow period. They have a very important technology. We knew they would come out of the decline, and we added to the position.

Generally, with a volatile stock like this, we add on dips, and when the stock runs up a lot we trim it. We use the volatility in our favor because we can hold a stock for a long time. There may be a short-term disappointment, but if the fundamental business is good, we would buy more. We've had FTI at some level in the portfolio since we first purchased the stock in 2001.

MJ: So is what's going on with the company more important to you than what's going on with the markets?

TZ: Oh, definitely.

MJ: Do you pay any attention to what's going on in the market? Do market cycles change the way that you manage the portfolio?

TZ: No, not really. Now earning season is coming up, so I was thinking there would be some opportunities. I wanted just a little more cash if there are opportunities, so I can take advantage of them. Today the market is up, and we're trading a few stocks. But that's it.

MJ: You have a relatively large universe of stocks that you can invest in, correct?

TZ: It's definitely over 1,000. Maybe 1,300 or 1,400. We compare ourselves to the Russell mid-cap and the S&P 400 mid-cap, and our average market cap is usually between the two. There are a lot of stocks that we can select from. However, in the 15 years we've been running the fund, we have only owned about 160 stocks.

MJ: Total?

TZ: We don't need too many stocks, and we don't need a lot of new ones. Last year we were up over 40 percent, and many stocks needed to be sold based on valuation. They were replaced by cheaper stocks to keep the portfolio attractively valued. In some cases, we had owned the "new" stocks previously.

MJ: And you try to meet with the management team or the CEO for everything that you invest in?

TZ: Before we buy anything we usually have at least a conference call with the company and before we buy a significant position, we usually meet them. Now because we are fairly big, they also want to meet us. So after we have built a new position, they show up here.

MJ: So you've invested in 160 companies, out of 1,500 or so. And not every company makes the cut. You must meet with a lot companies each year.

TZ: Yes, and we also meet with competing firms. Sometimes we find that the competition is even more attractive. Like BorgWarner, for example, we have owned since 2002. I used to have Magna International, a Canadian competitor. Then I ran into a friend, and he said, "Oh, I have a visit with BorgWarner. Do you want to join me?" I said, "Yeah, sure." I was so impressed with BorgWarner. I thought, "Well, this is better than Magna, because they were still small and more focused." So over time I reduced the Magna position and bought BorgWarner.

MJ: That's pretty cold. You don't get attached to companies after spending so much time with them?

TZ: I don't think that happens to me. You have to be convinced that it fits your investment criteria, and there's always the valuation that guides us. One stock we own now, Edwards Lifesciences, they make heart valves, tissue heart valves. We bought them fairly soon after they spun out from Baxter and owned them for a long time, like ten years or so. And then they were high priced based on any valuation ratios we looked at. So we sold it. Then last year, the stock came back on our radar, and because it had come down quite a bit and appeared attractive again, we bought it back.

One thing I looked at before we bought them last fall was the relative price-to-earnings ratio (P/E). On a chart you can see the relative P/E ratio was stable for a long time. Then it jumped up a lot in 2012 when we exited the stock. Then, it started to come down. The relative P/E went from 3.3 to 2.9 to 1.7. Last fall it was at 1.2, which was relatively cheap compared to what it had been. We bought it back, and we have done quite well since that time.

MJ: So is it always P/E and valuation making the decision? What else drives your "buy" decisions?

TZ: In many cases, it's the theme of "must-have" products. Companies that make products that you can't easily replace. Over 50 percent of the stocks in our fund are probably in the "must-have" products category. Certainly Edward Lifesciences is one of those, and we were able to get it at a good relative P/E. We also have some industrial stocks like BorgWarner. Clients of that company need their products in order to give longer warranties, in order to keep their market share, and in order to make automobiles more efficient. There are many advantages to these products. And of course it goes without saying the companies also need to have good balance sheets.

The stock has to meet our investment criteria: Is the balance sheet okay? Yes. Is it mid-cap? Yes. Is the valuation attractive relative to its own five-year history or relative to its competitors? That's when we buy.

Now we have bought a brand new stock. I can't mention the name, but there's no data history available right now, but we know on a price-to-revenue it's very undervalued, relative to similar companies, even to a similar company that was going to buy it. We know the CEO quite well. We know what the CEO has done before. Based on the price-to-revenue being low, knowing the CEO, and knowing the business, we bought it.

MJ: And that would start out as a small position in the portfolio?

TZ: About 1.5 percent.

MJ: So how did you get the idea to buy this stock? Was it because you knew the product, the CEO, or the market?

TZ: Everybody knows the product, and we know the CEO well, and we know the industry. We had a competitor in the office recently.

MJ: A competitor of the company?

TZ: Yes, a competitor of the company that had been on our watch list, so a combination of all of those factors made us look at it, really.

Ignoring the Herd

MJ: There's obviously a lot of recycling in your portfolio. What else inspires you to look at a company?

TZ: We read the papers a lot. Reading that there's a new spin-out—we have been very successful with spin-outs. Edward Lifesciences is a spin-out. We've owned Boston Scientific twice: First, when they spun out. We made a lot of money the first time. The second time it took a little longer, but last year the stock was up over 110 percent. We don't own it anymore. That was both a recycle and a spin-out.

FMC and FTI was a split of one company. We had Monsanto a year after they spun out, and it was in the early 2000s. At the time, the company was...

MJ: ...not universally hated, I'm assuming.

TZ: It was hated quite a bit. When I had it, it was 19 going on 15 or lower. They had an investor day in St Louis. Only four or five people showed up for the whole day. The analyst who organized the trip even showed up late. After the meeting, he put an "underperform" on the stock. But I was really impressed with Monsanto. I saw what they could do in terms of research. They can take a trait from a plant that can grow in the desert and mix it with a plant like wheat or corn, so you need less irrigation. This is really important because water can be a scare resource, and of course there's a shortage now in California. They probably wish they had more plants with drought-resistant traits and geared toward desert climates.

Anyway, I was fascinated with Monsanto's capabilities, and I liked the acting CEO, Scott Smith. The stock went from $19 to $15. And then it went to $25. And then *Barron's* ran an article about Monsanto with Frankenstein on the cover. A client called me and said, "You'd better be right on that stock." It was a really negative article. Then the stock went to $35.

Some people thought it was too late to invest. But at $35, the recommendations came out from Wall Street. Nobody was there when the stock was $15 or $19. When it went to $60 or something, we sold it.

MJ: You went against what everyone else was saying. Do you think that makes you a contrarian?

TZ: I have to say yes.

MJ: Are there other stocks where you have gone against popular opinion?

TZ: The craziest recent one was less than a year ago. It was an extreme case of contrarianism. Here is my picture book [pulls out a bound book of stock charts and financial data]. Alcoa was kicked out of the Dow. I didn't know it was a mid-cap name. I looked at the chart, and it was about $9 billion or something, $9, $10, $11 billion, in that range.

MJ: Your cutoff for mid-caps is around $12 billion, correct?

TZ: It could be $12 billion or $13 billion. I haven't bought anything that was bigger than $13 billion. In one of our accounts, if a company goes to $15 billion we have to reduce the position, which usually is a good time anyway.

MJ: But Alcoa was at $9 billion?

TZ: Around that. I looked at the price-to-sales ratio at the time, and I would say it was probably .3 or .4. I knew the five-year range was .3 to .9. Revenues were $22 billion. The difference between those was impressive. On a price-to-sales basis, the stock was pretty attractive. It was also funny because Tony, our trader, he didn't want to buy it. I mean, he has to do what I say, but he said, "That stock always goes down!" It was a few days before the earnings came out, and he said, "They report earnings and then the stock goes down initially, and then it goes down in the aftermarket trading, and then it goes down the next day." That had been the pattern for several quarters.

I said, "Tony, at the end of the day, I want the stock to be 1 percent of the fund." It was very liquid, because people were dumping it because it was thrown out of the Dow. They all had to exit it, so it had very good liquidity. We bought it at under $8, and it's over $16 now.

MJ: That's pretty contrary.

TZ: I had also just seen an interview with the CEO on the Charlie Rose show. At that time I was impressed with the interview in general. I thought it was interesting what the company does. But, at that time when I saw the interview, I didn't realize Alcoa was a mid-cap stock

MJ: Normally you don't think of Dow stocks as being mid-cap stocks.

TZ: Right! The investment idea initially came to me because I punched in a wrong symbol. I was looking for something else, and when I saw the chart I was, like, "Wow! Look at that!" I was almost afraid to tell people how I came to the idea. But the investment was also a sign of my experience. Somebody else might have just ignored it and put in the correct symbol. Instead, I was excited. I said, "Oh wow, what's happening here?" Then I did the research, and the stock met our investment criteria.

I went on the website. The first thing you think is that Alcoa is a commodity company. They make aluminum. Then you find out on the website that 60 percent of what they do is value-add. They are selling special titanium aluminum to airplane companies like Boeing and Airbus. The space program uses a lot of their product. About a month later, the Ford-150 truck starts using the aluminum to make trucks lighter. Then because Ford does it, GM wants to use aluminum. It's sort of feeding on itself. From all negative articles, all of a sudden there are all these positive articles. Now, with the stock up 100 percent, most people like the stock, and The Street is recommending it.

MJ: Is it hard to be a contrarian? As a mutual fund, you have to disclose a lot more information than, say, a hedge fund. Do you ever get pushback from your investors?

TZ: Oh, you wouldn't believe the pushback. I get these hostile phone calls. Another stock we had was Cooper Tire. I was on a panel at Columbia Business School in New York, and I had to pick one stock to recommend as a top performer. It was in March 2014. Before we started working on it late last year, I didn't know much about Cooper Tire at all. I saw that another company tried to buy them and pay $35 a share for the company. Then it didn't happen for various reasons. It didn't happen because the Chinese joint venture partner didn't want to be bought by an Indian tire company. It was a huge mess. I said, "Well, this was a learning experience for management." They had to go through all this. It was even difficult to do a conference call with them because the companies were suing each other. They didn't want to really talk to us, but we did have a call at some point and we spent time with the CEO and were quite impressed with him.

For me, it was almost a no-brainer, because when something like a merger is proposed, people jump on the bandwagon. People think it might go higher during the merger so they buy, but when it doesn't happen, they dump and dump and dump. At the end of 2013, it was $22 or $23. I think when I recommended it in March, the stock was still below $25.

Then I got hostile phone calls from some people that had a short position in the stock. They were mad at me that I recommended it. They laid out a totally negative picture of the company. Afterwards, I said, "Oh, my God, what if they are right?" I questioned myself. I wondered if maybe I made a dumb mistake.

MJ: Did you sell the stock when you got those calls?

TZ: No. Now we have touched $30.

Dealing with Volatility

MJ: But things haven't always worked out like that. I know the fund lost over 40 percent in 2008. Did you still hold your positions or did you sell?

TZ: We didn't sell and we didn't have big withdrawals. We selectively added to some positions where we had confidence. I remember one stock I actually bought more of on March 9, 2009. I know because my son got married, and I was in Chile. He got married on a Saturday, and that Monday was the bottom of the market. I was there with my little tiny computer, and I wanted Tony Smith, our trader, to see that I was watching everything. Electronically I put in a buy order and bought 5,000 shares, just so he could see that I see what's going on in the office.

The stock I bought was Belo, and Gannett acquired Belo last year. We didn't know that they were going to be bought at the time, but we did know the CEO of Belo. We also knew they were always the best in their market for nightly news, which is very important.

We bought Belo for, like, 60 cents on March 9, 2009. When Gannett bought Belo, they paid $14. Actually, we got more than $14 per share.

MJ: So if you weren't selling, the 2008 losses were mostly because your companies got dragged down with the rest of the market?

TZ: Oh, yeah. We actually outperformed at the beginning of 2008. The first eight to nine months, we did outperform because we didn't have anything housing related and we didn't have a lot of financial stocks. But on the next stage of the crisis, a lot of the hedge funds had to sell whatever they had to deleverage and get liquidity. There was so much selling pressure.

MJ: Did you get any pressure from investors to sell at that point? Were there ever any moments where you were like, "Oh, my God, I've got to do something"?

TZ: I remember I was on my bicycle going through Lincoln Park on a stormy evening, and I thought the market is like being on a sailboat. Big rolling waves. I just have to get to the other side, going through this market thing. We just have to get back to land.

I met with one client in October 2008. It was a really difficult meeting. It was a foundation. The people who were in the finance committee did not hire me, and there were some new members and they thought I was doing everything wrong. They thought I should buy large-cap companies that were safer.

MJ: Participate in the flight to quality?

TZ: Yes. I should buy Microsoft or something. Luckily, I wasn't fired.

MJ: Well, they do have the old adage: "No one gets fired for buying IBM." There's never been a temptation to move to investments that are "safer"?

TZ: We always try to buy a safe stock where we have conviction. Even with Belo, we thought that they had good TV stations, good management. They will make it through. We just stuck with what we knew, and the portfolio bounced back.

MJ: It sounds like conviction is one of the most important aspects of your strategy.

TZ: You trust your convictions, but you also double-check everything.

MJ: Ronald Reagan: Trust, but verify?

TZ: Yes. And the biggest positions are 4 percent of the portfolio. We don't want to go too high. We don't want too much risk in one particular company.

Managing Risks and Finding Opportunities

MJ: Is position size one of the primary ways that you manage risk in the portfolio? What about things like stop-losses?

TZ: We watch position size pretty closely. When I worked for Sears, there was this 15 percent loss control system implemented. Imagine that! You would have nothing left in the fund in 2008 or 2009 with a 15 percent loss control. So, academically, it never made sense. But it was a good experience for me because I became quite paranoid. You try to get stocks at the bottom and minimize the downside.

MJ: What about sector allocations?

TZ: In term of sectors, we tend to be overinvested in technology because we find a lot of ideas in that segment. Much of it is mundane tech, though. If it's high tech, we really need to understand what they do.

MJ: Are there sectors you're not keen on? You already mentioned financial stocks are not a big play for you.

TZ: Right now, we don't have anything in utilities because it doesn't meet our criteria. But at some point I could imagine that when interest rates go up and the stocks come down, maybe we find something then.

We are reasonably diversified, but we tend to underweight financials. We want to understand what we own. And I think we learned in 2008 that a lot of the banks didn't even know what they owned. The CFOs at the banks didn't truly understand the leverage and the products they were selling.

We do invest in different kinds of financial services companies. We had H&R Block and we had McGraw-Hill. For some time, McGraw was actually a financial stock after they got out of the book business. We bought it in late in 2009. Because of the headlines, we were able to get it at $27 a share. We did quite a bit of talking with the company and a lot of research. We thought the company had enough cash to deal with all the lawsuits, so we bought it. But it was not technically classified as financial. The symbol changed from MHP to MHFI, I think. We were so successful with that investment that, in the end, we sold it based on valuation. We probably sold it maybe a year ago, but we owned it for a long time. Now, it's over $22 billion.

We also have the Northern Trust right now. We bought that quite a few years ago. Probably late in 2011 the stock was low as it had been in 2008–2009. So, again, we got a great opportunity there, and we still have it.

MJ: So, I guess, the fact that you don't overweight in financials, it's mostly an opportunistic play. You'll invest in them when you see there's a good opportunity.

TZ: We will take an opportunity if we see it.

MJ: You are really making a research play, betting that you know something the market has not priced in yet. There have been some people that have said the market has become so efficient that there aren't really informational advantages anymore. Do you agree or disagree?

TZ: I don't think it is. I don't believe it.

MJ: And what about the fact that there's so much more access to information now? How can someone still get an advantage?

TZ: There's access to a lot of information, even more than I need. But I think what's ignored is common sense. When everybody was selling Alcoa, it was incredible. Looking at the website and what they were doing was intriguing. The company was really well positioned. So, how can you say the market was so efficient when there was all this tremendous selling pressure and the stock went under $8 then, and today it is $16.50 per share?

MJ: Do you think investors have lost their ability to tell the difference between a bad company, a bad market, and a bad situation?

TZ: People get emotional sometimes when stocks go down. Maybe it's a window-dressing problem. Like Alcoa, it got kicked out of the Dow. So, suddenly all the ETFs [Exchange Traded Funds] that copy the Dow can't own the stock. And then, hedge funds, maybe they're worried about what happens in the next week or the next two weeks or maybe they have to cover their positions, protect themselves. And the stock goes down. When we buy a stock, we ask ourselves, "Where could it be a year from now? And is it at the lower end price-to-revenue range, and does it have a pretty smart CEO?"

Maybe when you look second by second the market is efficient, but what happens between today and tomorrow? Or next year? I don't believe it.

MJ: So, there are still bargains out there as far as you're concerned?

TZ: There are always bargains. Especially when companies report earnings. Some blow up because they are two pennies short on estimates or because they lower the outlook. People that were already nervous about owning the stock, they cannot face meeting a client one more time with an underperforming stock. So they exit the position. And they take a loss. But that's not my situation. I can see the same situations as opportunities.

At the end of the day, if you do what everybody else does, you can't make any money. You don't outperform if you do the same thing as everybody else.

You need some imagination to look at a stock. Two or three years from now, if management cannot fix the problem, could another management team fix the problem? Maybe they have a production problem? Maybe they should lower their price? How can they restructure the business to make it more productive, or would it be a good business for another company to buy? We have to check that out and think about it. In every case, it's a different situation.

Managing Emotions

MJ: Have there been stocks that stood out in your mind that just didn't work particularly well?

TZ: Oh, yes. There are always stocks that don't work, and sometimes it's tedious. And sometimes, you think they should work and they still don't, or they take much longer than you think they should. And I think it was in 2010, we had Boston Scientific. It was my best stock maybe in 2002–2003, and then my colleague said, "You should look at it again." And I said, "Oh, my God, what happened?" It had been a large-cap stock and became a mid-cap stock again. So, we bought it at $5 or $5.50, and it went to $7. But then it went down again. It was down for some time. Last year, it was up 110 percent, and it was probably one of our best stocks last year. But it was frustrating.

MJ: But, you kept it even though it wasn't performing well.

TZ: We even added to it.

MJ: Strong conviction.

TZ: We had the same frustration way back when with Yahoo! Yahoo! was my first research trip after 9/11. I could see that Yahoo! did something very impressive. I bought it in 2001. A colleague I worked with at the time said it could go to $5 per share. And I said, "Yeah, you're right, it could go to $5. Anything can happen." After 9/11, you think, yeah, that thing can happen. But I bought it at $10 or $11. It went to $20 or $22 a year later, and then it went back down to $10. A very frustrating round trip. I bought more at $10. But later, it went up and up and I sold it.

MJ: I guess sticking to your guns, even when things aren't going exactly like you want is a very important part of your strategy.

TZ: It could be called perseverance. It could be called patience. My husband called it something different. But it sort of means the same thing.

MJ: In a way, isn't patience what many investors lack now?

TZ: We do quarterly phone calls with investors, and I have to talk about the fund. Some people ask, "Why does she still own this?" Yeah, I still own it. Sometimes it would be easier to get rid of a stock and find a new one. Often, when we get rid of a stock, the company gets taken over or something positive happens. So, that is frustrating also—when you exit something because you can't take it anymore and then it gets better.

We constantly double-check and recheck the valuation. Is it getting better or worse? Is it more undervalued when we first started? And would I buy it today... If I didn't own it, would I buy it today? So, take that negative stuff in the back of your head away and instead ask: would I buy it today?

A couple of years ago we owned Lexmark. They had a disappointment on earnings, and the stock went down to $16. We had a lot of arguments about it and frustration here. I said, "It's a new stock today because the price is different." If we didn't own it, it would be attractive today at this price. In the end, we bought more. Today it's over $47.

So, when you have a stock go from $25 or $35 at the beginning of 2012, all the way down to $16, that's very frustrating. Really annoying.

But hindsight is perfect. Yeah, we should have sold every share that we had, but that's hindsight. But these are the mistakes that we made. We make a lot of mistakes. But with all the mistakes that we made, over 15 years, we look pretty smart. I think it's how you manage your mistakes and how your winners balance out with your losers.

MJ: Has your approach to managing the fund changed in the last 15 years, either due to the way the market behaves or due to changes in the fund strategy?

TZ: We are still fairly concentrated. We have about 50 stocks, but we have had to hire more people to watch everything.

For quite a while we had 35 to 40 stocks, then 40 to 45 and now, we're sort of around 50-ish. And we take our time exiting and entering a new stock.

MJ: There hasn't been a major market correction in more than 30 months. Are you at all concerned about the markets at this point?

TZ: I got concerned after the first quarter of 2013. During that quarter we were up 14 percent. I said, "Oh, my God, this is what usually happens in the whole year." The full year, we were up 44 percent. Through June 2014 we're up 9 percent to 10 percent, now what? We need to keep the valuation attractive. We're very focused on keeping valuations below the Russell Mid Cap and the S&P 400 Mid Cap. And so, our P/E for 2015 is quite a bit lower than the benchmark.

MJ: As a successful long-time investor, what is the best piece of advice you can give to other investors?

TZ: I think you have to research thoroughly and work yourself into a company. Understand it. Be curious. Ask a lot of questions. Double-check yourself and ask what could go wrong. Don't get carried away. Use the valuation. And then double-check the valuation. Is there any reason that the next three years or four years will be substantially different from the last four, five, or six years in this business. Do a lot of thinking. You have to just constantly think about every scenario. It's like a puzzle.

MJ: So, you have to kind of try to figure out where things are going and not just look at the past?

TZ: Absolutely. Now, we have the situation of drought, and water is becoming an endangered resource. How will it impact some of our investments that we have today? Or the situation with Ukraine and Russia. There will be different companies that would be impacted by that. How significant will it be?

CHAPTER 4

Getting Extra from Ordinary: Investing Long and Short in Micro- and Small Caps

Fran Tuite, Portfolio Manager, RMB Capital Management LLC

B ill Moyers once said, "Creativity is piercing the mundane to find the marvelous."[1] And yet, when most people think about investing, they gravitate almost immediately to the extraordinary. Missing the next big thing—an Apple or Google or Microsoft— feels like a fate worse than death. Investing in mundane businesses is not only not sexy, it's not as profitable, right?

Wrong. Over the last 13 years, Fran Tuite has made a tidy sum investing long and short in companies that clean uniforms, manufacture drinking glasses, and manage waste. Of course, she had Apple in her portfolio at one time, but you won't find Uber or Airbnb in her investments. Tuite's focus is on mundane companies with annuity businesses and ordinary firms going through extraordinary circumstances, such as a spin-off, buyout, or turnaround. And since the 2000 inception of her strategy through May 2014, her investments have produced a compound annual return of 9.56, outperforming both the HFRI Equity Hedge Fund Index (5.40 percent) and the Russell 3000 (4.47 percent).

Growing up as one of six children to botanist parents, perhaps Tuite learned early on to examine how the everyday world influences us. Her family largely expected her to follow in their life sciences footsteps at Purdue and the University of Cincinnati, but a career aptitude test revealed a talent for finance, which changed her career path. An unfortunate three-martini job interview could have ended her investment career before it began, but a long love affair with sports (specifically rowing) had taught Tuite perseverance. She found a mentor in the investment industry, and the rest has become a 20+ year investment history.

In fact, Tuite attributes much of her success in investing to her athletic background. The day Fran and I sat down for this interview, she was fighting a case of jet lag, having just returned from London the night before. There, she raced in the annual Henley-on-Thames rowing competition, bringing home a gold and silver medal. In a sport in which the average female competitor nears 6' tall, you would not expect Tuite, at 5'4", to be successful. "The coaches usually want tall people and big, strong people," Tuite says, "But I'm a lightweight." All the same, she has successfully competed nationally and internationally since 1976.

Her first foray into finance was at Proctor & Gamble, but she quickly determined that corporate finance was not a great fit. Hired by the college professor who nurtured her interest in investing, she entered the investment world at Johnson Investment Counsel. A brief stint on the sell side at William Blair sent her quickly back into the arms of the buy side, and she joined Harris Associates to work on its sole hedge fund offering. Tuite later followed her Harris mentor to Sirius Partners, before taking the reins of her own fund at Talon Asset Management.

Throughout her investing career, the core values that Tuite obtained from sports—consistency, patience, and discipline—have been very much in evidence, both in her portfolio management, and in the companies in which she invests. With a concentration in small- and micro-cap companies, some with a market cap as small as $40 million, management teams become incredibly important. With a highly concentrated, 18- to 20-position portfolio, Tuite really gets to know her companies and their management teams and considers them her partners. If they need help expanding or changing their board, she provides it. And if they don't exhibit her core values, she moves on.

Tuite has built her strong track record from a combination of singles, doubles, triples, and home run investments. Her strategy has generated profits in every year but 2008, when a net long portfolio and the large-cap "flight to quality" caused a –26.65 percent decline.

She tends to invest in companies with strong cash flows (annuities) and smart management teams. Libbey Glass is a great example. There, a constant flow of new glassware orders from butter-fingered restaurateurs is the key to consistent cash flow. However, Tuite's favorite investments, the ones she considers her "home runs," tend to exhibit the same three characteristics:

- the potential for improved operating leverage, either through improved revenues or restructuring and cost cutting;
- an out-of-whack capital structure that the company can deleverage to accelerate earnings through debt pay down; and
- companies with an opportunity for the multiple to expand.

Martinis and Cigars

MJ: Tell me how you got interested in finance.

FT: I always wanted to be a doctor or veterinarian. Finance was not a profession I knew anything about growing up. It was only when I got into college and realized that I wasn't going to be a doctor that I tried to figure out what I should do. I took an aptitude test actually. It said you're really good with finance and accounting and numbers. I changed my major to finance and accounting, and ended up with a professor who inspired me. I just fell in love with investments in my senior year. I devoured every book I could read about investments. I had my eyes opened. This is what I wanted to do—be in investments.

From there I tried to get a job in investments, which was really hard. I had one offer from a bank trust department from two guys who took me out to lunch and were drinking hard alcohol at lunch.

MJ: The proverbial "three-martini lunch?"

FT: Yes. So I said, "Oh, this just isn't me, I am an athlete." I ended up going to Procter & Gamble and getting a position in their finance training program.

I did not enjoy working for Procter. It was very corporate. No pants for women, stockings, the whole thing. It was a big bureaucracy. And finance is not the guts of Procter. The company is all about marketing and branding.

So I went back and got an MBA, a CPA, and the CFA designation, all at the same time. I went back to my UC professor and he hired me after I got my MBA. He was running an investment business on the side while teaching, and he offered me a position as an analyst for his firm, which consisted of three people at the time.

I ended up being with that firm for eight years, and eventually became Director of Research. It was very different from what I do now. It was more top down. Like, "We're going to have so much allocation to health care, so let's find the good stocks that are a little bit cheap, pick a couple of them and have one name in this industry."

But it was a great beginning. My professor was a great guy and had a great business, which is still very successful. Eventually, I got recruited by a head hunter to work for Harris Associates for one of the founding partners who had a hedge fund. I didn't know anything about hedge funds. I walked into working for this very eccentric man who smoked cigars in his office every afternoon and I'd have to go in and...

MJ: Sit in the fumes?

FT: Sit in the fumes. He was a self-made man. He never graduated from college, but he was super smart. He always had this chip on his shoulder because he didn't have a degree. He always tried to hire smart, educated people to work for him. That was my real foray into the long/short hedge fund business, in 1990.

MJ: That may be the first time I've ever heard that a career aptitude test actually worked for someone and said they should be anything other than a policeman or garbage man.

FT: It actually worked. I still remember the day I took that test and what it said, and how true it was.

MJ: Did you know other women in finance at that point, role models if you will?

FT: I didn't know at that point that investing was so male dominated; I had no idea. I was raised that there's no difference in what a woman could do. I never even thought twice about it when I got into it. It was only later, going out to conferences where I was interacting more, that I realized that there are no women here. These conferences, you'd be lucky if there are one or two women out of a thousand people there.

MJ: The last conference I went to, I was wearing an orange dress in a sea of dark suits. It looked like that movie *Pleasantville*. So that's still true, even today.

FT: I go to conferences all the time and there are more women, but I always try to do the percentages just for fun.

MJ: It sounds like you had very strong mentoring relationships in sports and in finance. How important do you think mentors were to getting where you are now?

FT: I think they're really important. I wasn't looking for mentors, but I found them or they found me. You never know how exactly how that works. I think the real importance of a mentor is really just allowing you to believe in yourself. Not necessarily teaching you anything specifically, but teaching you that you're good enough, smart enough, that you have value and that you can do whatever you want to do. If you don't have self-confidence, you don't go anywhere.

One of my best mentors was Peter Foreman, one of the founders of Harris Associates. He had this hedge fund that he started in the '70s. It was small. He hadn't done much with it. He decided he was fed up with the partners at Harris and he was going to leave. I, and a couple of others, went with him when he founded Sirius Partners.

Peter was probably the strongest investment mentor of my career. He instilled in me this whole idea of concentration. Know your companies. Differentiate yourself with the management teams. He taught me a lot about asking questions about capital allocation. He taught me a lot and believed in me. Peter gave me part of the fund to run so I could establish a track record. He believed in working you really hard, but overpaying you.

MJ: Better than the alternative.

FT: Definitely. I feel really lucky and really blessed that I had that opportunity to work for someone who believed in me and gave me such an opportunity to make a living. The kind of compensation that one earns in this business can be significant compared with some of the other professions that are out there.

A Sporting Chance

MJ: So mentoring is critical. And I know sports continue to be a major theme in your life.

FT: I think sports are really important. I've been incredibly successful as a rower, even though I'm small, because I'm very consistent. When I look to hire people, I always look at their sports background as well. For me, it really developed the core values that I practice every day. I never miss a workout. I work hard and follow a plan, have goals in mind, and work from here to there. I have this competitive spirit about winning and achieving goals that I think is very helpful in the business world.

MJ: Does it make any difference to you whether someone plays team sports or individual sports? Or are you just, like, "sports is sports?"

FT: I think sports is sports.

MJ: For the companies that you analyze, do you ever find out whether your CEOs have a sports background? Do you use that as a filter?

FT: For me, when I invest in a company, I see it as partnering with that management team. Getting to know them is really important in my process. It's one of the three core steps to my investment process. There's the business assessment, valuation piece, and then the management assessment.

Most of the companies I invest in are smaller, so I spend a lot of time trying to develop some kind of relationship or rapport with them, understand what motivates them, how they see risk. Do they ski black diamonds or do they go down the bunny slope? Are they golfers? What's their golf score?

Staying "Active"

MJ: If you treat every company as a partnership rather than an investment, how much of a role do you take in company structure or day-to-day operations?

FT: I always spend a lot of time analyzing a company's board before I invest to see how it's structured. Are there gaps? Are there holes? Do they have the right skill set? Is it big enough? It's an important part of our investment process to examine that, and then we'll always have conversations around it. I'll always find out what they're thinking in terms of, are they looking to add? What do they want to add? What do they need and then do I know someone that could fit that?

I've not always had female directors that I could recommend, but when I do, I definitely try to help add diversity.

My approach is one of not going in with guns blazing. If I feel like there needs to be some change, I try to work with management teams or boards. I really think that I may have the big picture, but my skill is not running a business. To presume that I could tell this company they should do this, that, or the other, I think is really inappropriate for the most part.

MJ: Maybe you're more of a "facilitating investor" as opposed to a traditional "activist investor?"

FT: I don't know what the right label is. If I see a hole, I try to find out if management thinks there's a hole, too. If they agree that there's some hole, then I see if I can help in some way in filling that hole. I tend to sell stocks if I don't believe they have the right team in place and I don't think they're going to go in the right direction, as opposed to trying to force a change where we disagree on what needs to happen.

MJ: You mentioned that where you can try to get a woman into a board situation that you will, if you have an appropriate candidate. There's quite a bit of research these days that talks about how companies that have more diverse boards perform better. Is what you're doing more of a push for diversity or is it a push because you see a discernible difference in the performance of companies with diverse boards?

FT: I find that it's very important to have diversity because it's really healthy to have different viewpoints. You don't want all lawyers. You don't want all financial people. You don't want just operations. You definitely need diversity in a board. I'm a big proponent, if they don't have it, of trying to encourage them to go in that direction. Or investing with companies that already have some diversity.

MJ: If you see a company with a completely homogenous board, is that a red flag for you?

FT: It definitely is a factor in looking at it. I have invested where the board is not perfect, but I feel like they're going to move it in a better direction. The board area is a really important area of focus for us. I've gotten more active in the recent years. My network is expanding now so I know more women who might be potential board directors. I don't have a big list, but I have a few.

MJ: Do you think the reason there isn't more board diversity is a supply issue?

FT: I do think there is a supply issue, but also having women at the table to start with. I saw Carly Fiorina speak at a BNP Women's Leadership event. One of the things that she did, when they were hiring, was to make sure there was a woman in the mix. They don't have to hire a woman, but they always had to interview a woman or diverse person when they were trying to fill a position.

If you have guidelines like that, it forces you to work a little bit harder to add that woman to the board. Maybe you don't have to hire them, but at least if you include them, that improves the process.

MJ: Do you think the situation has improved in the 20+ years that you've been investing?

FT: I think it has improved, but it's still pretty dismal.

MJ: If anything, all of the Facebook, Silicon Valley, and Google diversity stats show that as well. So, for the majority of the companies we've been talking about, they are small- and micro-caps, correct?

FT: I like that area. I can invest in any capitalization in the fund. It's an all-cap strategy, but I've tended to really focus on small- and micro-caps because I think they are more inefficiently priced. I think there's just more opportunity. I have invested in large caps over the years, and right now we have one large cap in the portfolio. We have one mid-cap. The rest are all small or micro. The smallest company has a $40 million market cap. For small caps it can go up to one to two billion. Our sweet spot, though, has run between $500 million and $600 million. You have a little more liquidity there and more substantial companies. However, we focus on companies with market caps between $50 million and $2 billion. We did have Johnson & Johnson and McDonald's and Apple at one period in our history, but...

MJ: I think everybody has owned Apple at one period of their history.

FT: Probably. But we owned that one at $11, if you can believe it. Even though I'm not called a small-cap fund, that's my strength and that's where I've earned most of my returns.

The Lure of Tiny Companies

MJ: In terms of why you invest in small caps and micro-caps, you mentioned the inefficiency and the opportunities there. Obviously, liquidity can be a significant issue, and so can flights to quality. How do you balance that with the opportunities that are there?

FT: Our time horizon is three to five years in any of our positions. We have a couple of names that would take a while to get out of, but there's an art to portfolio construction that helps with that. Flows, in terms of some of the high-frequency trading and ETFs, really can wreak havoc. There's so much money today that's not fundamentally driven. It can create really big volatility in illiquid names.

We learned to live with high volatility in a sense and take advantage of it. We try to buy on weakness and sell on strength. There are so many small-cap names that no longer have research coverage. A lot of the big banks have just moved completely out of these names. Some of the small regional brokers have picked up a little bit of slack, but the quality of a lot of their research isn't as good. They may just be writing kind of a press piece, copying from an investor book. But that creates so much opportunity for us.

MJ: There are roughly 30,000 companies in the small and micro space. How do you cut through that much noise to get to a portfolio that's roughly 18 to 20 positions?

FT: One, we only need 20 names, and so we don't have to go through necessarily every single one of them. There are four of us on the team, and everybody uses a different process in terms of generating ideas.

A lot of what we're looking for are companies that may be in a transition. That's what creates the undervaluation. And those companies don't screen well. Screens are just not always the best idea. I like the "New Low" and the "New High" lists for generating longs and shorts. They help us find things that are out of favor or in La-La land.

I read everything. I have my watch list of companies I follow and want to own, and just need the right price. I go to a lot of conferences. I look at spin-outs. I look at companies coming out of bankruptcy. There are a lot of different ways that I generate ideas.

MJ: Are there any positions that stand in your mind because of the unique source of the investment idea?

FT: There was one name that we owned in a portfolio when I was at Talon. One of the partners that founded the firm knew a guy from St. Louis that was on a board of a company. He said, "Well, you should talk to him because he's on the board and maybe you'll get some information." He was not the best example of a leader.

So I met with Oglebay Norton because we had the connection to a board member. The board member came in and he talked about growth, growth, growth. When I asked about return on capital and cash flow, he really couldn't answer any of my questions. It was clear those were not areas of focus. I didn't buy that stock, and it ultimately went into bankruptcy. When it came out of bankruptcy, the company had a new management team. I ended up investing in it then because I had liked the business originally, just not the management team that was in place at the time.

Our investment in the company ended up being very profitable. The company was bought out by Carmeuse at 16 times cash flow. We thought it was worth 13 or 12 times cash flow, so we got way more for it than we expected.

MJ: Did you have any desire to short it the first time around?

FT: I should have but I didn't. When I started the fund, it invested both long and short, but I was still getting my feet wet on the short side

But that's the type of investment where I've had my most success—in an investment where you have a company that has a potential for improved operating leverage. The margins can improve from either revenues going up or restructuring and they're cutting SG&A's [selling, general, and administrative costs], so they're able to expand their margins. Second, they also have a capital structure that is maybe out of whack. They can deleverage and then can accelerate earnings through the debt paydown. Third, there should be an opportunity for the multiple to expand. It's a triple play when you can get those three things. The multiplier effect of those three factors is huge. Instead of making 10 or 20 percent, you can make 100 percent or 300 percent or 400 percent.

MJ: Those are certainly the home-run positions. How many of those do you find, and would you say that the rest of them are singles, doubles, or triples?

FT: We always want all the home runs, but we can't find them all. Usually, when we put the portfolio together we do have a mix of singles, doubles, and these home-run opportunities.

MJ: And the fundamentals you just mentioned are very important, if not everything?

FT: Absolutely. For example, finance is an area we don't invest in just because it's very hard to analyze the fundamentals of a finance company. Even though I'm a CPA, they have a lot of reserve adjustments in finance or things that are hard to really measure. They're highly tethered to an interest rate cycle, and we don't think our skill is in forecasting interest rates.

Own What You Know

MJ: Which would be a macro forecast.

FT: We stay away from macro bets. We try to find just one-off names that are going to survive in any kind of market cycle.

Right now, we have a fertilizer company that's in the portfolio. One could say that's something of a commodity, in terms of fertilizer prices, but it's a unique asset that has a limited capacity. We like that about it. It's very depressed now because of some Chinese influence. We feel that long term, we need to feed the world and so ultimately fertilizer prices will improve. It's more of an "out of favor" call as opposed to a macro call that fertilizer prices are going to turn tomorrow.

MJ: I know you don't really do energy plays either.

FT: Another commodity. There's a special expertise that we don't feel we have in energy. I just want to invest in what we know, where we can add value.

We're not gamblers. We're really long-term investors, and we need to understand the business. Most of the businesses are pretty simple and straightforward. We've done some health-care companies where they have a steady cash-flow business and where they're exploring some other areas. They have some downside protection in their base business, but then they're doing something a little more esoteric. However, we think it's a good risk-reward in terms of being protected with the core business. We don't invest in drug companies where there is a binary outcome, where it's either approved or not.

MJ: So it sounds like much of what you own, you can explain the company to anyone?

FT: If we don't understand it, we shouldn't be invested in it. I can't say that I'm an expert in the specifics of technology, but we have a technology company now that is a spin-off company from Dover. It's called Knowles, and it has 100 percent market share of the component in hearing aids. Then it has about 80 percent share in the microphones and speakers in iPhones and tablets. There's a big movement to having more speakers in smartphones and tablets. It has spent more than all of its competitors combined. So it's a leading position. The company has a really good management team. It's a local company, too. We love investing kind of in the Midwest where we find people with good core values and we have good access to management.

I understand the business and I like the management, but do I understand how a microphone is made? No.

If you don't understand the business model, then you can't invest. In my opinion, you can't make an educated investment unless you really understand that business. Like I said, maybe not every nuance, but you have to know what really drives it.

MJ: And for a position like this, you're a long-term investor?

FT: In every Wall Street report you read, the investment time horizon is six months to twelve months max. A lot of investors hold a position for less than a year. If you look at some of the turnover in these funds, it's quite high. We're looking at three to five years as a holding period.

I would say there are at least five or six companies that have been in the portfolio seven years. We sell when the risk reward is not there anymore. But if you buy a good business and a good management team, they continue to create new opportunities that can keep driving that stock price.

MJ: What about short-term volatility?

FT: We do have volatility. We have a small-cap name that is up 33 percent in the last month. It's 8 percent of the portfolio, so if it moves a nickel, it's crazy. They do esoteric personalized testing for people. It's a diagnostic company. We have owned it for seven years. But investors were worried about reimbursements for labs, so it went down. Now the results are really good, and investors are not as worried about reimbursements. The stock has been running. The company just made a small acquisition, and it's gotten some Wall Street press. It's just been on fire.

The company is called NeoGenomics. It is super volatile, and one of my analysts kept saying, "Why do we have so much of this? The volatility kills us if it moves two cents!" The analyst that follows the stock says, "It's great. It's cheap. We own it for all these reasons. We should have more of it!" The two of them were going back and forth. Now, it's everyone's favorite stock because the volatility is helping us.

MJ: If you've owned it for seven years. You must have had it in 2008. What happened to it then?

FT: It was crushed. In 2008, small caps were really crushed because investors just didn't know what to do and they didn't want to own things that were illiquid or small, so we had a tough year.

MJ: It didn't occur to you to sell with the herd?

FT: I think what really helps us is having a concentrated portfolio because we know your companies really well. We know what we own. The market changes price every single day, every single second of the day, and that doesn't change what the business is worth. The market is just moving around it. Once investors get caught up in emotions in the market, they will lose because the emotions will take them up in the wave and crush them down.

Finding Annuities

MJ: I know that you have a position in your portfolio right now, Libbey Glass, that has been in the portfolio for a while. Is that investment indicative of how you look at the long side of the book?

FT: I learned about it when I was working at Sirius Partners. Libbey is a glassware business, and the biggest part of its business is food service. It sells to white linen types of restaurants.

Once a restaurant picks a glass pattern, it generally stays with that pattern. Employees and customers are always breaking glasses, so Libbey gets this annuity business because the restaurant is going to continually buy replacements. It's more about the service than focusing on the price of a glass. Beverages are one of the highest margin things that a restaurant sells.

There's also been a big trend in drinks to have craft beers that have uniquely shaped glasses or to have whiskeys or margaritas with a different glass. Libbey has this great business in food service. It's very high margin. It's very predictable.

Libbey also have a retail business where it sells Libbey glasses at Walmart, Target, and Crate & Barrel. That's a little bit more competitive, and consumers don't necessarily buy the same glass. When they break it, they want a new set or a new shape. They don't have 12 pieces. They have four, six, or whatever, so it's not quite as brand sensitive. It's not as high margin, but it's a great business. There are not a lot of competitors. There are tariffs that protect the company in the United States. The company has been around forever. A glass factory is highly capital intensive with a high energy requirement, so companies aren't making glass factories as much anymore.

The factories are also very labor intensive, so Libbey has started to move offshore where it can lower some of the labor costs. Libbey has a plant in Mexico and one in China. As a result, it has reduced labor costs $30 per hour for labor in Toledo to $5 in Mexico and $2 in China.

MJ: And you bought it at $10 per share?

FT: I bought it at $10, and I bought a little bit at $12 and a little bit at $14. Then it went down when their balance sheet got in trouble. I sold it at around $5 or $6. I actually had a loss on this position. Then I bought back at $2. I bought more at $14 or $15. The stock is now $25. My target now is 40 bucks.

At one point the stock had a ten times cash flow multiple on it, back in the early 2000s. It was five and six times when I was buying it. It's at six now. I think it's worth eight times, but the market is not there yet. It has all this additional operating leverage. That's where I get to $40 per share because they're going to have margin expansion at a higher multiple. We'll see if I'm right, but so far so good.

MJ: Have you ever taken profits from the position, or are you still letting it roll?

FT: This is one of my rules. I'll have a 5 percent maximum concentration at cost limit in the portfolio and a 15 percent maximum concentration at market limit on any position. It went over 15 percent of the portfolio, so I trimmed some. But other than that, I haven't sold any of the stock. Now, if I only thought it was worth $30, I would be selling it. But when I have a good risk reward, I'll continue to hold it and just manage the position in terms of not going over 15 percent of my portfolio.

I convinced my mentor, Peter, to buy Libbey for his own portfolio. He actually asked, "Why do you have that arbitrary 15 percent concentration limit?" He thinks it should be 20 percent or 25 percent if I really like the stock. I think it creates even more volatility, and 15 percent is practical risk management.

MJ: Are there any other positions that really stand out for you. Ones that you are particularly thrilled with how they turned out?

FT: I've been invested in the uniform industry since 1983. Uniform rentals are a pretty mundane, boring business. Basically they're large laundries, and they have these trucks that go out and pick up dirty uniforms, and bring them back and wash them and take them out. It's a weekly cash business, essentially.

People that wear uniforms work at gas stations, hospitals, casinos, and airlines. There's been an effort to help people feel good about who they are by wearing a uniform with one's name on it, for identification and safety. There are many positive reasons to wear a uniform.

It's not something you would think about as a business to invest in, necessarily. But I started getting interested in this industry in 1983, when a company called Cintas went public in Cincinnati, where I was living. Cintas was run by a great management team, and all it did was uniform rental.

I learned to understand the dynamics of uniform rental. The essential quality is having route density. The company needs to be able to fill up that laundry facility. It has a fleet of trucks on the road. It can't afford to go to Timbuktu and bring back two uniforms and then go somewhere else. To be viable, it needs really dense and full routes. Transportation costs are pretty high.

The business is done by a long-term contract. Amoco signs up for three years to have all of its uniforms done, and it is committed. Uniform rental is a predictable, annuity business.

MJ: Do you like annuity businesses in particular?

FT: Absolutely. I think whenever there is predictability of cash flow, there is a higher multiple. Even if it's not growing at 20 percent, the cash flow is there for the investors.

I know the uniform industry well and know how companies should be run. I've invested either long or short in all the companies that have ever been public in the industry.

The one that I'm invested in today is the one called UniFirst. It was the number three player out there. It was a family company based outside of Boston. It has two classes of stock, which I don't love.

MJ: Why don't you like that?

FT: It doesn't allow for a full independence of a board because there's some super voting. I learned about this company through my industry experience, and I've been invested in it for seven or eight years. It's mundane, but it's a good business. The management team has been able to improve the margin from about 8 percent to 15 percent by getting a little bit bigger and improving the operating leverage. It also is taking on more technology to barcode their uniforms and is more efficient. Management also is focused on fuel savings for the fleet of trucks.

It's all about the details in these businesses. It's a hundred things that make it successful. UniFirst has been a great investment.

MJ: What about the other side of the coin? The investments that haven't been as successful?

FT: In the early 2000s I invested in a company that went bankrupt, and it was a disaster. It was timber and a pulp business. Talon had another hedge fund that did distressed investing, and both of our funds invested in this company. We went out to see them a couple of times, and we felt like we had asset values that would protect us if things turned down. The company could at least be taken over for the asset value. We thought the management team was good. We were basically wrong on all accounts. It went to zero. We sold it all the way down.

A bidder ultimately decided they could buy the company cheaper in bankruptcy, so they let it go down. We sold it before it got to zero, but it was a big hit for us. I think it wasn't as good a business, clearly, as we estimated. It had some unique assets in terms of controlling timber assets. It had a big pulp operation, but, as you know, the decline in newsprint has hurt any kind of pulp demand.

MJ: Are there any unifying themes with the companies that haven't worked out as well for you?

FT: I think we're decent on the management piece, and we're usually good on the valuation piece. Occasionally, we buy a business that's not quite as good as we think it is.

A Bumpy Ride for Short Selling

MJ: Hence the 20 positions and a 15 percent concentration guideline, I guess. And of course, you have short positions. What's your philosophy around shorting? Is it alpha, is it hedging, is it both?

FT: It's an interesting question because it's been so tough to short in recent years. I think that was part of the disagreement I had at Talon and the reason I left. I was shorting some housing before it broke, and they were very critical of me.

MJ: Then they thought you were a genius...

FT: I left before I was a genius.

MJ: And that drove you to leave Talon?

FT: We had two funds there. I was the first hedge fund at Talon, and then the principal hired another manager to run a distressed hedge fund. He had been working at a big firm, and when he started, he had a longer track record than I did. Talon raised a fair amount of money for him. "Replace your corporates with this fund (even though it's distressed) and look at the differential you'll get on return." It was a big product for Talon, and management was giving him a better payout than they gave me.

I said, "I want the same pay." The principals gave me all these reasons why I shouldn't have it. His fund was bigger. I had short positions that weren't working. I ended up leaving. Talon was reasonable enough, in some ways, to let me take my track record and the clients I had brought when I left to join RMB. It happened over a weekend, essentially

But in fact, my mentor, Peter, doesn't really believe in shorting so much either. And if you look at my attribution, I've made almost all my money on the long side, really, over the years. My goal is to make money on the shorts, but it's very hard. My goal is to hedge with the shorts and to protect the downside.

MJ: The market has lifted companies with bad fundamentals for a while. Is that part of the problem?

FT: Yes, I think prices can go up irrationally for too long. We're long-term oriented, so we're not traders. I think that hurts us to some extent. It's like the opposite of my longs: they are highly promotional, bad management, overvalued, and bad businesses.

MJ: How did the shorts perform in 2008, just out of curiosity?

FT: They were good, but we run a net long book.

MJ: What is your average long market exposure?

FT: Around 50 percent or 60 percent net long. So the short positions helped, but not enough. Small caps went down a lot more than the shorts went down.

I was running ten to fifteen names on the short side. The one thing that's changed is we've added a short analyst and now are running more names, 20 to 25 companies. There are more names but smaller positions. I don't know that it's helped us because I know we had a couple of doozies that were up 300 percent. Like Zillow. But we still believe it's flawed.

MJ: Is there any short that stands out in your brain as having worked particularly well for you?

FT: We've had a couple of really good ones. We had one called Home Solutions, and it was basically a fraud doing repair work in New Orleans after Hurricane Katrina. It went to zero. I shorted Overstock a couple of times, and it worked great. But last year, it went through the roof, and I finally took the position off. As I took it off, it went from $30 to $15. I rode it from $15 to $30. It's been one of those positions that runs over you.

We have a takeover right now in the short book that's really hurt us this year. A company called Questcor that's been highly publicized as a crazy stock that has a product that doesn't really work that well. It's overpriced. It's been written up negatively in the *New York Times* and *Barron's*, but the stock's still has just gone through the roof.

MJ: Does the short side of the portfolio worry you more than the long side of the portfolio?

FT: Probably. Because we have more names, it's harder to know as much about them. They can work against you for a while, and you can't foresee that. We haven't given up, though. We still believe in it. Ask me next year.

Shooting for Consistency

MJ: When Steven Eisen closed his fund in mid-2014, he said fundamental investing was dead. What do you think of somebody saying that?

FT: People have said that in different market cycles. When we had the tech bubble, for example. The reason I left Sirius Partners was because my mentor, Peter, felt like he didn't understand the markets anymore. He had his own money, and it was in public equities, private equity, venture capital, real estate, and funds of funds. He said, "I don't understand the markets anymore. We're not going to do any more public equity." That's when I left to start my own fund. But I believe long-term that fundamentals do matter.

MJ: Is being a good stock picker how you account for being positive 12 or the last 13 years?

FT: Absolutely.

MJ: But, unfortunately, you may be right, but you may not be right right now. That's always the interesting thing. I know 2014 started out rough for you. Do you ever see yourself getting away from your core strategy...

FT: No.

MJ: OK, that's easy.

FT: I think the second half of the year is off to a really good start for us. For some reason, somebody did some seasonal studies, and we've never seemed to have good first halves of the year. In the last five years, we have always had a better second half.

Last year we had really strong performance in the long book. Way better than the markets. The shorts just annihilated us. Our longs were up. We had incredible performance. But this year we've had some give back.

We had Fiesta Restaurant Group, which was a spin-off that got expensive, but we didn't want to sell it last year because it was short-term tax gains. It gave back a lot. It should have been sold. If we weren't so tax efficient, we would have sold it. We're starting to see some bounceback in the second half already.

Shorts are working better, and some of the longs that got hit in the first half are coming back.

MJ: Despite the fact that you had such a great year on the long side and not so great a year on the short side, you're still very committed to the short book from a risk management standpoint?

FT: It's what our portfolio is. It's not to be a home run. We are really committed to our tax efficiency. In 2013, for example, almost 100 percent of our returns were nontaxable. The shorts unfortunately helped a lot with that because they're all losses to offset all our great gains.

MJ: There's always a bright side.

FT: Our goal is to achieve 10 percent to 15 percent after tax rates or returns. Would we like 20 percent or 40 percent or 50 percent? Yes. But what we're trying to achieve for our clients is a long-term rate of return that fits into an environment when there are low interest rates and they need some protection. Who knows what equity markets are going to do? I think that's what our partners and investors are looking for.

MJ: Consistency, but not necessarily sex appeal.

FT: Yes.

MJ: So how are you positioning the portfolio going forward?

FT: We tend to stay away from fads or trends because, a lot of times, investors get so excited that the valuations just don't make sense. Often in the early stage, their business models don't make sense or they're already priced beyond any rational business model. So we're never focused on those forefront ideas in the market that may be attracting capital.

We look at more of those as short candidates. We've spent a lot of time on some of these recent initial public offerings (IPOs), shorting them. Especially since the JOBS Act was enacted, companies can go public with less information. We've found a lot of lower-quality business models. We have some great shorts in the portfolio. Some have already started to work. We have a lot of confidence in all of them, because the businesses just don't make sense.

In terms of where we see opportunity, I think it's more of the same. Random areas, I couldn't say one particular sector. We have an alfalfa seed company. We have a little craft brewery. Maybe that's a little bit faddish because people are drinking more craft beer, but it's pretty small in terms of market cap.

MJ: And unless there's a disease that wipes out hipsters, you're probably OK on that one.

FT: Right. I have to say we're finding fewer long ideas right now. That drives us. If we just can't find ideas, that says something to us about the market.

MJ: But I'm guessing since you don't really do top-down analysis, it's not necessarily the direction of the market that keeps you up at night.

FT: Right. I just don't like not making money. It pains me to be down or to underperform.

MJ: Is it the absolute loss that gets you?

FT: I'm an absolute investor, so I'm focused on making money. Would I like to be a relative performer? Maybe. But for me, I'm motivated to earn that 10 percent to 15 percent rate of return for my investors, which is what I promise them.

What I love about my work is that I'm doing this for the client. The client comes first. Certainly we want a job, and we want to do well. The hedge fund model obviously pays well, but it only pays well if you perform. It's all about trying to do the right thing.

CHAPTER 5

She Blinded Me with Science: Investing in Biotech

Dr. Fariba Fischel Ghodsian, Chief Investment Officer, DAFNA Capital Management, LLC

P rior to the adoption of the Pure Food and Drug Act in 1906, quack medicine was largely the norm. With potions consisting primarily of water, alcohol, opium, and herbs, these "patent medicines" did little to advance good health, ease suffering, or heal disease. Do you have depression, epilepsy, constipation, kidney and bladder problems, or just general disability? Try H.T. Humbold's Genuine Fluid Extracts.[1] Lumbago, gout, or a sprained ankle got you down? There's Stephan Sweet's Infallible Liniment, made from, you guessed it, snake oil.[2]

Today, biotech has come a long way from cure-alls. As of 2012, there were more than 1,466 biotech companies in the United States, with 318 of them publicly traded.[3] Advances in medical devices and pharmaceutical products provide more effective therapies for everything from diabetes to cancer. With an annual growth rate of more than 10 percent and the chance for enormous profits, it's no wonder that investors often flock to this innovative sector.

And while biotech investors no longer have to worry about snake oil, picking the next big drug or medical device company isn't as simple as examining a price-to-earnings ratio (P/E), market valuation, or a corporate balance sheet. A complex labyrinth of clinical trials and regulatory approval, not to mention insurance reimbursements and drug uptake, can create volatility for even the most experienced investor.

Biotech takes patience. It takes intestinal fortitude. And it doesn't hurt if you hold several advanced degrees and your own patents, too.

With a BS in chemical engineering from Technion, Israel Institute of Technology, an MS from the Massachusetts Institute of Technology, a PhD in Biomedical Engineering from Oxford University, postdoctoral work in protein modeling from Harvard University, and an MBA from the University of California Los Angeles, Dr. Fariba Fischel Ghodsian has lived and breathed biotech for more than 20 years. One of the first biotech securities analysts in the industry, Ghodsian has been in biotech almost from its birth. In fact, she started in the field before there was even an official "biotech" moniker. At that time, biotech was either lumped into chemical engineering or called, with no irony, food engineering.

Ghodsian started her investment career on the sell side, working for firms such as Wedbush Morgan Securities, Lehman Brothers, and Roth Capital Partners. After winning the *Wall Street Journal's* "Best of the Street" analyst award in 2002, Ghodsian made the leap from the sell side to the buy side to join her husband, Nathan Fischel, MD in running their hedge fund, DAFNA Capital Management LLC. Since its inception in 1999, DAFNA Capital funds have outperformed the NASDAQ Biotech Index by a very wide margin.

The passion for biotech is immediately evident in conversations with Ghodsian, and her knowledge of the space is encyclopedic. She moves deftly between the discussion of cancer treatments, Gaucher's disease and clinical trials, patents and diabetes. Her broad knowledge of the sector has certainly produced a winning track record, and her investing tenants have survived all phases of market testing. Her approved method of biotech investing includes the following principles:

- Drug and device efficacy is the most important aspect of biotech investing.
- Prioritize companies with drugs and devices for unmet medical needs or targeted therapies.
- Be data driven. Do not rely on hype, hope or logic.
- Seek out companies with platform technologies to minimize downside risks.
- Trade around drug company events and announcements where possible to minimize volatility.
- Good drugs can make up for bad management, but good management can't make up for bad drugs.

The Study of Food Engineering

MJ: What originally generated your interest in biotech?

FG: I started as a chemical engineer. I was interested in math, and I was interested in life sciences. The closest we had at the time was chemistry, so that's why I went into chemical engineering. Frankly, I also liked chemical engineering because I wanted to be in a male-dominated environment and to show that a woman can do it as well.

But chemical engineering was very broad. You could go into oil, or the chemical industry, or other areas that were not as exciting for me. I got more and more interested in the medical areas. At the time biotech was a very new term.

MJ: Can you tell me about some of your early work in biotech?

FG: After I finished my bachelor's degree, we moved to Boston. There wasn't even a biomedical engineering department. They had a program called food engineering. Then it evolved into more biochemical, biomedical engineering.

MJ: I don't even think I would have gone to a food engineering program. That reminds me of a lunchroom somewhere.

FG: I know! But that was it at the time, funny enough. I got my master's at MIT, but by then I knew for sure that I wanted to do something more medical related. I actually remember in one of our classes, we got a professor from food engineering, and he talked about his research in drug delivery. Basically, he used polymers that they inject under the skin. They would release a small amount of medicine over a long period of time. I got excited about that project and went to visit that professor. I decided to do my master's thesis with him. My project was actually, in a way, an artificial pancreas. The initial idea was that you can have a polymer system that you inject under the skin, like a Depo [Depo-Provera], and it would release insulin. The idea was that you could have a system that has a feedback loop, so that when glucose goes up, you can release more insulin. In the same polymer, you would use insulin, and you have an enzyme that would react to the glucose level in the blood.

MJ: It's like having a built-in monitor.

FG: Exactly. When there is a higher glucose level, the enzyme would react with glucose, which would decrease the pH inside the polymer. If the pH goes down, then the polymer ports would open more, and more insulin would be released. We developed that, and that's what my patents are based on. Obviously, it's easier in concept but much harder in practice, because the enzyme could get deactivated after a period of time, and in diabetes it has to be very exact. If you overshoot, obviously, it's very dangerous. If you undershoot, it's not effective.

MJ: As opposed to something like Depo-Provera, where it just releases constant amounts of hormones all the time.

FG: Yes, there you don't need feedback.

MJ: Of course, if Depo fails, the worse thing is that you get pregnant. If you mess up your insulin, you actually can die.

FG: From hypoglycemia, yes. While I was at MIT, I married Nathan. He was doing his residency at Harvard, and I was doing my master's at MIT. After that, we decided to go to England. It worked out that I could actually carry the project that I was doing at MIT and finish my PhD at Oxford University. At Oxford they only had an engineering department, and so I started to work with a professor there who was in control engineering, not biomedical systems per se. But he got excited about the project. He became my advisor, but he didn't have any biological knowledge. So we also worked with someone from the School of Pharmacy in London that had biological knowledge. At Oxford we did a whole mathematical model of how this system works, and how much enzyme do we need in order to reduce the pH in order to release more insulin. We collaborated with MIT and did animal studies with my old professor there. I finished my PhD in 2 years, which was probably one of the fastest PhDs there.

MJ: When you finished your PhD, you went to work in research at biotech firms, right?

FG: I did a postdoc at Harvard Medical School. My research was mathematical modeling, but with a focus on protein design. At the time, there was excitement to do rational protein design, rational drug design.... Before that we always joked it was irrational, and now the idea was that you could rationally design the molecule. My work there was to take the same molecule and design it so it has less side effects, it has more efficacy, and so forth. But you have to know which part of the molecule you are tweaking to get what you want. It was more of a broader drug design approach. I also did a project with Joslin Diabetes Center for an insulin molecule that would have better properties. I tried to still stay in diabetes research. Then after that we came to Los Angeles.

MJ: So you have a Bachelor's, a Master's, a PhD, and an MBA.

FG: Yeah, and a postdoc. It was grueling.

Losing the Lab Coat

MJ: So you worked at a start-up and you worked at Allergan, I know. What were those two experiences like?

FG: At Allergan, I was a research scientist. I worked in the lab in drug delivery for the eye. It was nice, but I think research moves very slowly. I think my personality was more that I wanted to be broader, to understand the different areas. I think that's why I thought that maybe it would be more interesting if I was in business development. Then you see what other companies are doing and other approaches. You're not just in your own office. I think that was partly what pushed me to do an MBA. It's something that I actually looked forward to doing. As an engineer and scientist, you just don't know the language of business. You don't know finance. All of that was very foreign to me.

So I went to UCLA for two years, completed the MBA, and I met the company that I joined: Medclone. It was a venture capital-backed biotech company with a monoclonal antibody for lupus. I was the second person there, which was nice because I wore many hats. I did the regulatory filings at the beginning, because there, we were only two people and the CEO was not a scientist. As a business development person, I got to see other approaches, other companies, and learned to negotiate for licensing. I got to see a broader landscape of autoimmune diseases.

The company unfortunately didn't make it. It was 1994, and at the time the market was weak and it was hard to raise money. We tried to do an IPO [initial public offering], and it didn't happen. Then one of the venture capitalists introduced me to Wedbush Morgan Securities in downtown LA. I think it's the largest Los Angeles-based investment bank. I interviewed with them, and I got a job as a biotechnology analyst. Now, I was their first biotechnology analyst, but they had obviously heard that biotech was the up-and-coming area. They were looking for someone.

I happened to be at the right time at the right place. Being a biotech analyst was fascinating. I loved it. The space was much broader because I went from eyes to autoimmune disease, and now, I was seeing everything—all of the biotech companies, all of the different approaches from gene therapy to rational drug design. You see all the projects and all the diseases. I ended up going from knowing a lot about something very narrow, to knowing a little about a lot of things.

MJ: My mom would call that the difference between being a mile deep and a foot wide and being a foot deep and a mile wide.

FG: That's a good way to say that. Since then, I have stayed in the investment field. I went to Wedbush in September 1994. I was in a few other investment banking groups, always as a bio-tech analyst. Later I joined Nathan on the buy side. I truly enjoy the field of investment, but again, I think the excitement of the investment is because it's tied to the industry that I love.

MJ: In 1994, you were not just one of the first biotech analysts for your firm, but anywhere.

FG: There were not many biotech analysts at all.

MJ: And you went from being one of the first to winning the *Wall Street Journal*'s "Best on the Street" analyst award for biotech in 2002. Where were you working at that time?

FG: At that time I was at Roth Capital. I had a detour through New York working with Lehman Brothers, but we decided we wanted to stay in LA. Then I worked with Roth Capital for a few years. I managed the health-care research there.

MJ: So clearly biotech had grown by that point.

FG: It had definitely grown much more. I think also initially there were many generalists. The analysts they had were more from a finance background. Biotech is a very complex field, so we've been seeing more and more PhDs and MDs come into the field. Now when you look at the sell-side analysts and the buy-side, there are a lot more specialists.

MJ: So do you think it was easier for people who had biotech knowledge to learn the financial analysis part of investing than it was for the people who had the stock and analyst background to learn biotech?

FG: Definitely. The MBA helped me. I didn't know accounting at all. It helped me learn to build a financial model, income statements, and look at balance sheets, and so forth. But in reality, most of the biotech companies, then particularly, didn't make money. You have that model in order to follow the company, but in reality that was not the basis for investment. The basis for investment was the drug that was in clinical trials. Whether or not it could become a multimillion-dollar drug.

MJ: So you weren't necessarily researching P/Es and valuations, you were researching regulatory filings, and...

FG: Regulatory filings, clinical trials, the platform technologies, the drugs themselves. In fact, I'll never forget the first company that I covered. Again, I was their first biotech analyst, and it was my first initiation of coverage. The only revenue the company had was interest revenue. I remember that the head of research came back to me and said, "Wait, something is wrong with their model. How can a company not have revenue?" and I thought, "Well, welcome to biotech." You're not investing in a revenue company.

MJ: You had to teach them how to even look at a company. Did you get a lot of pushback from people on that, or did they trust your judgment?

FG: I think they trusted me. Again, I had a wonderful time at Wedbush. Obviously, I learned a lot from them about Wall Street. For them it was a learning experience about the whole sector. And they really trusted me. My first three or four companies, they all did very well. When Wedbush introduced me to funds, they said, "This is the analyst that walks on water." Obviously, at some point you fall in the water, but they knew that I had that reputation because the first few covers that I put on, they all did very well. That builds up trust.

From the Sell Side to the Buy Side

MJ: So what made you decide to leave the analyst side and actually come to the dark side of hedge funds?

FG: For one thing, I think it's a natural career path that you go from the sell side to the buy side. Back in 1999, Nathan started the fund. We were thinking about going to New York. He took a sabbatical from the hospital, and he worked with a small biotech fund. One of the investors gave him a few million to start a fund, and Nathan was helping them analyze some biotech and biomed companies. During the first few years, the fund largely outperformed the biotech indices, both when they went up and off the charts in 1999, and when they came down later on, so the fund grew substantially.

Nathan had been nagging me, well, encouraging me to come and join him. Frankly, I was very resistant because I thought that a husband and wife might not be looked upon well. I had my own career, my own path, but I think two things led to me joining the fund. One thing was that the fund really was growing well, and Nathan at the time was still working as a physician. He really needed someone to be head of research. He had hired a few analysts, and he needed someone to manage them.

Also, the other thing was just the complexity of it. Let's say, if I wanted to pick up coverage on a company, obviously, I could not mention it to Nathan because of regulations. You really had to have a very strong Chinese wall. We were extremely cautious with that, but it just made sense that we do it together. It's also nice to be your own boss. I think that when I got the *Wall Street Journal* award, I thought, you know what, I achieved all I wanted on the sell side. It's like the athlete that gets the Olympic gold, and they think that's the best time to leave.

MJ: What continues to fascinate you about investing in biotech? Because, from 1994 to 2014, that's longer than a lot of marriages last.

FG: It is an amazing field. You see more and more companies with innovative ideas, new technologies, new drugs for unmet medical needs. You see different tiers of medicine being pushed forward, and you're part of it. I know that when I did my MBA, I was asked if I would do anything else apart from biotech, and I said, "No, no way. I don't want to do anything apart from this industry." I think it's exciting when you feel you are helping patients. Again, sometimes when a company has positive data, even if we're not invested in it, I get really excited because it's not just the money. It's really that fact that the industry is moving forward and that we are making a difference for the patients. I think at the end of it, that's really what inspires me and what encourages me to be in this business.

I mean, money comes with it. But the nice thing is that there is no conflict of interest. If you are invested in a good company that has a good drug, you also make money. Sure, we are in the business of making money. We have investors, and obviously our own money, all of it, is invested in our funds. Of course, we want to make money. But the great thing is that you can do it with a goal of developing good drugs. The two are totally congruent.

MJ: It's a mutually beneficial relationship.

FG: Exactly.

MJ: What are the biggest changes you've seen since you started analyzing companies in 1994?

FG: At the time, I think there were maybe really a handful of companies that had drugs that were on the market. Now we have a lot of companies with sales, and many are profitable. We have a number of profitable biotech companies that have surpassed even the large pharmaceutical companies in terms of market cap. In 1994, let's take monoclonal antibodies, which is a very important class of drugs in biotech. I think the first monoclonal antibody got approved a year or so after I started at Wedbush. Many of the monoclonal antibodies had failed, but now it's a very important class of drugs.

MJ: Has the drug approval process changed at all, or do you feel like it's pretty similar to what it was back when you first started?

FG: You know there are some improvements. The FDA sometimes goes through a cycle. There are periods of time that they are more lenient, and then something happens and they become very stringent. They have the obligation, obviously, to bring good drugs to patients, but also they have the obligation of safety for the patient. Sometimes it looks like they are too stringent, but in some cases they are proved right because there are drugs that are approved in Europe and not in the United States, and the FDA saved people from it. The famous case was the drug called Thalidomide that was for nausea in pregnant women. Many patients in Europe took it, and the babies were born without limbs. Now that drug later on became a very successful cancer drug. By and large, I think the FDA is doing what they have to do.

MJ: What about in terms of the length of time it takes to get drugs approved?

FG: The length of the process has improved. They developed what they call accelerated approval. Let's say for cancer drugs, it's based on some biomarkers like response rate and so forth rather than survival. Proving survival takes longer and also is harder. You need more patients because there's more variability in survival, whereas response rates are more clear. They developed an accelerated path for difficult diseases, for unmet diseases. They also developed priority reviews that reduce the time from the regular ten months to six months. Then, just recently they came with another approach that they call breakthrough designation. They have given this to a limited number of drugs for unmet medical needs and that are still in the early stage, but have shown some compelling evidence of efficacy. This pushes them faster through the regulatory process.

MJ: Do you primarily invest in companies that are developing new drugs and new devices?

FG: We focus a lot on unmet medical needs and targeted therapies—companies that have a drug or device for what we call an unmet medical need, which are diseases where either there is no therapy at all, or the existing therapies are not really effective. There is really a vacuum there where you need better therapy for patients or an approach to target patients who can best benefit from a specific drug. Many of these diseases are very serious. Cancer, obviously, and some other neurological and liver diseases fall in that category. We also like some of the orphan disease drugs, because if you have a drug in a crowded market, then slow reimbursement comes into play. If it's an unmet medical need, it means that it truly needs a new therapy. If the drug comes to market, you won't have as much pushback for reimbursement. Market adoption, all of that, becomes very automatic.

MJ: Are there other types of companies that you look for besides drugs, devices, and the unmet medical needs category?

FG: We look for diagnostic companies, also. Unfortunately diagnostics, overall, has been a difficult market. We do look at that also because eventually good diagnostics lead to better therapies and better patient care. We don't look at services.

MJ: Generally speaking, what is the size of the companies that you tend to look at?

FG: You know, our sweet spot is probably somewhere from $100 million to $2 billion market cap, but we definitely go below that and over that as well.

MJ: Both public and private companies?

FG: No, mainly public companies and very rarely private companies.

MJ: Is there a reason you shy away from private companies?

FG: Just that the development path is longer. This year and last year we had a lot of exits, but sometimes it takes a long time. Our fund is such that the investors can take their money after a three-month notice, but they can take all of their money if they want. We don't want to jeopardize our liquidity.

We still follow private companies and invest in IPOs. In the last two years, we have had a very strong biotech IPO market, but sometimes the IPO happens at valuations that are below the private round of financing.

Efficacy Is Everything

MJ: What makes an investment attractive to you?

FG: The proof of efficacy, first of all. We start with the drug or the device itself. It should be something that has shown some proof of efficacy. Now, for some diseases if you show proof of efficacy in animal models, it may be enough to make us think that, yes, this is most likely going to be a real drug. For some diseases you really need human data. So it varies. We also like companies that have a platform technology. It happens often enough that companies have one lead drug. They may have a few drugs in the pipeline, but one drug is the main drug.

If that drug fails, the stock can go down 80 percent. Now if it makes it, it can triple or more. Obviously, you look a lot at that benefit-risk ratio. When you see a company dropping so much, it's nice to have a situation where we have a safety net. To me, that safety net comes with companies that have a platform technology. If one drug fails, you still have the technology platform that mitigates some of that risk. Unless the whole platform fails, then of course you don't have a safety net.

MJ: Can you give an example of a company like that, where their drug failed but the platform technology saved them?

FG: I used to follow Isis. They have a platform for antisense. It's a way to block genes that you don't want expressed. They had a drug that failed for toxicity, but that was more related to that specific drug. It wasn't related to the overall technology. The stock took a hit, but it was much less than if it had been a single drug company. They actually recently got a drug approved.

MJ: So a little bit of optionality within the firm is important.

FG: Optionality and versatility.

MJ: It sounds like you're trying to take some of the risk off the table by looking at companies that aren't one-trick ponies. Is that the best way to put it?

FG: Yes, but the best long position that we have had is a cancer company, Pharmacyclics (PCYC). They have a drug that is now approved for two types of lymphomas and leukemia. When we met the company, they had a few patients who had used the drug. It targets a specific pathway in cancer called BTK. They showed remarkable improvement in a few very sick patients with hematological cancer. Again, this is a case where we saw unmet need. These were late-stage patients who had exhausted all the available therapies. For us, that was enough proof of concept. I think we bought the stock around $5. The stock at its peak recently was $150 per share. I think over a span of three-and-a-half years it went from $5 to $150. It has been one of our most successful investment stories.

Truly, you could call the company a one-trick pony company. It has one drug. But this one drug is very versatile and can be used in many diseases. As more data came, we saw more and more that the efficacy is holding and the toxicity profile looks very benign. Obviously as more data came, we felt more and more comfortable with that.

MJ: Did you add to the investment as the stock was going up?

FG: We have a rule that when we invest, we can only invest 5 percent of the portfolio. We can let it go up to 10 percent based on market gains, but we don't go beyond 10 percent. That is part of our risk mitigation.

MJ: And certainly going from $5 to $150 would be more than a 5 percent to 10 percent gain.

FG: Oh, yes!

MJ: It wasn't something you went in at 5 percent?

FG: I think we met them when the stock around $6, and then it actually took a hit below $5. They had a bit more data, but people took profits and the stock took a hit. That was our opportunity to build it into a 5 percent position. As the stock went up, we let it grow to 10 percent of the portfolio. Then we had to sell shares. Otherwise, literally, it would be 100 percent of the portfolio. But it's still one of our largest positions.

MJ: You've had it for how long now?

FG: Close to four years. We still feel it's a great drug and the valuation offers a lot of upside along with their partner, Johnson & Johnson. They have studied the drug for many hematological diseases and also for autoimmune diseases like rheumatoid arthritis. Sometimes you have one drug that gets approvals for several indications. Physicians also sometimes use it off-label because they know that it has efficacy for other diseases.

MJ: What's your typical process for researching a company?

FG: Between the two of us, we know almost all of the biotech companies, because I was on the sell side for many years, and Nathan was in the medical field as a physician. We followed them, but sometimes the company's drug development is very long. You have three phases of clinical trials: Phase 1, Phase 2, and Phase 3, and then it takes more time for approval. During that process, you may choose not to be in a particular stock, and to revisit it later. That is part of our approach.

We have a database of all of our companies. We record all of our talks to management and all of our scientific research that we do on the companies. We look a lot at the *New England Journal of Medicine* and all the other medical journals. We look at the scientific publications, at the conferences presentations. Conferences like ASCO, the oncology conference, and so forth.

The way we think about investing in a company, it could be either because a company comes to visit us, or we go to an investment conference and we meet with the company, or we see publications that make a company sound interesting. Then we ask the company to have a call with management. Ideas can come from different ways.

MJ: Do you always talk to management? Is that always something that's required?

FG: Let's say it's a company that we may have known some time ago and then suddenly we see a drug that was either not on our radar screen, or that we didn't think would work. Suddenly one morning they have great data. We have had cases like that, at least two cases I remember. They had great data and the stock was up 50 percent. Our trader calls us, and we look at the data and say, "This is amazing data actually." In cases like that we may later have the call, but we do the trading first.

MJ: A lot of what we've discussed has been about the actual drug and the process for the trial. When you talk about a

typical fundamental, bottom-up value investment, the management team is pretty important. It sounds like management may be secondary for you.

FG: If I have the choice, I'd prefer a good drug. But I can say that there are also some instances where management can rescue a failed drug. For example, Alexion had a drug that didn't work for several autoimmune indications. Then they came up with an idea to develop it for a very rare genetic blood disease. The drug mechanism of action exactly fits that disease. The drug worked, and it's one of those rare diseases where they charge a couple of hundred thousand dollars per year. The company now has a market cap of over $30 million, so here is a case where management salvaged the drug by putting it in the right conditions.

If a drug doesn't work and the management has the insight and the knowledge, they can try to do a clinical trial that may work better. But overall, if the management is good but the drug is not good, we would not invest. If the management is not good, but we like the drug, we may invest.

MJ: You said you remembered two investments where you invested due to the data before you talked to management. Can you give me an example of one of them?

FG: One of them made it through trials, but then they decided not to bring it to the market. One was for rheumatoid arthritis, one was for depression. The depression failed Phase 3 trials, actually. But Phase 2 looked compelling. Both made very lucrative partnerships with large pharma. We made money from both of those positions.

MJ: Even though they didn't ultimately make it to where you were able to ride the drug to market?

FG: Some of our companies, like PCYC, we have stayed in it all the way. But sometimes we invest in companies, and have made money on the company, but the company itself later failed. We went into the company at the right time, and then we came out at the right time.

MJ: Not all of your companies have to get to the finish line.

FG: No, definitely not.

MJ: Are you looking at P/E ratios and valuations and other traditional investment metrics, or do you focus more on the actual biotech research? I know a lot of these companies don't even have revenues in some cases.

FG: Mostly we look at the research side. For biotech, P/E ratios are less used because we typically don't invest in the largest cap companies. Sometimes we do, but in general the very large cap companies, let's say the Amgens, they have many different drugs. It's not one or two drugs that are leading the company. We usually prefer companies that are really driven by one or two drugs where we can do focused research work on those and make a decision. For medical devices, we look more at valuation metrics such as sales ratio and P/E.

"Honest" Shorts

MJ: Talk a little bit about your short investments. Looking at your data, you have either broken even or made money on your shorts most years, which has been hard to do of late.

FG: We still see so many opportunities on the long side that, by and large, we take long positions. On the short front, we short only if we truly think either the company is misleading or that there is a disconnect with The Street. We call that an honest short.

If we do all our work and we come to a conclusion that we don't think this drug is going to work, then we take a short position. Of course, that should also be paired with the valuation of the company being high, because if you're wrong on your short investments, there is no limit to how much it can go against you. If you're wrong on your long investment and it goes down, it can only go to zero. On shorts, it's infinite, the money that you can lose. We really are much more cautious on our short investments.

It also happens that sometimes our traders tell us a stock is up because they have data. You look at the data, and the data is actually not good. Sometimes the press releases can be misleading. They say they have positive data, but they actually failed on their primary finding, or something like that. These could be opportunities for shorting companies.

There was a company that had a drug for Huntington's disease. They did a three-month trial. I looked at other clinical trials for that disease, and usually you need much a much longer trial—usually a year or more to show their effect. You look at the other trials, and you see there are one-year trials, and here they are doing a three-month trial. Then their valuation goes up because people get excited that they may have positive data. But it's almost impossible for them to show benefit within three months. I don't know why the management was doing it that way. Sometimes companies try to take a shortcut and it backfires.

MJ: Do you remember your most profitable position on your short side?

FG: Antigenics. They had a therapeutic vaccine approach for renal cell carcinoma. It was more for early-stage patients, because I know for therapeutic vaccines the patient should have a healthy immune system. They kept pushing the data and delaying it. We looked at the evidence. We didn't think there was any evidence that the drug would work. I think that was one of our largest short positions.

Another was Genta with an antisense for melanoma. Again, we just thought that they didn't have evidence that the drug worked. I think either they hadn't shown clear benefit over the control group, or the design of the trial was compromised. We thought that the FDA would not approve the drug. Even though they want to approve drugs for cancer, we just felt they could not approve this drug. You also have to understand the FDA. The FDA wants to approve drugs, but they also don't want to give hope for something that doesn't work. Patients are desperate. I totally understand it. They are desperate to try new drugs. If they feel that this drug does not offer benefit, and just offers hope...

MJ: Then it's basically snake oil at that point.

FG: Exactly. That's not fair to the patient. Sometimes they actually offer more toxicity and you don't get benefits.

MJ: Any short positions that really surprised you, that didn't work out well, and you had to exit quickly?

FG: I had a painful short position, yes. Dendreon. A prostate cancer therapeutic vaccine where we thought there was minimal benefit. We didn't think that the FDA advisory panel would recommend it for approval. The FDA often has the advisory panel before they approve a drug. The FDA may or may not follow their advice, but the panel gives them advice on approvability. Their drug was an autologous cell therapy, which basically means you process the patient's own cells and give it back to the patient. We felt the data that they had didn't support approval.

We had, luckily, a very small position and bet against approval. Some of these panels are very fascinating to watch, but in this case the vote in question was, "do they think this drug should be approved?" Then, somehow the voting question got changed during the meeting to something like, "do you think there is any evidence that this drug may have benefits?" So, suddenly the panel voted yes. There was some evidence, but it wasn't robust enough for approval. But the stock went up three or four times. Small position, but painful.

We were ultimately right, because the FDA didn't actually approve the drug. But that was three months later.

Later, they did another full study that the FDA asked for, and the therapy made it to the market. But, then the drug was just not taking off in the market place, and it was expensive to manufacture. They priced it high, and physicians didn't really believe in the efficacy. By then, competition also closed in as two other good drugs came to the market.

The Biotech Roller Coaster

MJ: You bring up an interesting point. I think when a lot of people think about biotech, they think of this roller coaster-type of investment. How do you manage that kind of volatility within a portfolio? Obviously, the position sizing helps. How else to you help to manage that?

FG: Some of our positions are very long term. Some could be years, some could be months, and some could be days. We do try to go with the roller coaster to some degree. Obviously, you cannot always predict it. Let's say a company has positive data and the stock jumps a lot. We look at it and it looks positive, but it's not so amazing. We may take a pause here, come out, and maybe enter at a better time. Many times we do try to mitigate that roller coaster by trying to come in and out at the right time.

On the risk diversification and mitigation, the other thing we do is at the portfolio level. We are almost never leveraged, and our track record has been generated with an average gross exposure of 75 percent. Let's say there's a market correction and a stock drops a lot. We never have to sell a stock in distress, and many times we actually buy more. The other thing is risk diversification. We never invest in a thematic way. In other words, we don't go, for example, long on all the cancer companies, and short on the cardiovascular companies. Because sometimes suddenly one cancer company fails, and then the others fall in tandem because of the sentiment. We really analyze the companies bottom up, one by one.

MJ: What's your worst nightmare scenario in this sector of biotech? Is there anything that keeps you up at night?

FG: The worst nightmare is when an approved drug that is working well is suddenly pulled off the market. I think it was seven or eight years ago, Tysabri, a drug for MS, was pulled off the market.

It was a very powerful drug, and patients did very well on it. Basically overnight, the FDA pulled the drug off the market because a few patients developed a brain toxicity called PML, which was fatal. At the time we were not invested in Biogen Idec or Elan, the two companies that marketed the drug together, but it was still painful for the whole community.

MJ: So that's what would keep you up at night? Surprises?

FG: Yes. Biotech companies all have events. Sometimes it takes two years between one event and another, but they all have events like clinical trials, or regulatory approval, and so forth. Depending on our level of confidence, we decide if we want to take a binary risk.

Sometimes we go into companies before events. If we see that the stock has gone up a lot, we say the positive data is priced into the stock. Then we may decide not to go into the binary event. It depends how we view the benefit-risk ratio for that binary event.

In every binary risk, even if you're 80 percent sure that it works, there is always a 20 percent chance that it doesn't.

MJ: What do your short-term positions tend to look like, then?

FG: We may not believe in the drug fundamentally, but we may just be in it for a jump in stock price on the data. In medical devices, the positions are longer term because there are not that many events. In biotech, it's more event driven, so sometimes we may be in, come out, and later go back in again.

MJ: So recycling companies is a big part of your strategy?

FG: Oh, absolutely. I remember when I started at Wedbush, the first thing they told me was, "Okay, put together a list of 10–15 companies that you're interested in, and just watch them." They meant watch the stocks on the screen. See how it trades.

Some management teams are very promotional, so the stock seems to run before the news. When the news happens, the stock actually sells off because they have been hyping and talking about it. Some are overpromised and underdelivered. Some are underpromised and overdelivered. You get to know that. I remember that, after a while, I understood what they meant by just watching the stocks. You get a feeling for stocks that you have watched over many years.

MJ: How many positions do you normally have in the portfolio?

FG: Around 60 at any given time, and about 140 every year.

MJ: Long side and short side, or long side?

FG: Together.

MJ: What percentage of the portfolio would your top ten positions represent?

FG: It's probably, I would say, around 30 to 40 percent, I would guess. We have a couple of 7 percent to 10 percent positions, but more of it is 2 percent to 5 percent. Then we have a good number of 1 percent positions also, and sometime 1/2 percent positions. Some of the more illiquid companies, we take small positions.

The Future of Health Care

MJ: In terms of the health-care landscape, we've seen the implementation of Obamacare, for lack of a better word. There have been a lot of predictions about how that's going to change the way that people get health care and treatments. How do you see the health-care and life sciences and biotech landscapes being impacted by that over the next, call it five to ten years?

FG: In the stage of biotech that we invest in, typically we don't see Obamacare or health-care reform having much impact. There's some discussion obviously about pricing, but so far, we have not seen an impact on pricing. If anything, many of the cancer drugs are priced appropriately because there's a lot of research that goes into those drugs. There is more price pressure on the medical device side, and there was also an excise tax placed on device sales.

Many orphan diseases, frankly that's one area that I feel may start to be priced almost out of range. Some of the orphan drugs have become very profitable. Initially the idea was that, well, we should price them higher because there are not many patients. When you look at companies like Genzyme, they have turned many orphan drugs into multibillion-dollar drugs.

MJ: You do see some drugs out there that are literally thousands of dollars for a single pill.

FG: Exactly. Health care is a very paradoxical situation. On one hand, there is all that talk about reducing health-care costs. Now we should realize that drugs and devices are only a very small portion of the overall health-care cost. There's hospitalization, which is a bigger cost. And the whole malpractice insurance, that's another big cost. Physicians, in order to make sure that they don't get sued, do so many unnecessary procedures. There are lots of loopholes. I wish that the system would be fixed, and Obama would focus on some of those. Unfortunately we haven't seen much improvement on that front.

If you only focus on drug and devices—let's look at Gaucher disease, which is a very rare genetic disease. It's a over a billion-dollar market right now. There is an Israeli company, Protalix, they came up with a way to manufacture proteins that is much cheaper. They do it in a plant cell rather than in mammalian cells. The cost of manufacturing is a fraction of what Genzyme's drug costs. Their drug is approved in the United States and is on the market.

It's selling, but it's not selling a lot yet because physicians and patients are used to the Genzyme drug that has been on the market for many years. When you ask physicians, they say there's no pushback on reimbursement. Here is an example where there is another drug, almost identical, and it is approved in the United States, and it's doing exactly the same thing and it could be a fraction of the cost.

In this case, the company priced it at a 25 percent discount because they didn't want to make it a commodity. So why is it that insurance companies don't ask for that drug? I don't know. If they were so worried about cost, Genzyme's drug is about $300,000 to $400,0000 a year. Saving 25 percent is a $100,000 per patient savings. Somehow insurance pays for it. And patients say, "Well, this is the drug that has always worked. Why should I try something new?"

MJ: What about advertising? Would that help with those types of problems?

FG: Our edge really is in clinical trials and regulatory process. We typically don't invest in companies that have a drug on the market. Our bet is not on the launch of the drug. There is a lot of complexity in the reimbursement process, in the uptake of the drug.

MJ: So you're betting, then, on a different part of the market.

FG: Definitely on the biotech front. We are more on the clinical trial and the regulatory process. We look at the design of the trials, such as treatment time; the differential effect versus control and the inclusion-exclusion criteria; which patients are being enrolled. We look at the statistics, and all of that we're taking into consideration.

Most devices come to the market much faster. Obviously many of our device companies already have devices on the market. Even on that front, we have had some device companies that we invested in very early. Again, it was companies that were under the radar; one of them was Novadaq, a Canadian company NVDQ. It has an imaging technology that helps surgeons view blood perfusion and, at the time, was a very small micro-cap company.

MJ: Obviously, you have a tremendous background in this space, and even that's a bit of an understatement. For somebody who doesn't have a biotech background, do you think it's possible for him or her to be a successful biotech investor?

FG: I guess it's possible. You can talk to many physicians. You can try to read the literature and so forth. I think overall biotech is one of the fields that specialists have a better handle on. I think so many scientists and physicians are doing biotech investment that for somebody who doesn't understand the field at all, it's much harder.

Now having said that, I will never forget when I was on the sell side we went to see one of the largest East Coast mutual funds. I don't know if they still have this business model, but they had the business model that they rotated their analysts. I met with their biotech analyst, and he asked some trivial questions that I just could not believe. What is the disease? What is the target? What is an antibody?

I was shocked. How could somebody like that invest in biotech? Now they have dedicated biotech analysts. That was back 20 years ago. They figured out that for biotech they should not rotate.

Biotech is complex. The process is complex. Understanding the molecular basis of the drug, the clinical trials, the regulatory paths. Just knowing the full competitive environment. I think it's very hard for a generalist.

MJ: So is knowledge the secret to success?

FG: There are many ingredients to success, but to me the most important one is having a curious mind and being able to ask the right questions. To misquote Voltaire: judge a man—and a woman—by her questions rather than her answers.

Credit Investing

CHAPTER 6

Puzzling It Out: Distressed Credit Investing

Marjorie Hogan, Portfolio Manager and
Managing Member, Altum Capital

I still remember my first jigsaw puzzle. It was wooden and only had about eight pieces, but it was one of my favorite toys. On rainy days I can still recall the joy of working that puzzle, and the many that followed. Graduating from 50 pieces to 100 pieces to 1,000 pieces was milestone and a cause for celebration. If the puzzle had a lot of sky or ocean or other repeating patterns, so much the better.

When the financial industry began to create the first structured credit derivatives in the late '80s, it was in many ways a throwback to the puzzles of their youth. Pieces like interest rates, collateral, prepayment, credit, and legal structure fit together precisely to create an investable product. Unlike a boxed puzzle, however, the earliest credit market participants didn't know how the pieces fit together, whether they possessed all of the puzzle pieces, or how the puzzle would hold together over time. Miscalculating even one piece could, and at least once did, spell disaster.

In the 2002 Berkshire Hathaway annual report, Warren Buffett took a dim view on financial derivatives. "In my view," Buffett said, "derivatives are financial weapons of mass destruction."[1] After the financial meltdown in 2008, many shared his opinion, causing instruments like collateralized debt obligations (CDOs), collateralized loan obligations (CLOs), and mortgage-backed securities (MBS) to become, in essence, "three-letter words."

But like any tool, the outcome of investing in derivative credit instruments depends largely on the skill of the hand that wields them. That's where Marjorie Hogan comes in. A trained mathematician with a doctorate in mathematics from Stanford University, Hogan was lured to investing by dreams of a 9 to 5 job and Wall Street's need for modeling "rocket scientists." While regular hours turned out to be a pipe dream, the need for skilled mathematicians in finance was real. Hogan was hired in 1985 by First Boston, and in 1991 by Bear Stearns to develop models for mortgages and derivative credit products. Her job was to make investments that successfully account for all of the pieces of a complex credit market, and there can be little doubt after more than two decades of investments that she is a master of the debt market puzzle.

Since the inception of her Altum Credit Master Fund, Ltd. in July 2009, the fund has generated a compound annual return of 19.96 percent versus the HFN Hedge Fund Aggregate Index's return of 6.74 percent over the same period. Hogan was also one of the few people who both anticipated and profited from the mortgage meltdown in 2007 and 2008. In fact, she was the only one to bet her colleagues at Bear Stearns that such a meltdown could and would occur.

No doubt, debt instruments can be complex, but the credit market, at roughly twice the size of the equity markets, is simply too large for serious investors to ignore. In her decades of successful structured credit investing, Hogan has developed certain principles that help navigate the large and complicated credit markets:

- Look for distressed opportunities, because they won't fall as much in a bad market and they have more room to grow in a great market.
- Stay away from the crowds. Just because everyone loves a particular instrument doesn't make it a good investment.
- The devil is in the details—the legal structure and language that surround a product can be just as important, and sometimes more important, than what the numbers tell you.
- Take time off from the markets to clear your head and refine your thinking.
- You can sell in any market. Literally, any market. You may not want to sell and lose money, but sometimes it is just the right thing to do.

Working 9 to 5

MJ: Did you go to school specifically for mathematics or were you using math to get into finance?

MH: I went to graduate school to do pure math, and it seemed like I would be a professor. I really didn't have a goal in mind. I just loved math and wanted to keep doing it. Sometime near the end of graduate school, I decided I really wanted to go into industry. If I went into industry, I thought maybe the job would end in the late afternoon or early evening, and I would have more time for myself, which never turned out to the be case.

MJ: Because you always hear about people in finance being able to go home at 5 p.m..

MH: But I didn't know that. I started asking around among the professors, "What is there to do in industry?" No one had any idea, nor did they care. Most of them said, "If you don't want to be a professor, I don't know what to tell you."

I did find a professor in statistics at Stanford, Perci Diaconis, who had run off at 16 to join the circus and who is a world-class magician. He was a really interesting character. He said, "Maybe you should go to New York. These investment banks are hiring mathematicians. They call them rocket scientists."

I didn't know what an investment bank was, but I sent off a letter to Manny Hanny [Manufacturers Hanover Trust] and Chase, asking, "Are you an investment bank? Because I'd like to come be a rocket scientist."

I never got a response back, of course.

So, I went to Boeing. I found a really nice group there in the Boeing military aircraft company, with mathematicians creating real-world solutions. It was a great experience. I also took some economics classes and tried to learn some finance at the time.

When I was going to get married, my husband was in New York. Rather than him moving to Seattle, I said, "I want to come to New York anyway. I'm looking for investment banks."

This time I had better introductions to recruiters and introductions to some banks. It was the mid-'80s. They were looking for people just like me. So I joined First Boston.

It was an environment where they were desperately looking for somebody to build an options pricing model for mortgage-backed securities. They knew how to structure the securities, but not how to analyze them until I walked in. The first thing they asked was, "Can you price a complicated security?" Based on what I learned at Boeing, I put together a model that became "the model" over time. There was a real push to get more understanding of the risks that they were taking and their fair values. Whether we were overpaying for a security.

MJ: Would you say that the instruments were outpacing the knowledge behind them?

MH: Absolutely.

MJ: Did you find that interesting or a little scary?

MH: It's a problem to solve. I always like for there to be a real use for the solutions you come up with. That's what got me into risk management. That was the group that was not just creating models, but applying them as well. I was quite involved there with a large variety of products.

The risk management group was started in 1986 at First Boston and headed up by a person I knew from Stanford. It was a small group that worked with a lot of products. I think that was part of the fun of being in a bank in its earlier days. It was small and aggressive, and everything was new. We all learned at the same time. Always from the point of view of, what do the numbers say? Does that make sense? Then we would compare the numbers to the reality of how the market trades.

You would typically find traders saying, "I don't care what your models say, that is not how the market trades." They had some rules of thumb that worked locally. Then when the market moved a little bit, they picked another rule of thumb. They didn't recognize that it's part of a bigger pattern. The models weren't so wrong.

MJ: People can only draw conclusions from the data that they're exposed to.

MH: Exactly. I really loved that challenge aspect between what traders thought was right and what the model said was right.

There were errors in the model as well. Some of the inputs weren't perfect, and if they weren't perfect, the numbers were going to be off a little bit as well. That question was, which part was more right than the other? How do you come up with your best hedges? It was applicable across a lot of securities.

I guess that's how I got so involved in many different products at First Boston. But then there was a lot of turnover and change at First Boston. A large Solomon crowd came in, trying to make us more aggressive like Solomon Brothers. That's when we started a proprietary trading unit. I joined that division for the last year, but a lot of my old friends were leaving, and I was quite anxious to start someplace else that was away from First Boston.

I think I talked to Bankers Trust about joining them, but they really wanted me to do mortgage derivatives. I said, "I've been doing mortgages my whole life." Which was kind of funny. It was three years at that point.

But I really wanted to see a wider variety of things. At Bear Stearns, they didn't have much going on in derivatives. Everything was on the table. It was a great opportunity. Worse case, I find myself in a strong mortgage shop probably knowing more about mortgage research than anyone else. That's not a bad fallback. And I might get to do all this new stuff. So I joined Bear Stearns and, almost immediately, they honed it down to, "start mortgage derivatives for us."

MJ: Maybe the gods were trying to tell you something.

MH: It was funny that I had thought I had been doing it so long, and I wanted a change. In fact, it became really exciting, so it wasn't a bad way to go at all.

They had two mortgage derivatives trades on the books that I inherited, but they had decided they didn't want to do mortgage trading anymore. It was a business that they had tried, and they just didn't think they loved. They liked the cash collateralized mortgage obligation [CMO] business, which was a huge thing, and the interest only/payment only [IO/PO] business was a huge thing at Bear.

But now I was there, and Warren Spector said, "Okay, let's see what she can do." The mortgage market, the new issuance market, was going gangbusters. So the first business I proposed was to create things that looked like the mortgage market. To do swaps that look like you're buying a bond.

The challenging aspects were the capital rules, the hedging, and putting the model together. I walked in with just me. The Bear Stearns model back in the day was, until you're making money you got no support. I had to create the models myself, writing in FORTRAN, which was very outmoded even at the time, and come up with the technology for hedging. It was more like a mental experiment. How do you hedge something to term? If I put on a trade with a 12-year final, I've got to last the whole 12 years and make sure it's really profitable the whole time, not just for one week or two weeks.

That's thinking through the boundary conditions. What happens when the world changes and you're in a very different market? Will your hedges still be working in those conditions? I didn't want to go into this and realize I'd made a mistake and they were left with a bad position. I spent about a year thinking everything through and putting the model together. We eventually put our first trade on probably a year-and-a-half into it.

MJ: It sounds like putting together a puzzle.

MH: It is.

MJ: Except you not only have to put the puzzle together, you also have to know whether or not you have all the pieces for the puzzle to start with.

MH: Exactly. I was constantly rethinking my thought patterns. Will all these things work in line? Is there something I'm missing?

Building a Business

MJ: So even though you thought you'd done everything in your first three years, the mortgage derivative market continued to be intriguing for you. What reinvigorated you?

MH: I think it was the trading aspect, the fact that I'd be putting on risk. It wasn't just hedging a trading position and trying to make sure we don't lose money over a one-week or two-week period. It was the challenge of, are you really sure you're right?

There's going to be no exits for these strategies. It's got to last 10, 12, 15 years. I think that that whole aspect was what was so exciting and new.

Then there was the product development and actually running a business. I had to come up with something that was sellable. At Bear Stearns at the time, you were like your own little shop. In fact, in my first week people would come up and say, "What are you here for?" I would describe my business, and they'd say, "Best of luck to you."

MJ: Sounds entrepreneurial.

MH: Very. You were going to be charged expenses, so if you get too much help from the research team, they'll charge you. You'll have revenues, and you'll get paid on your net profits. I was trying to figure out what was affordable and achievable.

MJ: When did you finally start getting additional staff?

MH: It took two years. We started doing trades a little after one year, and became instantly too busy. I was working almost around the clock. At some point, I was told I could hire somebody. Of course, I had no time for hiring anybody, nor training them or anything. In the end, my husband recommended somebody. He said, "I know just who you want. She works with me at Citibank. If it gets to the point to where you can afford to support the family, and I can stay home with the kids, I'll introduce you to her. Otherwise, I won't."

MJ: Nice! A little bribery never hurt anything.

MH: But that's what eventually happened. He made the introduction. I hired her on the spot, and she accepted on the spot. She went back to quit and joined me almost immediately. That was Lynn Paquette, who's still with Altum today. I worked with her for the next seven years, from 1993 until 2000. Afterwards, she stayed and ran the business when I moved on to the next thing.

For the next couple of years, we worked seven days a week, roughly 18-hour days. I would go home and, after the kids had dinner and bedtime stories, go back in. Lynn would have been in the office the whole time. We'd work until about one in the morning, and then come back the next morning and start it again. It was a very intense time, but eventually we started to slow down to where we could take Sunday mornings off. It felt like I was getting my life back.

MJ: Was your husband staying home with the kids at this point?

MH: He did for a long time. I think maybe around ten years or so. We have four kids. Maybe around ten years ago he started teaching part-time at Columbia in the evenings again. Now he's with us at Altum on the bond team.

MJ: By the time you hired Lynn, had you had all four children?

MH: I think I waddled into Bear Stearns two weeks before I delivered the third. My first day there was nine days before I delivered. They didn't put me on the trading desk right away. They said, "We'll get more serious when you come back from maternity leave." The fourth child I had while I was on the job at Bear Stearns.

MJ: One of the things you hear in finance is that it's very difficult to have a child and still do your job because of the demands of both. But many of the women I've talked to say if you want to make it work, it can work.

MH: I think I had really good luck. I think there were bosses I could have had that wouldn't have been as great.

MJ: Because you started getting a team, or at least a team of one person, things must been going well for you. What were those first, call it, ten years like, 1993 to 2003?

MH: It was always different. Some people came up through the mail delivery room at that time at Bear Stearns. Then maybe they got put on a seat at the trading desk where they entered tickets. Then they would start to analyze some bonds. Then they might become a junior trader. Then, eventually, if they did well, they could become a senior trader.

They really knew their one product area very well, based on how it trades, but that's not a very flexible skill set. They can't usually switch to another area and start again. I think with us, we were constantly trying to learn new things and try new areas. That was really what was different about what was going on those first ten years.

MJ: Are there areas that stand out that you loved or really didn't like?

MH: Some people were putting on basically regular interest rate swaps cheap to the market because they thought they were going to buy something else that had better values, but the models were misestimated. The thought process was wrong there, because you're selling something that has a ready market at the wrong price. They blew up, of course.

Another product was Ginnie Mae adjustable-rate mortgage [ARM] swaps, which was when someone created something backed by Ginnie Mae at spreads of 30, 40 basis points or so over LIBOR. That's not where Ginnie Mae credit was supposed to trade. There was something fundamentally wrong. Everybody should want to do that trade. It was, again, a misestimation of the model. But everybody was doing it. We were under a lot of pressure to try and put on more of these trades. Customers all wanted them, of course. The sales people wanted them, and the Ginnie Mae ARMs trader wanted them. That was one where we just walked away from the business and did other things.

Typically, we would shut down almost every year for a couple of weeks and retool. We would think about what we could do that made sense and specialize our models. I think that's what saved us. We were constantly away from where the crowd was. We wanted to think about something that was less easily understood, but that had better value.

In the 1990s, we did a lot of swaps that amortized, like CMOs, to change their character in some way to help sell products that the desk wasn't able to move on their own. We would raise caps on floaters, or put maturities on, or something like that. Then later in the '90s, Bear started underwriting CBOs [collateralized bond obligations], either backed by emerging market debt, corporate or sovereign high-yield debt, or mortgage market value deals.

By the time 2000 came around, I was pretty keen on looking much more deeply into credit. That was the next frontier. All this time it was interest rate risk we were managing. I started to think more about credit risk. I moved into making markets in CDOs [collateralized debt obligations]. I was the first person to do that by almost three years.

MJ: Were there any areas within the CDO market on which you tended to focus?

MH: No, it was everything. It was all distressed after the dot-com bust, and I was interested in all of it.

MJ: What types of things did you focus on in those trades? Interest rates? Credit?

MH: It was mainly credit, but it was also refinancing and pre-payments of the corporate bonds or loans or emerging market, et cetera.

The People Part of the Equation

MJ: Were there other macro factors that came into play?

MH: The interplay between the timing of prepayments and what the manager can do was important. The manager is able to actively manage these portfolios of loans and debt. They can mess me up or help me out or remain neutral. Actually, one of my most fun trades was one where the manager was probably trying to mess me up. I think they were trying to protect the senior notes, and I owned the more junior note. They sold a lot of collateral to lock in prices because the senior note would be protected if all the collateral were sold, and I'd be largely wiped out.

Because of some strange rules, most of those proceeds were going to go to me. It was just a freak thing in the structure of the bond. The manager by accident, or accidently on purpose, managed to sell a lot of extra collateral that period. I was watching and saying, "This is too good to be true." I thought that was a decent trade with a little upside, but then I saw the manager actually making these voluntary sales as well.

I ran it past our in-house lawyers, and asked, "Am I reading this right? It's crazy. Can this possibly have been structured this way?" They all said, "It looks like that to us. I think that's right." When the due period ended, I waited out three days so they wouldn't reverse the trade, and then called the trustee. I said,

"Before you distribute the money, let's make sure we don't have a problem with how you understand the rules to read." It was a new trustee, and he said, "No, I've looked at it. It sounds like you get almost all the money, don't you?" I said, "I do!"

He said, "I have to tell you the manager is pretty upset about this. They've hired outside counsel to try and block this because they can't believe it works this way." But it did.

I focus a lot on legal documents. Lawyers don't always catch everything. They try to plan, but if they miss something or misstate something, that is a gold mine.

MJ: How does that happen?

People often start a deal by taking a block of language from another previous deal, putting it in, and then starting to write from there. Sometimes they put in contradictory things, or put something in they didn't mean to. The terms are at odds. One term takes precedence over the other. It is a fun area to invest in for all of these reasons, the interplay between the legal language and the underlying credit quality, and what's happening in the market.

MJ: So it's quantitative, but you also can profit off human error?

MH: It is very nitty-gritty, detailed work, looking for this interplay between the collateral pool and the legal language, intentional or not.

MJ: And you did that until 2004?

MH: In January 2005, I moved into proprietary trading, which was more of the same. I was given a very broad mandate. I think they said, "You can even do equities or whatever you want. You've done a wide variety of things. I'm sure you'll find something you love." I think one risk manager said, "You have the gift that keeps on giving. You always find something to invest in."

MJ: And the bonus was, you could just create something if you couldn't find something.

MH: I had a wide variety of tools at my disposal. The first couple of years on the desk, however, I just knew so many of these bonds that I continued with the same story.

By 2006, I was starting to think, it's time to wrap it up. Let's liquidate the collateral and start looking at what the next thing will be. I was hearing, and obviously anyone in America knew, about the housing bubble and loose underwriting.

The Big Bet

MJ: When did Greenspan first start talking about that? It was 2005-ish?

MH: I was going to say earlier, but maybe it was 2005 [author's note: It was October 2004].

I had a personal bet on it. I weaseled my way into this bet with the research team at Bear Stearns when I heard about it. Almost everybody thought housing prices can never fall year-over-year, any year. There can't be a bubble, and there can't be a mortgage wipeout.

There may be a pocket of distress, but you'll never have a year-over-year housing price correction. But I'd seen a lot of surprising things. So I took the other side of the bet. Anyway, I did think that was probably the next big thing. I assumed we probably had time before it happened, but I needed to get geared back up, which required more modeling. I needed a large infrastructure to get involved in mortgage-backed securities. I wanted to be ready for when the bonds were cheap. I loved horribly cheap markets. I went through the CDOs in 2001, and the RMBS [residential mortgage backed securities] back in '94, '95. Those were great markets, so I thought, "I'm going to be ready for this one. Let me put the team together."

That was right about the time that Bear decided to put together a large prop unit similar to Goldman's prop unit. I joined Wendy de Monchaux, my former boss in derivatives, on that team in late 2006, and started putting together a mortgage team. We had four of us. Li Chang was one of them. She's with me now. Then I hired the guy I had worked with at Boeing, the one who taught me all of these modeling tricks, I pulled him back from retirement.

He put together a home price appreciation model. Li put together the loan level analysis tool, and then a junior trader looked through bonds so we had some capacity to keep up with a rapidly moving market when the time came. We put this all together, but as this was happening, the mortgage market fell apart. We were watching it completely collapse as the models were coming together

MJ: So you didn't have any capital at risk?

MH: I was getting more urgent about wrapping up the CDO book. That's what I spent my time doing: watching what they were doing on the models and trying to wrap up my CDOs.

MJ: Just out of curiosity, did the guys ever pay up on the housing bubble bet?

MH: By the time they would have paid it off, Bear collapsed. It was going to be dinner, and everyone scattered.

MJ: So at the beginning of 2007, you're selling the CDOs and you don't have any positions in mortgage backed securities...

MH: I typically didn't sell the CDOs. I typically collapsed them. I would get the manager to sell collateral, and we liquidated from the inside. There was very little risk by the end.

The MBS models came together probably by July, and we were getting good results. But it didn't look like a cheap market. I had been in such attractive markets. I thought mortgage-backed securities should look screamingly cheap with all that's happening. The BSAM [Bear Stearns Asset Management] funds collapsed in August, and I thought, "This is something I don't want to get involved with, really, on either side." The market was jumping back and forth ten points every other week or so.

By January 2008, I'd put on large short positions in CMBS [commercial mortgage-backed securities] and leveraged loan markets. The CMBS trade widened all throughout January, particularly at the end. I remember the joy of coming back from some conference when it was collapsing. On the plane ride back from the conference, people on the plane were comparing notes. "You got the CMBS trade? I did too."

In March of 2008, the spread blasted out. I was cheering it on.

Then I noticed Bear Stearns stock was falling pretty dramatically at the same time. There was a real disconnect in wondering if Bear was having that serious of a problem and enjoying all the money I was making on my short positions. I started going, "Whoa. Is this the same thing?"

I didn't really understand until the last few days that we were in such dire straits.

MJ: I'm not sure anybody did. I was actually at one of the last cocktail parties their prime brokerage group hosted the week before everything hit the fan. I would say nobody in that room knew what was happening, or they didn't show it if they did know what was happening.

MH: I have a friend who is quite involved in day trading and writing options on positions in financial companies. She used to call at least a couple of times a day, saying, "Is Bear going under?" I was saying, "You're annoying me. Stop it. It's not going under. I've got work to do. I'm busy." I just had no tolerance for this question, which I thought was so silly.

But she was absolutely right. It was collapsing, and I just didn't see it. That Thursday night was when Bear went to the Fed and called Jamie Dimon.

Friday morning when I walked in, everyone was excited. The stock was up. We got this cash injection. We had a month to find more cash. Everyone was euphoric. My boss called on the way in, and I asked, "Wendy, what does this mean? Is this good news?" She said in the tiniest voice, "Marj, it's over. They don't understand, but it's over. You don't survive when you go to the Fed."

Sure enough, around noon, the stock started to plunge again. I guess more people digested what it meant.

That weekend I thought we were still going out at $20 per share or so. Then there was the news that they settled on $2 per share on Sunday evening. I had friends call from out of town, an old friend of mine from Bear Stearns, and he gave me the news. I said, "That's a ridiculous price. They can't be it. I'm sure there's a digit missing."

Most people on Monday left soon after they came back into the office. Once they figured out what was going on, most people went and looked for a job immediately. We had positions to unwind.

It was probably a month before J.P. Morgan even wanted to meet us and find out what we had. We stayed, but we all started to think about what we wanted to do. What's the next step? I thought, maybe it is time for me to think about starting a hedge fund. I probably should have done it for a few years, but I loved Bear, and it was just too easy to stay.

But J.P. Morgan had a large group that did mortgage-backed securities, and they wanted me to focus more on CDOs. I wanted the ability to move from product to product. I really wanted to leave, and finally I asked Wendy if I could be let go. I stayed through sometime in June. Then I went off to find something else to do.

The Birth of a Hedge Fund

MJ: And thus Altum was born.

MH: I wanted to go some place that had seed capital and the wherewithal to start a fund, but where they had nothing that interfered with what I would be doing.

I joined Capstone in January '09. I'd met them in probably August the first time, and then talked to them through the fall. They were not very deeply involved in credit, which meant they didn't really understand how bad the problem was in 2008. It would be hard to know on the outside whether what happened in the markets was an overreaction or something fundamentally, horribly miscalculated. I think that was their interest in me. They wanted to hire someone who could give them that insight. The kind of people that can provide that insight don't dislodge from Wall Street often. It was a talent grab.

MJ: They certainly had a lot of Wall Streeters to grab after 2008.

MH: Paul Britton is a very entrepreneurial guy. I think he just thought, "I've got to be doing something here. There's just too much opportunity in front of me."

MJ: And what did you tell Britton about the credit market? Did you tell him it was overblown or a fundamental problem?

MH: It was fundamental. It wasn't overblown. It was a horrible miscalculation. We can talk about who I think was responsible, or how bad it was, but it was a horrible miscalculation.

When I was starting to think about starting a hedge fund or joining a hedge fund back in 2004–2005, I instead went into prop trading. I knew I didn't know anything about starting a fund. I didn't know anything about what people wanted in a hedge fund. I wanted to go someplace where they were good at it and could help with that aspect. I knew how to trade, but I didn't know how to create a sellable hedge fund product.

MJ: Although you had built businesses before.

MH: But they were mainly trading and things I knew enough to figure out. I knew this was something that I didn't really know. I didn't know how to find investors or how to ask them what they were looking for. It's a professional market. I knew what I could provide, but I didn't know how to make a product that investors would like.

MJ: So the credit market has fundamental and systemic issues and you're launching a fund. How did you position that?

MH: I thought that would be wonderful. I like a long, nice recovery cycle. The Fed sped it up, the recovery, which wasn't exactly what I hoped for. For one thing, the recovery got going by even March. We didn't launch until July. I was kind of watching it all on the sidelines saying, "Wait! I'm not there yet!"

MJ: Yeah, the bottom was March 10th, March 11th, something like that?

MH: Traders were pretty aggressively putting on risk, mainly in the markets that were more liquid. The mortgage market had a quick run, not that it was by any means over, but it had heavy "risk-on" appetite.

The corporate markets and equities certainly were much the same: feeling that the economy was going to be saved by the Fed's stimulus. But almost immediately the CDO market was dropping. Even the underlyings of the CDO market were rallying, but the CDOs themselves were dropping in price because people were not interested in them.

So we started buying CDOs as well. It's probably two weeks into our trading when we picked up our first CDO. It was incredibly cheap, but we weren't set up for it yet. We had to do a lot by hand, and scrambled to put some tools together. That became a competing effort throughout the fall and winter of

2009 and into 2010, putting together better systems so we could do things more rapidly.

Corporates had a really bad October 2009, and the CDOs kept rallying because they were so cheap. Then mortgages had a horrible November. We sold out of our mortgages first, thinking that after what's happened in corporate, mortgages couldn't be far behind. We managed to avoid the correction in mortgages in November, and then bought again in December. By then, they were so cheap they were more attractive again. The cycles on corporates and mortgages were close, but not identical. They have a loose linkage, but they're not exactly identical. You can get some diversification by being in different markets, or you can see some patterns of what's to come by watching other markets.

Anyway, by the end of 2009 and early 2010, we decided that CDOs were just a better product than mortgages, and largely lightened up on our mortgages and focused on CDOs.

MJ: How did the capital raising process go? I would guess that initially people were, perhaps, a little scared of mortgages and derivatives? Or even full of hatred and recrimination?

MH: They didn't like anything with three-letter names.

MJ: Yes. Exactly.

MH: Capstone had had a fabulous experience with the ease of raising money up until then. They had a great marketing team that took me all around Europe, which was their focus.

We had really warm receptions. The head marketer would say, "This is exactly the kind of reception you get when you're going to get money out of these guys." As I'm taking notes at the end of each meeting, he'd say, "That was a good meeting. Write down $40 million. They're probably good for $40 million." I would write $40 million, and go on to the next meeting, thinking we're raising a lot of money here. Years later I went back to those notes. I raised $550 million.

MJ: On that one trip?

MH: On that one trip. But in practice, no money was raised. Afterwards, we went to Canada for a time, then Texas, then Brazil. Back to Europe again. February 1st, I got my first $1 million investment.

MJ: Nice.

MH: I told this guy, you're always number one to us. It was just so wonderful to answer the assets question differently. When investors ask, "Is it all seed capital?" I could say, "No. We have somebody who believes in us as well." It was a wonderful thing, but it was only $1 million. Finally, the money started getting more serious just past the one-year mark. People kept saying, if you get a one-year record, that's all people are waiting for. Then you'll get your hundreds of millions.

By the time we started getting serious traction with investors, we started getting more serious feedback as well. The pushback was that the setup wasn't ideal. The seed capital was a reallocation of Capstone's investors' money, and the strategy that Capstone ran was a very liquid strategy. Most people invested through either a monthly or quarterly full liquidity product. This meant our seed capital could be called on either a monthly or quarterly basis. We were in relatively illiquid product and looking for a longer lockup.

I came up with a plan that would let me do a management buyout basically. I just had to replace the seed capital because it was only allowed to be in an affiliated fund. Once I was separated, the fund wouldn't be affiliated anymore.

There were a lot of things that we had to get set up. By January 2012, we were all done. It was a fairly smooth transition.

Risks and Rewards

MJ: I think the credit and derivatives investment space is less accessible to many investors. Do you find that you have to do a lot of educating or reeducation?

MH: There are still people who come in and say, "I don't know much about structured products, but I know it's important and I need to invest." In the beginning, nobody said that. They just said, "Isn't that scary?"

And in many ways, structured products continue to be three-letter words. I always viewed CDOs as just debt. Everything was debt. It was emerging markets. It was loans. It was high-yield bonds, investment grade bonds, et cetera. All of that was CDOs. But that's not really how the terminology developed in the markets. CDOs became the mortgage market's resecuritization product, and CLOs became the better product. I had to learn to take it off my description of what we do because it was scaring people. CLOs became okay, and CDOs were not okay.

With CDO's I think there was a basic flaw. The technology that the rating agencies used when analyzing, for instance, a high-yield-bond-backed deal, said that if you had high yield debt across a number of different industries (hospitality, industrials, utilities, etc.), they're not going to all have stress at the same time. And they're not all identical, and the diversification protects the senior tranches. But with mortgage tranches as collateral, they were more identical than not. Putting 100 of them together doesn't give you much diversification.

MJ: Obviously, you still have the mortgage component within the portfolio, and interest rates have been low and stable since the fund launch. Do you model at all for interest rates or an interest rate increase?

MH: We don't have very much interest-rate exposure. Most of our instruments have underlying loans that are a floating rate.

I think the bigger thing is we could start to get some credit risk developing with UK homeowners, for instance. Right now they're paying rates that are linked to short-term interest rates. You have to assume that they'll start to fall a little more delinquent and have more defaults as rates rise.

There's also a belief that some homeowners will prepay and try and lock in a new fixed rate for another two or three years. There isn't a very long product like in the United States, where you can get a 30-year loan. In the United Kingdom, it's just a few years. But there's a belief that some people will try and lock that in, so there may be a prepayment that won't be to our benefit. It turns into a prepayment risk.

Then I think the bigger thing is just generally default risk. Not every corporation is 100 percent hedged to fixed rates. If they are 80 percent or 70 percent fixed rate and a little bit floating rate, they're going to have some trouble making the debt payment when rates start to rise again. This will happen throughout the system. Credit card holders, everyone gets a little more stretched when rates are rising.

I think the whole default experience will rise as rates rise. That's the bigger part of it.

MJ: I think there's a lot of disagreement as to what's happening in the markets. I was just at a conference where the guy speaking before me insisted we're only in year five of the 15-year secular bull market. Then I came home, and there was a study by Credit Suisse that said we're at the beginning of the end of the bull market. How do you structure your portfolio to deal with bull and bear markets?

MH: We have hedges. The way we structured the portfolio is, we don't use external leverage, or we haven't to date. There might be a reason for it at some point, but...

MJ: But your instruments are inherently leveraged.

MH: That's right. We buy bonds and have inherent leverage, but not repo financing. We also use hedges, and the hedges can be of varying intensity. In 2011 we raised them substantially in the second half, which obviously worked really well.

Nowadays, we have the hedges relatively light. Even though there's been a market pullback, I'm not that concerned that this is the end of the bull market. The end may be a year or two away. Then there will be a correction, but it may not be a deep correction.

We've been through something pretty horrible, and I think there's still a lot of caution in the system and genuine recovery to go. I do think that there will be a pullback and a more substantial correction and that as rates rise we'll normalize, or at least I'm optimistic we'll normalize.

The European market has been lagging, and I think does have more room to run. The financial institutions are all still doing cleanup. Then, in addition, these hard assets that aren't even securitized yet will give rise to better securitization or better opportunities. Yeah, I think that recovery will be ongoing for a while.

MJ: So has the European component of your portfolio changed over time?

MH: It's been growing. I think that it will grow again for another couple of years and then probably start trending back maybe even into late next year. I think there will be some good opportunities in the United States again.

MJ: How do you deal with risks in the portfolio, particularly the liquidity risk? These are not particularly liquid instruments...

MH: If there's a serious problem, the markets become frozen, and some of the less liquid instruments can be almost completely frozen for months. Eventually, the market gets going again, but really takes the catalyst of a forced seller, someone who has to sell, to define the market and open it back up again.

That can happen several months into a frozen market. We saw that in the second half of 2011. Finally, probably it was the middle of November, when some of the European CLO mezzanine bonds started to trade again, and at very poor levels.

I think for many people that is a pretty big concern. That you can go through a stage like that. Typically, not every market is going to be terribly distressed or terribly frozen, but the worst ones can be.

MJ: Is that a problem for you or are you generally not selling into that market?

MH: We don't want to sell into that market. We have structured our fund so we offer quarterly liquidity with 45 days' notice. That's really generous liquidity terms. But if a significant redemption happens, and we're in a frozen market like that, we may have to sell bonds for the investor and they'll get the proceeds of that sale.

We're trying to come up with a way where investors can redeem because it's their money. We'll sell their bonds for them over about 90 days. They know they'll get whatever they get. Some people will have to do this. Some people will say, "I need the money and I don't care that it's a stressed market. I don't have a flexibility to last any longer." They should be able to take their money, but ongoing investors shouldn't be penalized.

Learning to Lose

MJ: You sound like you have empathy for those that stick it out and those that want to sell.

MH: I had a large loss around 1993 or 1994. The market blew up, and I personally bled $16 million dollars in two weeks.

I remember what that felt like. It was horrendous. You just don't want to be in that situation.

MJ: Did you feel like that loss changed your perspective?

MH: It did. It was three months into the year. I was up $8 million and then bled $16 almost immediately. I was down $8 million, but I had another nine months to go, and that turned out to be a good year for me. In fact, the senior managers, I mean, this is the old Bear Stearns for you, they called me in and basically slapped me on the back and said, "Well, there's your red badge of courage. Everyone goes through it. Until you've done it, you don't know what it feels like. It will affect your trading." They were very supportive. They said, "Don't do it again, but you're not fired because you did it once. It happens."

MJ: What changed for you after that loss?

MH: I had a risk that was developing that was growing daily. I knew I needed to liquidate a position to rebalance, and I just didn't want to lose money by selling in a weak market. Day after day, I didn't hit the bid. Bids just weren't close enough to my price and I didn't do it. Finally, Warren Spector came in and said, "You can sell positions. I'll show you." He just started hitting the bid even down half a point.

I was like, "Oh, you're killing me! You're losing all this money!" But he got rid of the position, wiped his hands, and said, "There, you can always sell a position." I think that showed me there is always a market. Just force yourself to do it. It will be worse tomorrow. If you're in a bloodbath, you can't assume you'll outlast it. Maybe you're wrong. Maybe you shouldn't even try. It may not come back. It may be that you miscalculated. You have to have willingness to be disciplined.

MJ: I always tell people a trader's famous last words are, "It's too late to sell!" You're saying it's never too late to sell.

MH: I think that's right. Everyone thinks that they'll just ride it out and then it will come back and you'll be the hero and all.

That's the thing: you can always sell your position. Sometimes it's the smarter thing to do. Just get out of it, clear your head. I guess that's what I took away from what Warren showed me.

MJ: Today if you had something in your portfolio that wasn't performing, would you hesitate to hit the bid?

MH: Would I hesitate? Yes. But I would do it. I think you have to make it to another day. If that means sell and lose some, you still have to do it.

MJ: Another thing I noticed is that your position sizes tend to be pretty small. Is that another layer of risk management, since smaller positions tend to be easier to liquidate?

MH: Not completely. We seldom see a block of bonds that we want to buy that's large enough that we have to take 50 percent but not the whole thing. It happens sometimes, but it's really rare.

I do think part of the risk management is to find cheap bonds.

If you buy something that just looks incredibly attractive versus where the overall market is, whether on income or to maturity, you have some comfort that it will fall less when the market has a panic or if something goes wrong. We tend to find cheaper bonds are smaller bonds.

Large players will pay a lot more for bonds than we will, and they only want large bonds. They can't be bothered looking at smaller pieces. Some of the larger funds will say, "If it's not a $20 million block, don't show it to me. I've got too much money to put to work." When bonds come out individually or in small sizes, they tend to be cheap. It's a little bit less liquid, although they're not untradable. They are social sizes.

Distressed Is Best

MJ: So small positions are part of your strategy, not necessarily part of your risk management.

MH: That's exactly right. I think buying distressed bonds is part of our risk management, as is buying cheap bonds.

Throughout my career, one of the themes is to go into markets where the run hasn't largely happened yet and stay out of the more frothy areas that everyone is comfortable with. It's going to be a more competitive market with lots more people involved. I'm mainly looking for markets that haven't had that much exposure yet and have a lot more room on the upside. I think that's part of risk management.

MJ: I guess that explains the period of time pre-2008 when you anticipated the buying opportunities in the mortgage market?

MH: It's about what's coming next. Warren told me one time that some of his best trades were shorts and that I should think harder about putting short positions on in the market. My focus has always been bottom fishing and looking for something cheap. I can analyze a bond in great detail, but short positions tend to be more of a macro trade in our space.

When I was thinking about the housing market being a bubble, I could get ready for the bottom fishing opportunity. It really didn't dawn on me so much that I should be focused on "the big short."

MJ: Do you feel like there's more risk involved in the cheap and distressed bonds that you're buying? Obviously, there's additional liquidity risk, but what else?

MH: There are more legal risks and misunderstanding risks. The whole legal aspect becomes much more relevant in a distressed bond. It's also more the timing of the corporate event or the underlying event. In a well-performing bond, you just need the general pool not to do too badly, and you'll get out on schedule and you'll get your decent yield. Whereas in something like this we may have a dramatic difference if the bankruptcy wraps up in one year or two years.

MJ: How do you find these great distressed deals? I know you have large quantitative systems and a lot of relationships in place...

MH: The models that run overnight are doing a very complicated but a fixed set of analyses for us. For one thing, they're cleansing the collateral pool and filling in missing data and correcting data, and then telling us what the system has done.

MJ: Data janitor work.

MH: That's right. The second thing is running option-adjusted spread models and saying what fair value ought to be.

All of that is waiting for us in the morning. But when we hear about a bond, it's from a relationship. People call up to tell you they have seen an interesting bond. It's like a stream. It's flowing by all the time. You may not be interested in this bond. You'll not be able to get to this other bond because you have too much on your plate. But when you are interested and you grab it, you need to pull up all the information that was run nightly. You look at that, but then you also have to do your own screening. Did they do a good job of this? Is there something else I should know? Reading that legal document, trying to get a sense of where the risk is or what the opportunity is in this situation. Most of that isn't done by the machine.

MJ: I don't know that many people realize how large the credit markets are. In fact, they're bigger than the equity markets. If people ignore the credit markets, do you feel like they're ignoring the lion's share of what the market is?

MH: That's absolutely true. I also think it is a more risk-controlled part of the market than the equity markets. Volatility is much higher in equities than in any of these fixed-income markets. It's definitely not a do-it-yourself thing. All of this is not something you can do on the back of the envelope or with Excel spreadsheets or anything. But people should be involved in these markets. You have more control over the alpha part of the trade, whereas in a liquid market product, it's mainly beta that you are getting exposure to.

CHAPTER 7

The Simple Things: Relative Value and Directional Credit Investing

Olga Chernova, Managing Principal and
Chief Investment Officer, Sancus
Capital Management

One of the favorite topics of magazine editors and blog writers is simplicity. Look online or in your favorite publication and you are likely to find a host of suggestions on how to strip away clutter, wasted time, unnecessary expenses, or anything that adds complexity or waste to our lives. Perhaps that's why Leonardo da Vinci is rumored to have once quipped, "Simplicity is the ultimate sophistication."

And yet, in investing we tend to value the complex. We create impenetrable jargon to talk about intricate models and complicated instruments, creating an air of opaque complexity around investment strategies and products. In no area is this as evident as the credit markets, where structured products baffle even some professional investors.

But not Olga Chernova. A firm believer in finding simplicity within complex instruments, and of recognizing the hidden complexities in simple instruments, Chernova's goal is to create an accessible, understandable, and profitable strategy. "Most of the concepts in structured credit should be able to be explained in very, very simple terms," she says. "If someone can't, perhaps that is a reason not to invest."

Raised in Russia until just after the fall of the USSR, Chernova moved to the United States in 1992 at the age of 16. She quickly ascertained that finance was the heart of a capitalist economy and pursued a BA in Finance at Northwestern College and an MBA at Columbia University. Chernova was immediately attracted to credit derivatives at Goldman Sachs "because of the simplicity" and established a track record there and at J.P. Morgan before launching her own fund in 2009. In 2010, she was named one of "Tomorrow's Titans" by the *Hedge Fund Journal*.

Over time, Chernova has developed a set of rules and best practices that help her cut through the market noise and maintain discipline in her investment strategy. These rules, honed over 15 years of trading experience, have clearly served the fund and its investors well. Since its inception, her fund, Sancus Capital Management, has generated a compound annual return of 11.6 percent versus the HFRX Hedge Fund Index's 2.69 percent return over the same period.

Not every year has been simple, however. In 2011, the Greek debt crisis sparked an annual loss of 5.1 percent in the fund. However, Chernova says that, if faced with the same ominous signs today (a potential default, the collapse of the Euro and systemic financial institution risk), she would make the same decisions. Her strict adherence to her disciplined strategy and her belief in capital preservation are indeed two of the hallmarks of Chernova's strategy. Her other keys to success?

- Don't assume popular and "straightforward" instruments are simple. Bonds, for example, can have embedded options that many investors may not understand.
- Maintain discipline around your trading strategy, including the use of stop losses and liquidity and leverage parameters. Rules help you take a step back and clear your head.
- Continuously evaluate your investment thesis to ensure the conditions you need to make a profit are still in place.
- You aren't the only smart person in the world. If you are making investments that no one else is doing, review your thesis to determine whether you are early or wrong.

From Communism to Capitalism

MJ: Coming from a communist country, what led you to pursue the uber-capitalist profession of hedge fund manager?

OC: I came to the United States after graduating from high school in Russia. I was 16, and that was a very exciting time because communism had just collapsed, and Russia opened up. It was about the first time that people could travel. I came to the United States, and everything here was interesting and exotic to me. I really wanted to learn how this country worked.

It seemed like there was no better way to learn about the country than to figure out finance. I picked the subject pretty much instantaneously after I reviewed what was offered at my college. The classes were mostly focused on corporate finance and less so on capital markets.

After finishing my studies, my first job was in corporate finance at a firm in Japan. I really enjoyed it, and I probably would have never have turned to trading if I hadn't met a senior executive from Cargill, which is a Minnesota-based commodity trader. He told me that if I liked finance, I should go and work for a firm where finance was the main focus.

He also pointed out that very rarely do finance people get to run manufacturing companies, which is where I was working. It's usually engineers. I thought it was good advice, so I joined Cargill, and this is really how my career in financial markets began.

MJ: How long were you at Cargill?

OC: I was at Cargill for a little bit longer than a year. It was at Cargill that I realized that having an MBA would open up more doors for me. It was a very popular degree at the time, more so than perhaps now. I really felt that getting an MBA would give me a broader range of opportunities, rather than just being based at Cargill in Minnesota. I applied to a number of schools and went on to get my MBA at Colombia University.

MJ: At Columbia did you focus more on the capital markets?

OC: At Columbia, I focused on the financial markets. I had a somewhat unusual experience because in a sense my experience was the reverse of what usually happens in an MBA program. People typically study the first year, and goof off and network their second year. I was super excited to be in New York. I loved everything about it. I was goofing off my first year, because it was a pretty easy program. My undergrad major was finance, so a lot of the things that year were repetition.

However, my summer internship was at Goldman [Sachs], and I was offered a job at the end of my internship in credit derivatives. I became much more serious and decided that, since this is what I am going to be pursuing for my career, I wanted to get more substance.

My second year, I went to the Vice Dean in the business school and I asked him if I could take classes in financial engineering at the Engineering School. He said, "Yes, sure, no problem. As long as you pay your MBA tuition." Which I did my second year. I also ended up working part-time at Goldman during my second year.

As a result, my second year was very, very busy. So it was pretty much the reverse of what happens to most MBA students.

MJ: So you went from Russia to Minnesota to Japan to Minnesota to New York?

OC: Yes, exactly.

MJ: I assume New York must have been your favorite since you are still there?

OC: New York is definitely my favorite.

MJ: So you went to Goldman after getting your MBA. What was your life like there? What types of things were you doing?

OC: At Goldman, I decided to pursue my career in credit. My internship was a typical rotational program. The interns were shown different areas of the firm. I was always pretty mathematically inclined. Back in Russia I participated in math contests, so I wanted to be involved in derivatives. I was very attracted to the fact that, while they seemed like complex structures, they could be deconstructed into simple building blocks. Then those blocks could be rearranged in a different manner that produced different solutions.

It seemed very elegant and simple, like solving puzzles. I was interested in both interest rates derivatives and credit derivatives, but credit derivatives were pretty much brand new. In 1999, ISDA [International Swaps and Derivatives Association] came up with a standardized definition, and it really gave a catalyst to the nascent credit derivatives market.

MJ: Because it was a new field, what did your peers look like at the time? Were they mathematicians like you?

OC: A lot of people came from the interest rate derivatives desk. They mostly had mathematical backgrounds. And it was tiny. I think we pretty much knew everybody who traded similar products on The Street.

MJ: Were there a lot of other women in the credit or interest rate derivatives area? Were you one of many or one of few?

OC: I was definitely one of few. I think it's always been the case, and still, 20 years later, there seem to be fewer women, especially on the trading side. You would see more women perhaps in the sales roles. The trading was always very loosely populated with women.

MJ: Did you find that at all odd? Or intimidating?

OC: This is a very interesting question. I think I generally have thought very little of the fact that I am a woman in this industry, mostly because of my upbringing. One actually good and very progressive thing about communism was the fact that they were very gender neutral. When I was growing up, I grew up completely free of any kind of gender bias. Never was I told, or was it even mentioned anywhere in society, that because you were a girl you may not be able to pursue a career in math or anything quantitative. I found that this was very helpful to me and very liberating. When I worked at Goldman or J.P. Morgan, I knew there were not very many women, but I never even paused to consider why.

MJ: And you stayed at Goldman before eventually transitioning to Dillon Read and then J.P. Morgan? How was Goldman different from J.P. Morgan?

Goldman Sachs was amazing. It was extremely well run, but at the same time, very decentralized and very entrepreneurial. It felt like you were running your own little business on your desk. I definitely felt that no reasonable idea would be declined by management.

I had a number of different trading roles, although always in credit. I traded a lot of different products for Goldman. I went to

London to develop a high-yield credit derivatives trading market in Europe. At J.P. Morgan, I worked on the prop desk, in a much more senior role. I was a managing director already at the time. It was a very useful experience but in a very different way. I was part of big multistrategy group, and I was also part of the risk committee. I spent a lot of time with people from different areas, such as equities and interest rate trading. I learned a lot from those different perspectives.

Educating Investors

MJ: How does one go about building a high-yield credit market?

OC: It was 2002, and Goldman wanted to expand the business to London, to the European market. I was focusing on high-yield credit derivatives. The high-yield market in Europe is generally smaller. We actually were trying to hire somebody there, but because the market was so new, there were very few experienced people. At the end of the day, we decided that I was going to go and try to kick-start it myself.

I had to learn a new set of corporates, a new set of bankruptcy codes and rules, which are all very different in Europe because you have so many different countries with different legal systems. I think it definitely was very useful in light of my later career and what we do now, to have spent time in Europe learning European markets.

MJ: What types of products were you working with specifically at that time?

OC: A very popular product was a cross-currency extinguishing swap. They are also sometimes called "perfect swaps." They were used by European CLOs [collateralized loan obligations.] In Europe at the time, there was not enough diversity to satisfy rating agencies. As a result, European managers tried to put in bonds denominated in sterling and also denominated in US dollars.

However, that was creating a foreign exchange and interest rate risk that was not acceptable for this type of structure. The idea was to come up with an instrument that effectively made your interest rate swap and your FX swap go away, with no mark-to-market, in case the credit defaulted.

It's effectively a credit derivative, just a little bit more complicated credit derivative, because it has an interest rate and the foreign exchange component. Those were the instruments that, at the time, I was trading the most, in addition to market making in simple CDS products. It pretty much enabled European CLOs to function.

MJ: Is that what you focused on for most of the time that you were in Europe?

OC: It was a big focus. Also, we were focused on developing regular market making in high-yield derivatives, offering investors alternatives alongside corporate bonds. We had to educate investors on the fact that credit derivatives had some potentially interesting features, such as floating rate risks, the ability to customize maturities, and no callability bullet structures.

MJ: So you took on the role of educator for these new products?

OC: Very much so. I worked very closely with the salespeople and attended many investor meetings. We were educating people and explaining to them what we were doing and how potentially the instruments could be beneficial to their portfolio.

MJ: I would say the credit markets in general and derivatives specifically remain murky for many investors, even today. What types of things did you stress to potential investors as the benefits of credit derivatives?

OC: What is really interesting about this market is the number of different instruments that people can use. In fact, I think credit derivatives came about because seemingly simple instruments, like a corporate bond, are actually not all that simple.

If you think of a typical high-yield corporate bond, it has a lot of embedded options and embedded risks. First of all, it combines interest rate risks together with credit risks. Most high-yield bonds are actually callable by the issuer, so the investor is basically short the call option. On the other hand, many high-yield bonds are also putable by the investor, so then you are long a put option. In addition to all of that, most corporates can take out about 35 to 40 percent of the bond issue if the company files for an IPO [initial public offering]. Some bonds have the right to pay the interest in kind. They are called PIKs.

So bonds are actually very complex instruments. They are very easy to purchase, but at the same time, they combine many options inside and have some complicated features that you may not want as an investor.

Credit derivatives came about to create a more simplified instrument, one that specifically focuses just on credit risks. Now, credit derivatives are a little bit more complicated to settle. I think sometimes investors get confused about, or at least don't differentiate, the operational risks associated with trading some of the derivatives structure versus actual investment complexity.

Investing during the Meltdown

MJ: So to misquote Sigmund Freud, "Sometimes a bond isn't just a bond." You went to J.P. Morgan in 2007, right before the financial crisis hit. What was that like?

OC: J.P. Morgan was obviously a very big organization. I think perhaps certain areas were more cognizant of the crisis earlier than others. The proprietary trading area definitely was. If you think about it, that's the area that is effectively betting the capital of J.P. Morgan on the best possible investments (hopefully). It had a lot of very good talent, and I think people were very, very aware of what was going on. It was easier to see this because it was a multistrategy unit, so you could really see stress coming through different areas of the market.

For us it was a very exciting time. I would say one of the best trades in my career so far was done during that time. It was actually done using 100 percent credit derivative products. They definitely came in very handy during the financial crisis.

In the spring of '08, we were very focused on shorting some of the financial institutions in Europe, given everything that we saw happening in the markets. In early summer, the European governments came in and guaranteed some of the most important systemic institutions. There was an instrument called iTraxx

Financial Senior Index. It was referencing 25 names, European banks and insurance companies. It tightened approximately 100 basis points because the government was guaranteeing the underlying financial institutions.

However, implied volatility in the options was still extremely elevated. Realized volatility was dropping very, very fast, but implied volatility was still sticky. In fact, if you look at the implied volatility, it was so high that it was interesting to sell options and straddles. Break even for the straddle pretty much covered the full historical trading range of the index.

Because the options were so mispriced, it was very interesting to sell volatility. But at the same time I was running the credit side of the prop desk. We were generally in the business of buying options, not selling options. Furthermore, based on everything that we were seeing, even though the governments were guaranteeing the largest banks, the financial institutions were still very over-levered and far from out of the woods.

We were uncomfortable selling straddles without buying back any of the payor protection. This is exactly when we looked at the market on sovereign CDS. It had just started to trade, and all the European sovereigns were trading super tight, anywhere between 3 to 7 basis points. We thought buying sovereign CDS was the perfect tail hedge for us selling straddles. The thought process was, okay, we are selling straddles and betting that volatility decreases, but if we are wrong and spreads widen again, which would only happen in an environment of great stress, then something must be wrong with the governments.

Now, it was a very remote possibility at the time. But nonetheless, it felt like it was a perfect hedge. This is what we did. We in fact put on our straddles, and we bought a bunch of sovereign CDS protection on European sovereigns. We monetized most of our straddles over the summer and decided to keep our tail hedge, even after we took options off. Our conviction was really growing that the market was mispricing sovereign CDS. People were laughing at us, saying, "You don't understand. The sovereigns can't default."

First of all, sovereigns can default, as we saw later on. But in this case, the bet was not so much on the default, but on the potential volatility and the tail risks. So we kept the tail hedge.

Then, a month later, Lehman happened. Our sovereign protection went from single digits to 100-plus basis points.

It was our best month that year. I really loved that trade because I think it was very creative and we were very fortunate to notice the mispricing. We were one of the few groups who recognized that the same volatility risk was being priced by two markets in very different ways. We were able to capitalize on this mispricing.

MJ: What other trades worked well for you besides that one? Obviously, the credit markets are where we saw a lot of the problems expressed. The mortgage crisis, the housing bubble, the leverage in the financial system, all of those things manifested in the credit markets. What were your other big trades?

OC: We definitely had a number of other trades that did well. Overall, that year we ended up being extremely profitable. The sovereign trade was not the only trade that worked. Another interesting thing was basis between credit derivatives and cash bonds. We traded a lot of the bond/CDS basis, first by shorting the bond basis into this widening of cash, and then, at the end of '08, going the other way and buying stressed bonds and hedging them with CDS, basically locking in positive cash flow and waiting for the basis to correct.

Credit derivatives are a perfect instrument for shorting. Because you are buying protection and you are buying it for term (five, seven, or ten years, depending on maturity of your contract), you know your borrowing costs. Your initial margin is locked in at the time of the trade. Nobody can shake you out of your trade, assuming you are not losing money overall and keeping your ISDA agreements intact.

If you look at shorting a corporate bond, it is very difficult to do. There is no term market. You can generally short for a month, sometimes three months, sometimes even up to six months, but there is no permanent lockup of the repo rate in the corporate space.

So you are constantly running a risk of refinancing. And guess what? The more people want to short something, the more expensive borrowing becomes. You eventually can be priced out of your short. It becomes so expensive for you to carry it that it becomes impractical. Credit derivatives don't have that problem, and that's why so many funds, even ones that don't specialize in credit, turned to credit derivatives during the crisis.

Because so many funds use credit derivatives to express a bearish view, the credit derivatives were moving first. They were the indicator of the initial stress. However, people's cash securities eventually caught up. Later in the crisis, after Lehman, this changed: credit derivatives stopped widening so much and cash securities—bonds, CLOs, converts—dropped.

Because part of the crisis was the excess leverage (banks were overleveraged, hedge funds were overleveraged, consumers were overleveraged), everybody was trying to run to the door and de-lever at the same time. Later on in the crisis, when people needed to unwind the books and sell assets, cash assets underperformed. At that point, credit derivatives probably had a more correct reflection of the actual credit risk. Other instruments reflected additional funding risk—the fact that people just didn't have enough cash in the system to pay for funded securities.

I think it was an interesting dynamic. This dynamic still happens in the markets. Derivatives tend to overshoot on the downside because they are a hedging vehicle of choice. At the same time, if a crisis gets into the next stage and becomes more severe, then derivatives actually start outperforming because people decide to finally sell what they own and unwind the hedges.

MJ: Did the fact that credit derivatives gave you an early warning help you choose your more bearish and profitable positions?

OC: Most definitely. I think by being active in the derivatives market, you can see all kinds of stress coming.

MJ: You mentioned that some of your colleagues thought that it was a little crazy to be betting against sovereign debt. Did you worry at all that you were wrong?

OC: In that particular case we were not worried. I think we were definitely analyzing our data. Any time we are critiqued, we consider the critique. You want to know what your opponents are thinking. We were debating and considering that they could be right, that there would not be a default of the sovereigns. But that's why we ultimately became even more convinced about the trade, because we did not need the actual default in order to make money. It was an increased volatility and tail risk bet.

I think it is very healthy to take contrarian views. We are not afraid to do that in our fund. Obviously not every contrarian view is always good. If we are the only people who are doing something, I get a little bit worried. We are not the only smart people in the market. But we are not afraid of being contrarian if, after a thorough examination of our opponent's criticism, we are still convinced that it is the right thing for us to do.

MJ: But trades where you aren't the only ones doing them can be a problem, too. Some researchers have identified that one of the problems with Long Term Capital Management, for example, was that they didn't know they weren't the only smart people in the markets and were therefore more correlated than they knew. If you worry when you don't see your peers in the same trades, do you also worry when you do see them there?

OC: I think with popular trades, it all depends when you enter them. Just because trades are popular doesn't mean that you won't make money. I think the danger with popular trades is when you enter them at the tail end of the trade, when most of the move has already happened. That is definitely something that we absolutely try to avoid. That's not what our investors are paying us to do. I think this is sometimes what happens to more retail-oriented, less experienced investors. By the time they hear about a certain trend, the trend may have already played out.

But you also bring up a very interesting point about correlation. We play a lot of the correlation in our strategy because we do some relative value trades. When you are running a relative value strategy, you eventually want correlation. You want convergence. You don't want to be the only person who sees this dislocation. If you are the only person who sees this dislocation, chances are the dislocation will continue to persist. You need other market participants buying into your theory. All you really want to do is to be the one forcing it earlier.

Support from Citi

MJ: Makes sense. So you made money throughout the financial crisis and then you started your own fund.

OC: When the crisis happened, it was very obvious that prop trading would no longer be what it used to be. That this is not the right venue to have this type of business, as part of a bank that is systemically important. I felt that I had a long career in credit. I ran several very successful groups, and I was ready to start something on my own. I negotiated my exit from J.P. Morgan and got a seed investment to start my current fund.

MJ: Your seed investment was from Citi, is that correct?

OC: Yes, it was Citi Group's fund of funds business.

MJ: And they funded you with how much money exactly?

OC: We got funded with $50 million, which was amazing at the time. We got the commitment to do the fund at the end of March 2009, which, if you look at the chart of the Standard & Poor's (S&P), was the bottom—basically the worst of the worst during the crisis. It was quite amazing that we got the money. I considered myself very fortunate.

MJ: Did you approach Citi, or did they approach you with the seeding opportunity?

OC: We approached them. We were introduced to them by one of the salespeople that covered us. He knew that I was leaving J.P. Morgan to start a fund. He said, "Why don't you talk to our funds of funds unit? I think there will be opportunities." They were considering seeding several funds and, needless to say, they had more applicants than they knew what to do with.

MJ: Did you continue to look at the same instruments and the same strategies in your own fund, or did that change when you left the bank?

OC: Our strategy remains very much the same. I believe we have a somewhat unique investment style. We combine fundamental high yield and arbitrage trading with more macro credit products. We also capitalize on dislocation and inefficiencies found in credit markets, because credit markets are very siloed.

However, our focus and use of specific products has varied over time. For example, right now, we focus a lot more on structured credit and CLOs, because the products have embedded complexity premiums. They are still priced significantly cheaper, and there are fewer market participants looking at them compared to more straightforward products.

That being said, right after the crisis, we used them less because there was no need to go into less liquid and more complex instruments when there was so much low-hanging fruit. We vary the allocations to different products throughout the cycle, depending on where we see opportunities and risk and liquidity trade-offs.

MJ: The typical universe of investments that you are looking at includes what instruments?

OC: We use pretty much all credit products that exist. We definitely use bonds, loans, CDS, CLOs, credit derivatives [CDX] indices and index options, and tranches, to name a few. Most often, we actually use a combination of these instruments, and this is what helps us create a nonlinear and very positively skewed return profile.

Our favorite trades are the ones that combine some fundamental cheapness together with some dislocation that is caused by trading flows that we believe might correct. In general, we focus on any dislocations that can be created by either regulatory or macro changes such as Dodd Frank or the Volcker Rule or banks having to shrink their balance sheets. That has traditionally given us a lot of trading opportunities and the ability to capitalize on inefficiencies.

A lot of it is just experience. Having traded credit since 1999, I see parallels in the cycles and know what instruments might be best for each stage. For example, I think 2003 and 2004 were very similar to 2009 and 2010. The economy was coming out of the crisis, and there were a number of great fundamental trades to be made, especially betting on lower defaults, steepening credit curves, and the reduction in volatility. I view 2011 and 2012 as the continuation of the financial crisis, just the second leg affecting Europe. It was very similar to 2007 and 2008: high cross-asset correlations and a lot of systemic risks.

I think 2005 and 2006 are similar to what we're experiencing now [2013 and 2014]. Perhaps fewer directional opportunities, increased focus on relative value, idiosyncratic risk increasing. The market is experiencing reduced correlations, and players are increasing leverage to achieve returns. I think the experience of having traded through the cycles gives us an edge.

MJ: So you use leverage? I know some of these instruments are inherently leveraged, but are you using financial leverage as well?

OC: We use both structural leverage, which is what you are referring to with the instrument being leveraged, as well as financial leverage. Structural leverage is one of our preferred ways of getting exposure because it has limited downside. You cannot lose more than you invested. So structured leverage, I think, is a very useful and powerful tool We do use financial leverage as well, either through the use of credit derivatives or repo.

We have an overall limit, a strict limit, of 4.5-times maximum exposure on the funds (including structural leverage). However, after running the funds for five years, the maximum exposure we used has not exceeded 2.6 times. Our financial leverage is significantly lower. That being said, I think leverage is a healthy and useful way to enhance returns. It just has to be very carefully managed on a daily basis.

A Disciplined Approach

MJ: A lot of people tend to be concerned about leverage. Some investors have moved away from portfolios that are leveraged. What would you say to people that are scared of leverage just because it happens to be leverage?

OC: There are people who say, "If we are not sure how to control it, let's not use it at all." I think, in general, that is the right approach. If you're not sure how to control leverage, you shouldn't use it. We have a concept of Capital Adequacy that we developed within our funds. It is a very robust way to limit the amount of leverage we can use overall in the portfolio. It ensures that we always have sufficient capital.

For example, we have a limit of 40 percent of AUM that can be used for initial margin via derivatives or repo or prime broker financing. In addition to that, we have a concept of internal risk capital where we take our portfolio and we stress it under quite extreme, worst-case scenarios. All positions are made to deviate and go against us with a correlation of one. If we have hedges, this scenario gives zero benefit to those hedges. It assumes that your long positions go against you, and your short positions go against you. If we reach our stress level limits, we cannot put on any new positions without taking off some of the existing trades off.

MJ: So you're saying leverage doesn't kill people. People using leverage kill people.

OC: Absolutely. It should be used responsibly. Prior to the crisis, people would lever risks 10 or 15 times. That is not healthy. But do I think that two to three times leverage in the current market is ok. We always look at overall system leverage. Corporate leverage is still pretty much under control. Households continue to de-lever. Banks are very strictly regulated. So really, the only part of the system that is over-levered is the governments.

MJ: So if leverage is a risk, but not a crippling risk, what are some of the other risk factors in your portfolio?

OC: There is definitely idiosyncratic default risk. One of the things we do well in the fund is to combine event-driven, single-name strategies together with basket macro products. Definitely on the single-name side of the portfolio, we are running idiosyncratic default risks and we have strict limits. We would not put more than 9 percent of the portfolio in any given name. We try to control idiosyncratic risks via diversification.

In addition, credit products have liquidity risks. This is something that we monitor. Again, the concept of the Capital Adequacy keeps us in check and makes sure that we always have sufficient cash to unwind positions, if we choose to do so. But liquidity risk is there. It may not feel like it right now because the markets are pretty liquid, but having lived through the crisis, I think we all know that this is something that can change quickly. We would not put on trades where we can't get marks from at least three different brokers, and we monitor trading volumes and bid/off as indication of liquidity. If something becomes less liquid, we consider unwinding, unless it is a short maturity trade.

We have interest rate risk, but minimal. In fact, this is a differentiating factor for many absolute return strategies as opposed to investing in the credit markets through ETFs or other bond market tracking funds. We use a lot of products that are not available to retail investors because they would need to have ISDAs and so forth, like CDS. Many such products are spread based and don't have much interest rate risk. Loans are also floating rate products that don't have interest rate risk. CLO tranches are the same, with the exception perhaps of the equity tranche, because those are exposed to 1 percent LIBOR. So we don't have much exposure to interest rates due to products we trade. In addition, the bonds that we use are usually lower rated and higher yielding. That further limits sensitivity to interest rates.

MJ: Obviously, the trades you have put on have often worked out well, like in 2007 and 2008. Is there anything that comes to mind that perhaps didn't work as well?

OC: Unfortunately, not all of our trades work. It is okay as long as we have vigilance and we cut the losers before they can inflict too much pain. This is where the risk limits come into play. But in addition to risk limits, what we generally watch very carefully is our original thesis. We develop the thesis as to why we believe a trade should work when we put it on. We look at the conditions that must exist for it to work. Then we monitor these conditions closely.

One of the trades we had that didn't work out was on TXU. TXU is an energy company with a very complicated capital structure. We put on this long/short trade between different entities in the capital structure. The basic thesis was, it was impossible for one entity to default without causing the default of another one. However, TXU had a very complicated capital structure, as I mentioned. It was also the largest leveraged buyout (LBO) in history, and was a company with very deep pockets and very good legal advisors. The legal advisors were determined to work very hard to try to keep the company out of bankruptcy and, at the same time, preserve the option value for equity holders.

What started to happen is the company started to issue debt from yet another part of the capital structure on a secured, ring-fenced basis. It was very obvious that the only reason to do so was to have one part of the company file for bankruptcy and while preserving the other. While we were not exactly sure when or how they would get rid of the default covenant, it was clear that they are moving in that direction. The whole thesis of our trade was basically becoming invalid.

When we saw these transactions, we determined that it was a very complicated situation and that our thesis was at risk. We unwound the trade before we had any significant losses. They did file bankruptcy later on. Had we kept this position, we would have ended up with much worse performance.

MJ: In addition to re-examining your thesis, you also use stop losses to mitigate risk, correct?

OC: Yes, that's correct. We use hard stop losses of 2 percent, irrespective of the size of the trade. No individual trade in the portfolio should inflict more than 2 percent losses. The reason we have this limit is to have discipline. One of the things that, at times, managers are accused of is falling in love with their own trades. If it's attractive today, it's more attractive tomorrow. All of a sudden, your fund is down 50 percent and you don't have any investors. Our theory is that a 2 percent stop loss forces us to unwind and forces a clean slate. If we decide that we love a position, we can go back into it later. But the stop loss forces us to stop and take action, rather than just sitting there and justifying our original thesis in our head.

MJ: Have you overridden that stop loss?

OC: We have never overridden it.

MJ: So you've capped single position losses to a large extent. What about things that are harder to predict, like the liquidity in over-the-counter [OTC] transactions. How do you minimize

liquidity risk, transaction risk, and counterparty risk in your transactions?

OC: We know transactions have both liquidity risk as well as counterparty risk. One thing I would say is that liquidity risk is present not only in OTC trades but also in cash securities. We track trading volume to determine liquidity. Trading derivatives are surprisingly transparent; DTCC [Depository Trust & Clearing Corporation] publishes trading volumes for derivatives, and you can very clearly see not only trading volumes but also the net amount of contracts written. Compared to TRACE [Trade Reporting and Compliance Engine] for corporate bonds, it doesn't show you all the individual traded levels, but it gives you more transparency into overall volume.

We have a rule in the fund that we would not put on a position unless we think we can get quotes or marks from three different counterparties. We also have another guideline that the entire position should be able to be taken off in five phone calls or less. In other words, if the standard trading size for either a derivative or a bond is two million, we would not want to place more than five phone calls to the dealers in order to take off the position. The maximum size that we would consider wise to put on in that situation would be $10 million.

Definitely after the financial crisis, one thing that you have seen is a reduction in the number of banks and counterparties. The market is more concentrated, and we don't want to be in a position where the market knows our trades. This influences the sizing of our positions, and is something that we monitor on a daily basis.

In addition, we monitor the counterparty risk. We keep track of the spread levels on our counterparties. If their spread level exceeds our limit, the counterparty is put on a watch. If spreads continue to widen, we have a second threshold where we have to make a decision to either hedge the risk or try to unwind or move trades away from this counterparty. This is also something that we monitor on a daily basis.

Eventually, credit derivatives will go on an exchange. But, in the meantime, the way we approach it is, we have 12 different ISDA counterparties. We're quite diversified, and we try to make sure that we don't have all of our trades with one dealer.

That was the reason why we decided to go against recent trends where funds consolidate all their trades with only one bank to achieve better margin. It might be operationally convenient to do that, but you are putting all your counterparty risk in one basket. We prefer to monitor more counterparties and have less exposure to each one of them.

MJ: You have mentioned rules a lot. It sounds like your strategy is a very rules and discipline-based strategy.

OC: We have tried to be very disciplined about our investments. I would say we have some "hard" limits that never change. But in addition, there are some rules we put in place because we believe they are the best practices and they come from the experience of trading. Some of them come from the institutions where I previously worked. I would say both our hard risk limits and our best practices rules enhanced our investment style.

Experience and Market Cycles

MJ: Speaking of learning, I know the fund has posted overall outstanding returns since inception, but I also know the fund struggled in 2011 and 2012. Can you talk about what happened then and what you learned from that?

OC: 2011 was a difficult year for us in the market. I think it was for many funds. It was the year where we had the Greek crisis and US sovereign downgrade. We had lots and lots of systemic risks. We had politicians making market decisions. It really was not clear which way it was going to go. As much as you trust individuals to protect the system and to make wise choices, the moment politics are involved, it's less controlled.

At the time in 2011, we had many relative value trades. In the fall, during the Greek crisis, we were entering into a big market de-risking mode once again, and many of our relative value trades dislocated. We had to make a choice whether to stick with our trades or perhaps de-risk. The only reason why we decided to cut the risk was because of the counterparty exposure. This was the time when, all of a sudden, the Morgan Stanley one-year CDS was starting to trade at about 800 basis points. I have not seen anything like that before. During Lehman's bankruptcy, their five-year spread was still trading below 400, at the beginning of September. There were many signs of extreme pressure at different banking institutions related to what was going on in Europe. I felt that this probably was a time where we had to reduce risk.

I made this call. I figured out that it's better to close our trades and move more to cash to protect our investors' downside, rather than running the risk of something going wrong and having another potential Lehman crisis on our hands.

Of course, none of that happened. You had [Mario] Draghi who eventually said that they would do whatever it takes to protect the Euro, which was a turning point for the markets. But we came quite close to a pretty unpredictable outcome. After the fact, it was clear we should have stuck with our trades. We would have had a very good performance in 2011. However, I feel that, given what I was seeing at the time, I would probably make the same investment decision again.

In 2012, we actually finished the year slightly positive, but this was the year of our business restructuring. Our seed investor made the decision to exit the seeding business. They redeemed from all funds that they had seed agreements with. At the time, they were 50 percent of our fund, and so we were faced with a very large redemption. In addition, some of the other investors decided to redeem once the seed news hit the market. People were concerned that such a large redemption could potentially cause illiquidity in the remaining portfolio. This was clearly not the case, but 2012 was a year that the fund size was significantly reduced. We were very proud that we never gated anybody. We gave 100 percent of the money back to the investors within the standard redemption period, and we still finished the year with a positive return.

MJ: So we've talked about sovereign debt and risk a few times now, first with your 2008 trades and now with Greece and its impact on the portfolio in 2011. What do you think of those sovereign risks going forward?

OC: I hope we don't have to live through 2011 again. High systemic risks don't pass without scarring the economy and reducing longer-term wealth.

With that being said, governments are still extremely lever-aged. They're in a very difficult position because they need to support growth and recovery, but at the same time, in the long term, they need to de-lever. Will there be situations where systemic sovereign problems come to the surface again? It is very possible.

The positive thing is that markets actually adjust. In September 2014, ISDA is coming out with new definitions to specifically address some of the limitations that were discovered in credit derivatives in light of dealing with sovereign defaults. People have seen how different instruments react and what their potential shortcomings are. If we go back to that environment, I think market participants will be more prepared.

Private Markets: Venture Capital,
Private Equity, and Real Estate

CHAPTER 8

In the Beginning: Seed and Series A Venture Capital Investing

Theresia Gouw, Co-Founder, Aspect Ventures

Napoleon Hill, author of the wildly popular *Think and Grow Rich*, once said, "All achievements, all earned riches, have their beginning in an idea."[1] In the corporate world, those words are certainly true. Think for a moment about the origins of Apple, Inc. In the 1970s, we weren't all breathlessly waiting for the next iPhone or iPad release. As recently as 1976, Apple consisted of three guys building hand-made computers that sold for $666.66 at places like the Homebrew Computer Club. Apple Computer Inc. incorporated in 1977, received $250,000 in funding from multimillionaire Armas Clifford "Mike" Markkula, Jr., and then doubled its revenues in each of the subsequent four years before going public in 1980 at $22 per share, creating about 300 millionaires in the process.

While not every company becomes an Apple, most successful companies experience a similar genesis. A founder or group of founders believes they've built a better mousetrap. They establish some credibility around the market and product. The company gets funded, grows, and finally goes public (or gets acquired), creating wealth for the founders, early employees, and the financial backers of the firm. Facebook, Google, and Amazon each began in a similar fashion, raising outside capital to take what started as ideas and turn them into growth and profits.

If you look at some of the more recent corporate success stories, chances are you'll see Theresia Gouw behind them. Take real estate site

Trulia, for example. Acquired by Zillow in July 2014 for $3.5 billion, Trulia was incubated in Gouw's old office after a $4.5 million Series A investment by her then-firm, Accel Partners. Her investment actually predated the Trulia website launch. Or look at Imperva, the enterprise security system that protects financial data. Gouw was the first (and only) choice for early-stage funding in 2002. That company went on to become the most successful initial public offering (IPO) of 2011. And what about Facebook? Gouw was a Series A investor in that company as well.

After obtaining her BA in engineering from Brown University and an MBA from Stanford University, Gouw became a product manager and engineer for enterprise software companies. She started her career in venture capital in 1999 at Silicon Valley-based Accel Partners and was later named to *Time* magazine's "Tech 40: The Most Influential Minds in Tech in 2013," alongside Bill Gates. In 2014, after 15 years and a string of successful investments, she launched Aspect Venture Partners with partner Jennifer Scott Fonstad, a fellow venture capital veteran. In many ways, launching the new firm was a "back to basics" move for Gouw. Frustrated with the responsibilities of managing a multibillion dollar firm like Accel, she and Fonstad wanted to spend more time doing what they love and do best: investing in and growing companies. Early-stage investors at heart, the move allowed Gouw to get back in the trenches, and the pair made eight investments in their first eight months.

With a high success rate and a very low loss ratio, Gouw has become one of the most consistently successful early stage investors in enterprise security and consumer-facing technology. Her secrets to success?

- Invest in markets and people that you know. Products and timing change, but if you know the markets and you believe in the founders, you can mitigate a lot of your investment risk.
- While you should have expertise in your portfolio company's markets, you should also be prepared to extend your knowledge into new areas that exhibit similar business models or technology foundations.
- Look for trends before they become obvious. If you read about something in a tech magazine, it's already too late to invest.
- Use your differentiated networks to find unique opportunities early. Be one of the first investors in the door.

- Successful early stage investing isn't just about writing checks. You need to be prepared to work hard to help the company grow, and you should be excited about that work.

Excelling at Accel

MJ: How did you go from engineering to investing?

TG: I always liked math and science. I am also the eldest daughter of first-generation Chinese immigrant parents. My dad was a little bit of a tiger dad, I have to say. It was always expected that I would do something. My family is all in medicine, but I was always very squeamish when it came to that kind of thing. Therefore, it was like, "The other alternative, if you're not going to be a doctor, is to be an engineer."

Then when I was working one summer as an intern at General Motors, I realized that the jobs that I thought were more interesting than being in a tech lab or sitting behind the computer were actually product manager positions. They were actually designing products, but they were also doing work to ensure the product and the market fit, and they were taking things to market, not just running tests in the lab.

At a very traditional place like General Motors, where there were thousands of design engineers in that building, and there were two women. All the product managers had MBAs. That was really what opened my eyes to, "What is this MBA thing?" When I went back to my senior year, I was like, "All right I'm going take my GMAT [Graduate Management Admissions Test], and I'm going to try to get an MBA." My career path was to be a product manager. In fact, when I wrote my business school application for Stanford, I said I wanted to be a product manager at Hewlett Packard or some other tech company in Silicon Valley.

What brought me to the venture and investment side of the business was really two steps. Step one was being a product manager. I was a product manager at Silicon Graphics. Then I ended up joining a couple of Stanford GSB classmates right as they raised seed funding from DFJ [Draper Fisher Jurvetson], which was my current cofounder's firm at the time. I joined them as the first product business development–customer-facing type person. I managed both the product managers and the product engineers, and I had the sales engineers and a couple of support people reporting to me.

That was how I got into the venture-backed side of the business, by being at a venture-backed company and helping to raise a few more rounds of venture capital. I was there for nearly four years. When I decided to leave and go to my next thing, I naturally went to the venture capital representative on my board and said, "Hey, you know, I really love start-ups. This time I think I'm ready to be a founder. If you have an engineer or technologist who wants someone who can do the from-the-ground-up go-to-market plan, I'd love to do that."

This was in late '98, early '99. The company that I was at was Release Software. We were doing electronic software distribution. So, encryption, payments, and crucial downloads for software. Our customers were firms like Netscape and Macromedia, as well as Symantec and Intuit.

One of our investors said, "I'm going to introduce you to three portfolio companies, and then I'm going to introduce you to three venture capital firms." He knew my background: that I had an engineering degree, I had a Stanford MBA, and I had just spent three years working in this Internet e-commerce company. He said, "A lot of firms are growing, and they're looking for people with backgrounds like yours, people who have experience with Internet companies, and e-commerce." That was really how I ended up getting into venture capital.

MJ: And you became the first female partner at Accel?

TG: I was the first female professional investor of any sort at Accel. I was hired in on a partner track in 1999. I was made a partner in 2000. I was made a managing partner in 2003.

MJ: What was that experience like, being the first dose of investing estrogen at Accel?

TG: I guess I was pretty used to being the only woman in the room, between my General Motors and engineering experience. Whenever there were things that were brought to the firm that had a certain kind of consumer or retail angle to it, I might notice the difference. Even if women partners are hard-core into enterprise software, the male partners in the room would always ask the woman, "OK, what do you think about this?"

On the one hand, you look at it as a positive. They care about your opinion. On the other hand, it's a little bit odd, right? Why me? I knew much more about encryption software than I did about shopping for makeup until I funded BirchBox.

MJ: Is that part of what prompted the decision to start Aspect Ventures with your business partner?

TG: Bottom line, I love doing early stage. And there's a lot more time to spend on looking for companies and working with your companies when you don't have international investment committee conference calls and firm management and all those other things like you do at a global, multibillion-dollar venture capital firm.

We launched Aspect in February of 2014, and, since then, we've made seven investments. We've announced five of those [including BaubleBar, Exabeam, and SupportPay]. We have an eighth one that's closing in the next couple of weeks. We're able to be more productive and spend a lot of time in the field, because we're not managing a large firm anymore. We're certainly not doing any conference calls with India or China or anything else like that.

A lot of my best investments over the years have been based on the same thesis: early stage seed and Series A investments. If you look at Trulia or Imperva, or even more recently, a BirchBox or a HotelTonight, those are all Series A or seeds. They take longer to grow, but you're in on the ground floor. That's what I love.

MJ: How many investments would you generally be involved with in a given year at Accel versus what you expect to do at Aspect?

TG: It's only been six months, right? In a year, as a rule of thumb, people who focus on Series A might do one, two, or three new Series A investments. We're very much on pace for that. And you might do double that number with seed investments. Seed investments are smaller. They happen more quickly. And because they typically don't include board seats, they don't use your board capacity until you decide to lead a Series A investment.

Back to Basics

MJ: It sounds like starting Aspect was a "getting back to basics" move. Do you expect it to lead to more investments, too?

TG: Jennifer and I would both say this has equaled the most productive time period ever in our careers.

And you're right. It's partially back to basics. We're actually finding more time to do stuff that we love. By the way, we each still sit on about six or seven of our boards from our prior firms. We came into this with about half a dozen board seats each, and those boards take time, as well.

But I would absolutely agree with your thesis, which is it's freed up a lot of time. That was our hope, and it's turning out to be true.

MJ: If you are saying you do one to three Series A deals, and roughly double that number in seeds, how many companies do you actually look at to get to those numbers?

TG: There's been at least several hundred already in the six months since we announced the new firm. Of course, as a new firm, the answer to that question is still being refined. The data is still being collected. But the answer, for us, is the same as what I always experienced at Accel, and Jennifer experienced at DFJ. Out of the companies that actually end up getting an investment from us, that's single-digit percentages of the things that come in. Depending on the time frame, it's one to four percent. It's also a very significant decrease from seeds to Series A investment.

MJ: Are most of those inbound funding requests?

TG: It's a mix. At this stage in our collective careers, me being in my sixteenth year and Jennifer being in her eighteenth year in the venture business, there is a fair bit now that comes inbound through referrals. Existing entrepreneurs have friends who are starting companies. Former entrepreneurs are starting second companies. People who used to work at one of our companies, maybe as a director or VP, are now ready to spin out and start their own company. Referrals come from other seed and angel investors. We've both been very active in the seed stage, so we get referrals that way. We get referrals from other venture capitalists.

I teach a class at Stanford business school, and I get some referrals from that. Jennifer's very active at HBS [Harvard Business School], so there are some referrals there. Jennifer co-founded Broadway Angels, and we get a lot of referrals there, from seed rounds especially, or from when those companies are ready to graduate to a Series A.

And some deals we look for proactively. I did an investment in a security software company [Exabeam] shortly after founding Aspect. It came to me through the referral of an existing security CEO, but I was proactive in saying, "Look, I'm very interested in something in this space, in this stage. Can you think of any?" That's basically how the process works.

MJ: So your network is critical?

TG: Differentiated networks are really important for differentiated deal flow. Otherwise, you're seeing the same things that everyone else does. And if you read about it in *Tech Crunch,* by then it's too late.

MJ: But isn't that how a lot of investors tend to operate? They keep looking for the same patterns over and over again?

TG: That can be a risk. We feel that's one of the things that differentiates us at Aspect. The combination of not always looking for the same thing, and being willing to and wanting to invest before something becomes obvious. We don't want to invest in the sixth company to start in the space. There's definitely a lemming effect in Silicon Valley sometimes. When a sector gets hot, then everyone feels like, "I have to have one of those."

Some people are very successful at that, but that's just never been my personal style. I've always been much more interested in having a thesis and then meeting all the interesting entrepreneurs and companies in that space. Then we see if there are one or two companies that seemed very interesting and unique.

I think a lot of people here have very similar networks. You have to be willing to look outside of those networks. I mean, of course, you have to be very close to people who are at Facebook or Twitter or Google because they are going to be very relevant. You have to do that, and everybody does do that. However, you also need to look a little bit more outside the box as well and cultivate differentiated relationships so that you're not one of ten VC's who are having that exact same meetings.

A Diverse Portfolio

MJ: One of the things that has gotten a lot of attention lately is the lack of diversity in Silicon Valley in general, and the lack of diversity within venture capital-funded firms as well. I think I saw that most VCs' estimate that between 4 percent and 19 percent of their portfolio companies have female founders.

TG: I think those numbers are probably pretty accurate. That range is not surprising to me. I think that I have anecdotally seen, and I'm actually working with somebody to get data, that that number has been growing over the course of my venture career. In particular, it's grown a fair bit over the course of the last five-ish years.

MJ: Well, that's sad because that means it was truly terrible before.

TG: Yeah, it was. I would say the low number was what it used to be, and the high year number feels like the way it's trending. I think it's actually going to continue to grow for two reasons. One is that, the number of consumer-facing businesses has grown, and there are more women represented in consumer-facing businesses than in traditional enterprise-facing businesses.

The other thing is there was Web 1.0, then there was social web, and now there's mobile web. If you look at the usage on social media and mobile, women are more than 50 percent of your active users. Women have more social network connections and more mobile apps on their smartphones than men do, when you adjust for the same demographics.

I also think there's a greater understanding by founding teams that having diversity of thought is valuable. Women are just one dimension—I think there are other dimensions of diversity, too.

MJ: Does the fact that you are a woman have any impact on your pipeline or the deals you see?

TG: It gets back to the point of our network and deal flow. I have an engineering degree and I went to Stanford Business School, and so I have a lot of same networks as male VCs. I have those contacts. But I was also the only woman at my firm, and the one of the only woman VCs anywhere.

As a result, if there is a founding team with a female on it, and it's in a sector that Jennifer or I have expertise in, there's no doubt that we're going to see that deal because we are preferentially situated in those networks.

MJ: I would have to assume using differentiated networks helps in competing for deals and in getting better terms on your deals. Being one of the first venture capital firms in the door should be more profitable than traveling with the herd.

TG: Being first makes all the difference. With Imperva, I was fortunate enough to be in Series A, and actually I spent time, through another one of my security software companies, getting to know the CEO and founder, Shlomo Kramer. He had started Check Point. and he had been very active in looking at a lot of other security companies. He was still a young guy, and I knew that at some point he was going to start another company. I spent months getting to know him and being part of the process. He would kick around ideas on security that he thought were interesting, and I would give him feedback and tell him whether I was or was not seeing other companies like that coming into the marketplace.

I remember making introductions and going to some meetings with him on Wall Street to vet the market opportunity. As a result of doing that, when he finally coalesced around one specific idea, which ended up becoming Imperva, I was fortunate enough to be able to lead that investment. He didn't show it to anybody else. He came in and talked to me. He said, "Look, this is how much I want to raise. I think this would be a fair deal. If you're willing to make that fair deal for me here, it's done. No one else is going to see it."

The majority of these deals, other people will see it and there will be some competition. If you come in earlier, if you've got a relationship, you can win preference. You want to be on that short list. You want to be one of the first firms in the door. Or you want to be the first or only one in the situations when you can get that. But you don't want to be number nine or ten. It's unlikely that you're going to win that deal. You have to have competitive and market-based terms, but at the Series A level, in terms of dollars, it's not that different. A 10 percent or 20 percent difference on a $5 million dollar investment round? It's not that meaningful from a dollars perspective in the concept of a hundred-million-dollar fund.

Building Value for Founders

MJ: The other thing that stands out is that you were building value for the founder of Imperva before the investment was even made. Is that important as well?

TG: Absolutely. We're in the business of making investments, and we make an investment upfront. But really then I'm entering, on average, a ten-plus-year relationship as a board member, from the Series A through the exit. I need to be actually adding value through connections, networks, and introductions. Or I need to be giving candid feedback and sharing those patterns I can see because I get to see hundreds of companies every year, whereas that founder is head down in their own business. If you're doing well as a founder, and you have good ideas, there will be lots of options. You should pick someone you're excited to partner with for ten years.

MJ: People have the perception that private equity and venture capital firms are somehow evil and that it's a one-way street. Think about all the press a few years ago about Bain Capital. The investor makes the lion's share of the money, and that's the end of the discussion. But what I've noticed is that a lot of venture capital investors are much more focused on these ancillary ways to build value and help companies be more successful.

TG: That's really true. With all due respect to our private equity buyout brethren, I do think venture capital is quite different. One, because, we are investing earlier. There is a lot more company building and work that we need to do. Everything from helping to recruit—if you invest in seed or Series A and there are four or five people in the company, you're going to be spending a lot of time helping that founder and founding team grow their team. You'll be making introductions to their first potential customers, and so forth.

I also think it is much more of a repeat situation with founders in venture capital, unlike typical private equity. You tend to work with the same founders more than once. The other thing is that a lot of times in private equity, the private equity firm is going in and investing and taking control over the company. The founder wants a generational transition or wants to leave and have professional management come in. It's a very different dynamic in that relationship.

My view is this: even if I don't invest in a particular company, the next time the founder starts a company, that next one might be the next great company. Every interaction I have, I want to leave that founder with something useful. Their time is valuable, my time is valuable. At the end of a conversation I say, "I hope at least that I asked one question, or gave you one piece of information or data that you find useful."

MJ: You're sowing seeds for something down the road. I've noticed that there have been a lot of seed and early-stage funds that have started up lately. Why do you think that people are getting more and more interested in that particular space, especially if it's more work and a longer-term investment?

TG: One reason is, especially for software-oriented companies, whether those are consumer or small business mobile software, with things like open source and Amazon web services, it's a lot more efficient to build a company on a seed amount of capital, a million-ish dollars or less. You can actually build something, take it to market, and show some early traction, whereas it used to be a lot harder. In the old days, when you had to buy Oracle and provision a big server, a million dollars couldn't even get the server, and then you still didn't have any software. That's part of the trend. There have been an increasing number of firms that raise seed amounts because they can show some traction and not have to sell as much of their company.

The other thing is that there have been a lot of people who have been active investors and angels through either formal outlets, like Angel List, or just as individual angel investors. When a company like Facebook or Google goes public, there are early employees who receive a good amount of employee shares and become millionaires. And they're very much in the loop. A lot of their former colleagues are leading the new start-up companies. The number of angel investors grows, and the number of seed rounds grows. A subset of those people, who are successful investing as an angel with their own money, will then go and seek outside institutional capital to raise a seed fund. You're seeing both of those trends coalescing.

MJ: Let's talk for a minute about how easy it is to raise seed capital now. One of the things that has evolved over the past couple of years is crowd-funding platforms like Kickstarter and Indigogo. I've seen two very different articles that discuss how crowd funding will interact with venture capital. One of them said, "Crowd-funding platforms are the venture capitalists new best friend." The other talked about how disruptive the technology is, and that they will disenfranchise early-stage funding because entrepreneurs can get it without having to give away much of their company. Do you have an opinion on crowd-funding platforms, one way or the other?

TG: I'm sure it's a good thing for entrepreneurs, and partially the same for venture capital, as well. In the beginning, a large portion of the things on Kickstarter were not necessarily venture-backed-type things. Filmmakers, artists, photographers, and things like that were getting funded.

In general, crowd funding is good, because it is allowing a larger number of founders and entrepreneurs to get their businesses off the ground. Many of these would not historically have been in the sweet spot of tech venture, which is where most of the dollars are in venture capital funds.

I don't know yet if there have been any breakout venture-backed successes that first started out on Kickstarter, just because it's early still. But I have no doubt that there will be. I could see how maybe the next-next Jawbone gets started on Kickstarter.

Not All Seeds Sprout

MJ: In terms of these early-stage and the seed-stage deals, what kind of risks exist that maybe wouldn't be in later stage VC or public market investing?

TG: In the earlier stage there's a lot more risk for failure. There's a lot less that's known. There's a lot less you can see, and a lot less data. On the other hand, history would show that if you are thoughtful and proactive about that, you can be smart and take calculated risks and minimize your losses. One or two break-outs, like Trulia or Imperva, can return hundreds of millions of dollars. You're investing at a very low basis with a low amount of capital.

Typically as a rule of thumb, we always say when you invest in Series A you're hoping to make a ten-times return, knowing that some of them will be much less, some will be much more. Most places you try to make a case like, "This is why I see how this can be a 10x investment at this stage." Whereas for growth and expansion stage capital, typically the hurdle is trying to make a two-times to three-times return, with much bigger dollars at a higher price and hopefully lower loss ratios, because you have more data.

MJ: Is there a certain percentage of seed and early-stage investments that just aren't going to make it at all?

TG: In the early-stage investing, I would say it varies a lot based on the macroeconomic environment you're in. Loss ratios in 2000, when no one wanted to touch anything in tech, were much higher. Loss ratios in 1998 and 1999 were much lower because everyone wanted to fund your next round. On average, for good early-stage venture firms, you might have a loss ratio, which is something actually going to zero, around one-third of your portfolio.

Then you might have 50 to 60 percent of your investments returning one time to three times your investment. It's that small percentage that everybody talks about that are your home runs. These that are not just 10 times return on investment, but maybe 10 times, 20 times, 30 times, 40 times, 50 times, or 100 times your investment. That's how you get that weighted average. I've historically had a much lower loss ratio, and I've been always very Series A focused. I don't necessarily think that you have to tolerate having that much failure just because you're in the early stage.

MJ: Why do believe that your loss ratio has been so much lower?

TG: The bear case argument would say, "Theresia's just not taking enough risks. She must not be looking at enough for those home runs." Then, you look at the returns, and there are certainly plenty of home runs in my portfolio. I think the reason why is that even at the Series A stage, there's taking risks and then there's taking calculated risks. If I believe that there are real market trends—either technology, business, or user trends, or some combination I've already seen—and that there's a big need for what this company is trying to build—and you know the team, the founders, and that they can execute, then the risk just becomes, can they get the right product market fit and timing? They might get outcompeted. Certainly there are still risks that things might not work, but you can take smarter risks by looking at fundamentals.

MJ: Are those the three things you think are the most important for a successful investment: the market, the product, and the people?

TG: I would put it in the order of the people, the market, and then the product.

MJ: Evaluating people can be difficult, however. There's no spreadsheet. There are no quantitative fields that you can analyze. How do you determine whether or not you've got a founder or an early management team that can do the job?

TG: I look for a couple of different things. I look for people who have tech domain expertise, basically industry knowledge and experience, because they worked in that industry at a company before, attacking that same market and the same industry. Or I look for where a founder is solving a problem that he or she has experienced, either in his or her personal or professional life. They're designing for themselves. My job is to vet that the overall market is large enough, that they haven't solved a problem for themselves that just five other people have.

The other thing that they have this true passion and belief that what they are doing is so important that they're changing the world in some way. They're driven to make it work.

MJ: How do you know if you're dealing with someone who is passionate rather than a zealot? That they will be able to change and adapt and deal with the evolution of a growing company?

TG: Being able to adapt is obviously critical. Part of that discovery happens through referencing and talking to other people. But part of it happens during the initial process, when you are talking to them. Are they are actually taking information, processing it, and making those thousand little tweaks, changes, and decisions to their product, their process, their go-to-market plan, their strategy, and their thinking?

It's typically a couple of months between meeting someone and investing, if not more. In some cases you might meet the person, and six years later they decide to start a company. During that process, you get to see a lot about how that person thinks. When they see data that tells them that they need to adjust what they're doing, do they act on that, or do they just stubbornly stick to their original vision?

MJ: Are there times when you've realized you don't have the right jockey on the horse?

TG: Sometimes you do. But I've always been more of the belief that, at the end of the day, there's a certain je ne sais quoi that comes from the founder. These are incredibly bright and driven people who again are great entrepreneurs and great founders. They really believe that what they're building is important. They want that company, that product, that service to be as successful, as large, and to touch as many users, people, or businesses as it can. The best founders come to you and say, "Look. I really love doing product. I really love writing code. I really love doing the sales and marketing piece, but I really need someone to help me. If that person's awesome, they can be the CEO, and I'll be happy being the Chief Product Officer or another title."

It doesn't always happen in that way, but that's the best case. Usually, we're somewhere in-between. People want to be successful. Great officers care more about the company that they're building than their own personal ego. They will bring in other people to help them be successful.

Areas of Expertise

MJ: I've noticed there seems to be a sort of dichotomy to the companies you invest with. On one end of the spectrum is security software like Imperva, which makes sense given your own entrepreneurial experience. The other end of the spectrum has more consumer-driven products, like BirchBox. How did you come to specialize in those very different sectors?

TG: I've done a mix of enterprise software as well as consumer investing throughout my career. For me, the commonality is seeing a market trend based on data, core technology, or consumer usage, user behavior, and desires, coupled with the right domain expert, passionate founder, or founders. Both of those companies, though very different on the surface, actually share those common characteristics.

I've actually done a quite a few consumer-facing companies. Look at HotelTonight or Trulia or BirchBox. What I saw there, in terms of the market structure, was large, existing incumbent industries. Real estate. Beauty products. Hotel travel. People used to buy these products on the phone or in person, and then they bought them on the Internet, and now they buy on mobile. Each one of those transitions creates huge opportunities for new entrants whose sole focus is a new user interaction model. Even though those all seem like very different businesses, those are the commonalities.

I can identify markets that are interesting, and then end up proactively finding and getting referred into all of the companies that are around that space. Before I invested in Trulia, I met with close to a dozen other companies in various shapes and forms that were trying to do online real estate. I met with a bunch of other companies that were trying to do different types of subscription commerce, which is one of the angles for Birchbox. So they are different, but also very similar.

MJ: Would you say that you're totally sector agnostic, then, as long as they have those core characteristics?

TG: I do feel that you have to have an area of expertise. Within enterprise software, I do have security expertise. I have expertise in both consumer-facing businesses that primarily rely on e-commerce. I also have expertise in businesses on the consumer-facing side that are more of a marketplace model. Trulia's main business is on the marketplace side, meaning they have a marketplace between consumers and real estate agents, who are the ones that actually pay marketing, software, and subscription service fees to Trulia. I've not done a bunch of mobile gaming companies, that's not an area of expertise for me.

MJ: Do you feel like this focus is helpful to you in terms of understanding the market opportunities and the companies?

TG: It helps at every stage of the deal. It helps up front with the deal sourcing. Because we've got the right network and because we've been in the industry, we know who the players are. It helps with recruiting. When I'm looking for VP of marketing, or a VP of sales for a security software company, chances are I've done several searches for those with my other companies over time. It helps in the sourcing of companies, and it helps with helping them grow. It helps with the strategic partnership that they might need to make along the way. It helps with knowing who the later-stage investors are in that area. The people who will want to do your Series B, C, and D in security software or e-commerce are quite different.

MJ: Basically, you have to be specialized, but also have a willingness to consider different types of companies that may not look exactly like what you know?

TG: Because technology is evolving and business models are evolving so quickly, you need to be agile and you need to be able to figure out how to extend to the next logical thing.

For example, because I had done a bunch of security companies that were for tech data centers, when the technology evolved to being security for mobile devices, I understood the core security technology. Even though it's targeting a different end device, and maybe even a consumer instead of a business. Maybe it's going after small businesses instead of enterprises or consumers. I know the base technology, or I know the industry and the business model, and there's a parallel to it. I try not to make it a bridge too far. But you have to be constantly evolving.

MJ: So you've mentioned Trulia, Imperva, BirchBox, and HotelTonight a few times. Are these your favorite children?

TG: Well, maybe that has become somewhat obvious. With Imperva, I loved being in on the ground floor. I told you the story about how Imperva got started. I invested in that in Series A. I think the Series A was $4 million with a single-digit pre-money valuation. At one point, at the high, we owned a third of the company. The US office was literally incubated in my old offices. I helped to interview the very first hires that we had. For me, it was just exciting. I was an entrepreneur, and now I kind of get to be an entrepreneur again. I love seeing the growth over time. It's seeing the customer perspective and the company growth and how the product grows and changes. Being with the founding team and staying there with the company all the way through the IPO and beyond.

And it was a very similar story with Trulia. I think that was a $4.5 million Series A at $11 million valuation. I remember it was very important for them that it started with double digits. There were four people in the company at the time. The site hadn't even launched yet. It was so exciting to see how it grew. Feeling like you're part of the early founding team. And you grow not only terms of numbers and people but being able to recruit world-class executives. And you watch them learn and grow and develop as executives and as entrepreneurs.

MJ: What about some of your problem children? The investments that perhaps didn't go as you hoped?

TG: Oh, sure, there's always some. Anybody who will tell you otherwise is not being honest with you. There's a company that I was involved with where I was on the board, a company called WetPaint.

The founder was a guy, Ben Elowitz, who is really talented and a serial entrepreneur. I knew him from Bain. He was a cofounder of Blue Nile. In the end, the business was bought. It was okay, but it wasn't a great outcome. It certainly wasn't the outcome that any of the founders or any of the investors would have hoped for. That was a case where the initial market that we all financed was the wiki market.

That market never materialized nearly as large as we thought it would. That was a case where we had a great founding team. I would work with any of them again. I think if you ask any of them, they would work with me again. We were the fastest-growing product in that market. But the absolute size of that market ended up not being very large.

MJ: So in baseball terms, that wasn't a home run. It was more like a single or a double?

TG: I would say single for sure.

MJ: What about ones where you didn't get on base?

TG: There were two investments that went to zero. They were in gen-1, consumer web companies that had great co-investors. One was Sequoia, and one was IdeaLab. Bill Gross was actually personally on board. In both of those cases it turned out to be that the ultimate end market that we thought would be there was not nearly as large as we thought it would be.

In one, it was a marketplace for trading as opposed to a marketplace like eBay for cash. It's not that big of a capital cost for people to pay cash and then get cash ten days or even 30 days later. The trading market didn't end up materializing. People just preferred using cash, even if that meant that they were out on account to other people for 30 days.

The other market (which actually was just too early, because there's going to be a second run at these companies) was in doing same-day delivery for e-commerce companies. It was just super early. From a company's perspective, it was too expensive to be successful. You needed to have route density. Even if you had three of the five biggest e-commerce or retailers on the planet, the number of people buying stuff online in 1999 or in 2000 in a specific neighborhood wasn't going to be dense enough to make those routes financially possible.

MJ: And now you have Amazon testing drone delivery.

TG: We were using people, of course. Partly the technology has evolved, but also just look at the scale of people participating in e-commerce and on Amazon. It's orders of magnitude more. You can limit it to certain geographies, and it could work.

I mean, look, an investment that one of my Accel partners invested in—a company that is called Quidsi—was bought by Amazon. When we first invested, they were doing next-day delivery, but then it moved to same day delivery in New York for things like Diapers.com and Soap.com. So, now it can certainly work.

The common thing on both those companies is that you're doing a seed investment or a Series A investment in something when it's still small and early. You're betting on the fact that the market will materialize. Sometimes it just never does, like in trading versus classic cash market places. Sometimes it does materialize, but not in the time frame that makes sense for your company.

My error has more often been being too early rather than being too late. And I'm okay with that. I guess everyone makes mistakes. I've learned over time that, in the area that I focus on, that that's the better type of error.

Predicting Markets

MJ: So the markets are one of your bigger concerns?

TG: Hopefully you can spend time and do research to get to know the person that you're going to be a partner with for ten years. The market data is just unknowable at that point in time. You do your best, but it's like you're trying to project ahead three, four or five years.

MJ: So the market is a bigger unknown than the people or the product, which you can evaluate to some degree?

TG: Don't get me wrong—there are cases where you make an investment and it turns out that one of the founders is more inflexible than you thought. More stubborn. Doesn't take deep breaths. Those things certainly happen. Usually those are recoverable if you identify them soon enough. You bring in other people around them who can see those things and make changes. Or you bring in another board member or an adviser who is able to convince them to change because they are CEO at a similar or parallel company, and the founder will take peer feedback that they view as less threatening.

There are things you can do to supplement or augment your team that makes those kinds of errors much more recoverable. Being wrong about market timing or the market existence, there aren't a lot of good options there to recover. You can only buy so much time.

MJ: But when you come in, you're always thinking about that future growth?

TG: I think you always have to. In terms of what's important to grow the company, it's your founder and your CEO who gives you that. They pull together the priority of what's important for the company. They bring forward the things that are board level or strategic, where we can help, versus the things that are everyday that they or their management teams need to do.

I'm also already thinking about additional financing at the beginning. In the end, great entrepreneurs are the same way. You need to be thinking about, "Okay, I raised X. Why X versus X minus $500K or X plus a million?" Because I believe that is what it's going to take me to achieve a certain set of milestones.

Those milestones, which are different for every business and every type of business, are what I know. This is where I can be helpful as a Series A investor. I know what those milestones need to look like for it to be a very attractive potential investment for a Series B investor. I understand the milestones for enterprise security companies, for consumer product companies, and whatever else my expertise may be.

I know what those milestones roughly should look like, and roughly the size and growth trajectory you need to be on against those milestones. I also know who the three to five most likely investors are for that particular type of company, because in my 16 years in the venture business, I've probably helped raise 250 plus follow-on financing rounds.

MJ: How many follow-on rounds of financing does a successful company need? Is there a magic number, or does it differ for each firm?

TG: It differs because some businesses are more capital efficient than others. However, at the size and scale of being a stand-alone public company, it's in the order of four to five rounds. Obviously, if the company gets acquired earlier in its life, it's less.

MJ: You mentioned that your general time frame for investments is between 10 and 12 years?

TG: Through to IPO. When I entered the business, it was eight to ten years, and now it's 10 to 12 years. Part of that is that companies are waiting longer to go public, and so they are bigger and larger scale by the time they go.

MJ: Do you ever find it difficult to be patient for that?

TG: I love what I do. I feel very fortunate to be able to work with these brilliant, dedicated, passionate entrepreneurs. So the time frame is not something that I ever really think about. I'm much more focused on the value creation at the end. I've never been one who's been very focused on what year we're in with an investment.

MJ: Certainly some of the VC firms that I know have been very focused on "timely outcome," shall we say?

TG: If you're earlier in your career, or earlier in your fund, then there is some pressure to show returns or liquidity to your limited partners. If you're in the fortunate position where you're more stable, you have the luxury to think about absolute value creation.

Arthur [Patterson] in particular taught me patience. He told me to take the long-term view. Don't be in a hurry. It's much more important to make the right investments. If that takes 12 years, then it takes 12 years. If it takes 9 years, it takes 9 years. Don't sell a company too early just because you're feeling like you need to have some liquidity.

MJ: Do you think that in the 16 years you've been investing, your investment philosophy or the type of company

you're looking for has changed, or has it just become more concrete?

TG: I think it's the latter. It's really become much more clear to me now that I've got a lot more experience.

MJ: How did being in Silicon Valley during the Tech Wreck impact how you think about companies and investments? It was a pretty lean period for venture capital after that...

TG: Absolutely. I guess what it taught me was a couple of things. One was that you need to be thoughtful about capital and preserving capital. If something isn't working, you need to figure out if it's the fundamentals of the business versus what is going on in the markets. If it is the fundamentals of the business, you know you've got to figure out a home for this company or move it into something else. If the business fundamentals are fine, and it's just that, right now, nobody's buying anything, that means you think about capital preservation and waiting until the market comes back to you. You think about being smart, about how you weather that storm versus whether you now know that what you thought there was going to be a market for, there really actually wasn't.

MJ: I would think separating the wheat from the chaff, the fads from the real innovation, is something that is obviously very important in venture capital. How do you think about whether something is a fad or whether it's going to have legs?

TG: That's a great question and a tough one to know. All entrepreneurs think what they are building is going to be long lasting.

One way to think about it is like this. For the enterprise software space, is this going to solve a business' top one, two, or three most important problems? If it is, then that's a good indicator. If it's not, then it's a nice-to-have versus the must-have.

In the consumer business, where everything is consumer discretionary spending and discretionary time, you don't have that same question. It's not just the number of users and the growth, but whether consumers are really using it deeply. How ingrained is it in the users' everyday life?

Think about gaming, like Zynga, for example. On one hand, you look at how many downloads, how many users, how many active users? How many monthly active users? How many daily active users? What you really want to look at is the people who are paying. Are they continuing to pay more and spend more every month and every week? Is the number of people who are paying growing?

MJ: So if you were going to give any advice to people who may be considering an early-stage investment, what would it be?

TG: Specifically in early-stage, tech investing, what I would say is this: number one, make sure you're investing in either a market or people that you know well. That's really what you're betting on.

The second thing is to make sure you are in a position to and actually are interested in providing specific and meaningful help to the company based on your own expertise. These companies are young. They need help, and they need help from their investors because there may be only two to five people in that company. They really are counting on you. You can actually have an impact on their success. It's the complete opposite of making a passive investment

CHAPTER 9

The Pragmatist: Growth Equity Investing

Sonya Brown, General Partner,
Norwest Venture Partners

The word pragmatic is derived from the Latin *pragmaticus*, meaning "skilled in business or law," and the Greek *pragmatikos*, meaning "fit for business, active, business-like, systematic."[1] However, in the late sixteenth century, the word took on a much different connotation and was defined as "busy, interfering or conceited." It wasn't until the mid-nineteenth century that pragmatic returned to its original definition. In truth, however, disagreement over the definition of pragmatic exists even today. Synonyms range from practical and matter-of-fact to hardheaded. People proudly claim to be pragmatists, but some consider pragmatism a crime against humanity.

We see these contradictions writ large in investing. On the one hand, we want common sense to rule our investment and business decisions, but on the other hand, we want to ensure that the "people factor" is given due consideration. It's one thing to close a failing business line or make changes to a senior management team if the numbers no longer support the investment. It's another thing entirely to be seen as "cold hearted" in the process.

There are few areas of the investment world in which pragmatists get as bad a rap as in private equity. Often vilified for cost cutting, restructuring, and aggressive growth targets, what actually happens in private equity investments is a bit more nuanced.

Sonya Brown is the quintessential private equity pragmatist. Omnivorous in regard to sectors, unbiased when it comes to gender in the C-suite, and happy to keep management teams in place as long as financials remain strong, Brown's bottom line is unfailingly practical. She looks for growing, profitable companies where she can make a difference. Even when it comes to driving, Brown's efficient streak shows: she won't tolerate more than a seven-minute commute, so time with work and family are both maximized.

Brown originally pursued a degree in media at Northwestern University after objections from her equally pragmatic father kept her from film school. One "Money and Banking" course put her on the road to investment banking. After cutting her teeth in the analyst program at Bear Stearns, Brown tried working at a public company, but a stint at iXL Ventures during the Internet boom (and bust) whetted her appetite for principal investing. It also dampened her enthusiasm for the high failure rates often found in early-stage venture capital. Brown went back to school, got her MBA from Harvard Business School and eventually found her niche in growth equity. She has been writing checks ever since to companies like Snap Fitness, Airborne Health, PCA Skin, and Physicians Formula.

Brown's investments have performed considerably better than most, but not all have gone perfectly. Airborne Health, for example, took to YouTube to complain about the negative side of private equity ownership before buying back majority interest in their company. Interestingly, Airborne sold another majority interest to a different private equity firm a short time later.[2] On the other hand, companies like Sparta Systems and Physicians Formula each returned more than five times her initial investment, making them "Hall of Fame" investments at Summit Partners—investments which provided some of the best returns ever at that firm. After more than 12 years of investing in growth equity, Brown has developed the following practical rules for principal investing:

- Look high and low for good deals. Publications, trade shows, and cold calling are part of a growth equity investor's deal flow repertoire.
- Be an omnivore. Look first for profitable, growing companies and figure out the business later.
- Twenty percent growth and twenty percent EBITDA is your daily mantra.

- There are more opportunities for investment downstream. Look to write checks in the $15 million to $100 million range for good growth equity.
- "If it ain't broke..."—If management is maintaining growth rates and doesn't want out, keep them.
- Be gender blind when it comes to acquiring top leadership. The best CEO may be a man or a woman (although it's often a woman).

I Don't Want My MTV

MJ: How did you become interested in finance? I don't believe it was a completely linear path, was it?

SB: There are a lot of women out there that don't think about the finance field. It takes usually someone or a catalyst to direct them to this career. I was a communications major with a radio/TV film specialty and a minor in business institutions at Northwestern University.

Northwestern was actually my second-choice school. My first choice was to go USC Film School. I got into USC [University of Southern California], but my father did not think that that was the best long-term investment. He pushed me towards the opportunity at Northwestern. They happened to have a great communication school, and they produce a ton of great people in the media industry. They also have the Kellogg Business School. They have a strong academic reputation and access, if you want to think about it that way, to business opportunities and professors.

I made the decision to go to Northwestern. I really wasn't focused at all on finance until either the end of junior year or the beginning of my senior year. I was taking a class called Money and Banking with an economics professor, Mark Witte. He was the best professor I had while I was at Northwestern.

He taught me about this thing called investment banking and encouraged me to go through the interview processes with Morgan Stanley and Bear Stearns and all those other guys. I happened to get an offer from Bear Stearns in their Chicago office where there was a partner that was focused on media. He was doing a lot in radio and advertising. He saw my resume and thought, "This is cool, someone who likes my industry. At Bear Stearns, we have a training program. We can teach her the finance stuff."

I ended up taking the position with Bear Stearns in their Chicago office and working for this managing director there that was focused on media. My job choice at the time was going to work for MTV as an intern for $12,000 per year or to go to Bear Stearns and make $34,000 to $37,000.

MJ: That's a huge salary differential. And thus you became a private equity partner instead of the next Sonya Spielberg Scorsese.

SB: I really enjoyed the team that I was working with at Bear Stearns. Then I had the opportunity to move to New York with Bear Stearns. That was a huge plus in my career. They decided at the time they were going to shut down the Chicago office, and they gave the people they wanted to keep the opportunity to move to New York. So I worked in New York at Bear Stearns in the media entertainment group, which at the time was run by Alan Schwartz. Alan later became the head of Bear Stearns.

MJ: What did you do at Bear Stearns at the time? We still hear about the shortage of women in investment banking. What was your experience like?

SB: I was an analyst. I was part of the two-year analyst program in the investment banking group. We were doing a lot of M&A [mergers and acquisitions] and IPOs [initial public offerings]. I was the class of 1994 to 1996 at Bear. We started as 50/50, or maybe 60/40, male/female, at that time. I would tell you that by the end of my second year, my analyst class had only 3 women left out of a 60-person analyst class.

MJ: Wow.

SB: Now, some of those were emerging markets analysts, and the whole emerging market team was let go after a debacle there. It wasn't all necessarily a male/female thing, but it was not a very female-friendly environment at the time.

MJ: But obviously you loved it.

SB: I did. I was working 100 hour weeks and not sleeping and getting high blood pressure at 23 years old. I would have said back then that I would have paid to have that job versus getting paid. Especially since we were working with folks like Disney and doing deals with others like Time Warner. It was pretty cool at my age to be doing all that.

MJ: Was it the fact that the people you were working with were in your area of interest [media], or the actual deals and work that excited you?

SB: I definitely liked the financial analysis piece and learned a lot about finance while I was there, having come in without a finance or real business undergraduate degree. I did have a learning curve that was probably steeper than others on putting together a three-statement model. But I did enjoy that work and the opportunity to interact with high-end clients at that level.

I did two years at Bear and then started my third year. I left about a third of the way into my third year to go to a REIT [Real Estate Investment Company] in Georgia. I got engaged to my husband, whom I had dated for three years. He was a West Point grad, based in Georgia at Fort Gordon. It was both an opportunity to be at the same location (we'd been commuting up until that point) and an opportunity to work for a public company.

At the end of 1998, I joined iXL, which at the time was a roll-up of Internet services companies. One of the investors had been a client of mine at Bear Stearns, and they introduced me to the CEO. I landed a job initially as Vice President of finance, and then as the right-hand "man" to the CEO in a business development role.

While I had that business development role we created something called iXL Ventures. I was part of creating that. That was my first time as a principal-side investor, although it was early stage investments and not the growth equity I do now.

Boom and Bust

MJ: You founded iXL Ventures at the height of the Internet bubble. Was the company formed to take advantage of the plethora of investment opportunities in technology?

SB: We lived the Internet bubble. I was there through iXL's IPO. I was also there when we were starting to deal with unwinding investments when the company needed cash quickly. We had to shut down the offices in Europe. We eventually raised some money from an Indian group. Ultimately we merged with another company, but we eventually went bankrupt. I hit the eject button and decided to go back to business school, leaving before the bankruptcy and the merger. I was accepted into business school for the class of 2001 at HBS [Harvard Business School] and ended up deciding not to go that year because of the stock options I had at iXL.

Subsequently, I began to see the writing on the wall. It was spring of 2000. My husband had applied to HBS that year for the Class of 2002 and was accepted. It looked like the bubble was bursting, so I reapplied for the Class of 2002 as well, and got in.

I left iXL and went to HBS. At the time they had a truncated 18-month program that started in January. I worked part-time for iXL for my first six months, helping them continue to wind stuff down. Then I ended up leaving iXL and finishing my MBA at Harvard.

MJ: What types of investments was iXL making at the time?

SB: We did a couple of things. We incubated a few businesses ourselves and then got outside money involved. For the most part, these companies didn't make it through the tech wreck—they were all very technology focused. We were incubating CFN, Consumer Financial Network. Gateway Computers invested $50 million, and GE invested $50 million in that one. We had a series of probably five or six incubated companies. Then we had another five million of cash from the balance sheet of iXL that we used to invest in $10,000 to $500,000 seed investments. Most of those companies also don't exist today.

MJ: It was definitely a frothy time.

SB: Yeah. We did make one invest that ended up doing well—Silverpop. That one actually just sold to IBM. Most investments were similar to the typical venture capital model: one out of ten companies do really well, and nine don't. That was probably our track record, too.

MJ: **When you were incubating these companies, were they in your offices? Were you working with the founding teams?**

SB: We were thoroughly involved as far as sitting on the board with those entities and helping them hire key talent. We had a similar involvement with both the venture capital investments and the companies we were incubating as far as sitting on a board, helping them raise their next rounds of financing, all of that. There were probably a dozen companies between those that we invested in directly with cash and those that we incubated.

MJ: **That's a pretty big change from working for a public company, working with all of these Internet entrepreneurs and growing companies.**

SB: It was brand new and I loved it. I wasn't sure that I would go back to business school. If the bubble hadn't burst, I might not have gone. But once I did go back to business school, I was very clear on what I wanted to do when I got out. I wanted to go back into the principal investing side. I wanted to sit on boards. I absolutely was looking, from the moment I started at HBS, at how I could accomplish that. I wanted to join a firm where I could be on a partner track and do principal investing.

Initially, I thought it would be in venture capital. I started looking and networking with folks like Greylock and other people that were on the board of iXL. I quickly learned that the Internet bubble damage had not yet been dealt with. The dust hadn't settled, and venture wasn't growing at that time. There was a lot of collateral damage from the bubble bursting.

No one was really hiring yet in 2002 when I graduated. If they were, the bar was so high. I didn't have an engineering degree. I hadn't been a CEO of a company. When I was having this conversation with folks on the venture side, they were saying, "Hey, we're not hiring. If you want to come and work in one of our portfolio companies, that would be great experience. Maybe in a couple years there will be an opportunity for you in the venture world."

I had no interest in going to work for a portfolio company. I really wanted to go directly into the investing side. I started to look up the curve. I didn't want to go to a buyout firm like KKR, but I did at least have the skill set, having worked at Bear Stearns, to go further down the spectrum. That's when I learned about growth equity in the middle market and found firms like GTCR and Summit Partners and TA Associates. I started to network and interview with firms like those. Eventually I had an opportunity to join Summit.

MJ: What was it that lured you so strongly to the principal investing space?

SB: It's the idea of building companies... of taking a $25 million revenue business and building it to $100 million. That is very attractive. Sitting on the board and being involved and thinking through how we can strategically accomplish that growth. Also, being involved in recruiting talent and helping to create the right team to accomplish something like that. It's great.

The Lure of Growth Equity

MJ: How did you find the growth equity space differed from that seed-stage investing that you had cut your teeth on?

SB: I found that I could sleep better at night. I didn't have to deal with issues of how we were going to raise that next round of financing. And having lived through that bubble and the bubble bursting, I realized that what I was doing at the time at Summit, the opportunities there with those firms that were already profitable, was huge.

MJ: Is that what led you to join Summit? The growth equity expertise?

SB: Some of it was the fact that I was learning what the opportunities were and what growth equity was. It seemed very appealing to have the cash-flow positive nature of these companies.

MJ: That always does make an impression. Did growth equity continue to be your primary focus at Summit?

SB: I did only growth equity—investing in profitable, growing companies with minority and majority positions. That was my career there for almost ten years. I was mostly a generalist, but eventually focused on consumer companies, leading the North American consumer practice.

MJ: Which did you prefer? Was it more or less advantageous to be a generalist?

SB: It actually is a real positive in deal sourcing to be a specialist, especially in winning deals against the competition when you get more senior. It's less important as a junior person.

MJ: From Summit I know you went to Norwest. What led you to join Norwest at that time?

SB: They had been recruiting me. The firm had been around a long time and had done growth equity opportunistically over the years, but they were just formalizing a team to focus on the sector.

They hired a growth equity partner from a competitor of Summit Partners, and at that point, Norwest became an appealing opportunity. Knowing there was another like-minded investor on board, I knew we could build our own team and our own culture, which would be growth focused.

And there was the benefit of the long history of Norwest. The firm has been around for more than 50 years. We could start at a place where we had a brand name and some history rather than going out and raising a new fund.

If we had just gone out to raise a new fund, we would have started with no history. We also would have started with probably a much smaller number. I don't know if that would have been $100 million or $200 million, but I know it would have been a much smaller amount of capital than what we have today, which is a $1.2 billion fund. Our $1.2 billion is commingled between our venture team and our growth equity team. Our minimum equity check is based on a $1.2 billion fund rather than a $200 million fund. That was appealing.

Also, when I joined Summit it was a $1.5 billion dollar fund. When I left, we were at $4 billion. The type of investments, from a size perspective, changed lot over those nine years. We were looking for larger and larger deals. It is a little bit like a pyramid: there are a lot of small companies and only a few big companies. Going to Norwest was like going back to where Summit was when I first joined it, closer to that size fund.

MJ: So for a $200 million fund, you could make very few investments at $25 million to $75 million before your fund was fully committed. With a $4 billion fund like Summit, you would have had to have to invest in a ton of portfolio companies to use up the cash.

SB: Right. We had moved our minimum equity check at Summit up to $75 million. It was $75 million to $300 million. We were playing in a totally different market than what I had grown up with, which with Summit had been more of the $15 million to $100 million size checks. That's exactly where Norwest is today, $15 million to $100 million, with our sweet spot being $25 million to $75 million.

MJ: What were some of the companies that fell into that $25 million to $75 million range, versus the $75 million to $300 million range?

SB: All but two of my Summit investments were below $100 million.

MJ: I would imagine what you do as a board member and how you add value can be radically different for companies of that size.

SB: We had the opportunity to be a bit more hands-on with the smaller-sized companies. With smaller firms we tended to be a bit more of the outsourced corporate development arm and almost the outsourced CFO at times.

Omnivorous Investing

MJ: So your focus has shifted a bit over your career. You've stuck with your preferred investment size, but I know you've shifted from technology to consumer products. What appeals to you about consumer companies?

SB: I was in technology with iXL. When I came to Summit I expected to be a generalist, but probably at least half of what the firm did was technology. My first investment at Summit ended up being a consumer investment. It happened more from being opportunistic than from focusing on that sector at that time. Once you start to do a deal in a space you learn a lot.

You're on the board there for a few years. That makes it easier to do your next deal.

MJ: I know a lot of private equity firms have been more focused on consumer products as well. Do you have any ideas why that may be?

SB: Back in the late '80s and early '90s there was a group of people on the growth equity side that focused on technology and a group of folks that focused on retail. At the time, consumer investors were retail focused because there were shopping centers going up everywhere. Retail was a big growth engine, and the economy was doing well.

Today, the interest is more around brand, the value of a brand, and what that can bring versus just retail. Retail has become passé, and e-commerce is in. Branded products are important. People see the value of brands that exist in the marketplace.

There have also been growth opportunities in consumer products and in sectors like tech or fitness. There has been some really nice growth in the consumer sector in which to invest.

MJ: So you mention brand. Is this the number one factor that makes a consumer company attractive to you?

SB: It's definitely an important factor. It's not the only factor, but it's a very important piece.

MJ: What are some of the other factors that make a consumer company attractive?

SB: Market size, market growth rate, and innovation potential. We see a lot of interesting companies that maybe have the same type of product, like jewelry. They're coming to market in an innovative way where they are doing something special with technology or they're doing something special with their go-to-market strategy.

MJ: Is there a sense that the consumer product and the delivery method/marketing method are converging?

SB: I think of it as omni-channel. The world today is definitely omni-channel, from my perspective. I'm focused on e-commerce companies, but I'm also focused on opportunities for omni-channel investments with retail, wholesale, and e-commerce components. There is less reliance on one channel. Adding the direct-to-consumer side gives you opportunities for more mergers or capital for mergers.

MJ: I know you have also continued to do some technology investments as well, like Sparta Systems. What makes that kind of company attractive?

SB: Technology tends to be a growth sector. I am a growth equity investor, and industry agnostic for the most part, but always focusing on growth. A common theme, though, across the companies I've backed are those that exhibit revenue growth rates of at least 20 percent a year and that are cash-flow positive. Technology tends to be a sector that has a lot of growth. Health care also is a sector that's had a lot of growth. Sparta happened to be a software company selling to pharma.

It wasn't that I necessarily had sector experience in pharma or health care, or that particular kind of software, but the firm was a profitable, growing company, with industry tailwinds, so it fit. Our view was, "Show us a profitable, growing company and we'll figure out the industry. We'll figure out the specifics of the company." We were looking for a needle in a haystack, trying to find companies that had 20 percent growth and 20 percent EBITDA [earnings before interest, taxes, depreciation, and amortization] margins.

MJ: So you were somewhat sector agonistic?

SB: We were focused on profitable, growing companies. Then we figured out the rest.

MJ: Is that how you also got involved in a business services firm like Aramsco? Because it fit your growth profile?

SB: We made that investment post-9/11. They were doing products and services for emergency response. It was very much a trend at the time, and looked like it would be going forward. That was their newest business line. They also had a traditional business model that was dealing with environmental protection and distributing products for that during the construction process. It was a combination of historical, steady business in environmental protection and then adding the sexy, new opportunity in emergency response.

Ultimately, the investment didn't pan out exactly as we'd hoped. The company had a nice growth opportunity in emergency response, but honestly, after a few years, people seemed to forget 9/11. The budget that everyone expected and planned for didn't come to fruition. That emergency response business started to decline.

MJ: So the market opportunity didn't materialize the way that you had hoped?

SB: Exactly. We had done a lot of due diligence talking to people in Washington. We did a lot of diligence around the company and opportunity. It's hard to control the government budget. It's hard to control politics. It's hard to control political sentiments, and what people said versus what people did in that industry.

MJ: People do have notoriously short attention spans.

SB: The market going away like that is always a risk factor. I think you see that in technology and other areas as well. If the market goes away, that's not going to be good for anybody. You obviously have to try to predict that. That's one reason why we look for really large markets and try to avoid smaller markets that could go out of favor or just literally go away.

Another risk factor is management. We look for strong management teams, but one of the funky things about growth equity is that management tends to be founders. Sometimes founders can scale and be great CEOs of $100 million-dollar companies, and sometimes they can't.

Through no fault of their own, maybe they just don't have the classical management training or have never worked at some place like Procter & Gamble. They just don't have some of those experiences that help them scale.

It's our job to vet that out up front. If we're going to put ourselves in that position and we don't think that management can scale, maybe we need to start socializing the idea of bringing in a CEO before we close an investment, or other resources to the team to get from $50 million to $100 million.

But management is bit more fixable than a market issue. There's not much you can do other than pivot into a new direction if the market turns on you.

MJ: Did Summit sell Aramsco because it was nonperforming or because it was time?

SB: We don't own things forever, right? Our investment periods are usually five- to seven-year holds. We look to exit things by then. As soon as we felt like we had clearly refocused the company on its core and had a strong business to sell, that was the right time to exit. Holding period is usually a determinant of when we sell a company, and that's usually within that five- or seven-year range. Sometimes you own them a little bit longer if you're riding it through a recession or working to build your business back up.

The Importance of Networks

MJ: Thus far we've talked about a pretty diverse portfolio of investments. How do you find the companies in which you invest?

SB: We look through industry trade magazines. We go to trade shows. We're reading newspapers. We're reading the local business journals. We are picking up the phone and cold calling companies. Some of it is coming through investment bankers that are calling us about opportunities with companies, and some of it is going to a trade show and meeting ten companies that day that look attractive to us, and learning more about them.

That was a tenet of Summit Partners: cold calling companies and not sitting around waiting for bankers to come to us with opportunities. Plus we were doing both minority and majority investing. Bankers tend to really only be hired specifically for the full sale of a company. We were reaching out to companies because we could do a minority re-cap of a company. We do things the same way now at Norwest.

MJ: So it's more proactive than, say, venture capital, where they are bombarded with founders looking for money.

SB: It's just different. The companies we are looking for are profitable and growing. For the most part, they don't need our money.

They're not the venture companies that need money to grow because they're not yet profitable in their early stage. Our companies are all profitable. Five million in EBITDA and up from there, and growing 20 percent is our mark. We may see them from a bank if they decide to do a full sale of the company. If it's just a minority re-cap, they may not even know that's an option.

We're reaching out to these companies to say, "Hey, we'd love to know more about you, would you ever consider taking on a partner maybe to buy a third of your company and take some chips off the table? We can give you liquidity—maybe put a little cash on your balance sheet or help you form a board to think about taking your company to the next level. Help you professionalize the organization or help you recruit talent and grow from here to the next stage. We can help you achieve whatever your goals are, whether that's achieving an IPO in the next five years or achieving a sale to a large strategic investor."

MJ: I know that you also tend to do spin-offs and divestitures like Physicians Formula, for example. How do you find those deals?

SB: We find those deals through investment banks, lawyers, and even business school classmates. Physicians Formula actually came through a business school classmate of mine. It's our job to be very well networked.

In the case of Physicians Formula, my business school classmate's father was on the board of directors, and he knew that they were going to be spinning that out. They were considering not hiring a bank. They wanted to just select a small group of private equity firms. My classmate knew I was working at a private equity firm, and he called and asked if we'd have any interest in taking a look.

MJ: Are there any pieces of your network that you consider more important?

SB: My business school network has been a very strong one and an important one in my career.

MJ: Are there deals besides Physicians Formula that came through that network?

SB: About half of my deals came through a mix of both cold calling companies and my classmates from business school, and the other half came through an intermediary like an investment bank or broker. Airborne was through an industry contact. That was more of an industry-related recommendation from CPG, or Consumer Package Goods. Someone that was a distributor in that space that I'd gotten to know at a couple of trade shows mentioned my name to them. They eventually did hire a small boutique bank, but it was the relationship with someone I knew that gave them my name initially.

Snap Fitness was a cold call. It was a company that was on the Inc. 5000 list. One of my associates cold called the CEO. PCA Skin was a business school contact. The owner was actually a business school classmate of mine who had acquired the company shortly after graduation. Kendra Scott was a cold call by me after my stepmother suggested I stop by her newly opened store in Houston, Texas, where I was visiting my family.

MJ: So that's a lot of points of origin. I bet most people don't think of private equity partners cold calling.

SB: That's one of the fun things about private equity and growth equity: the various skill sets that are really important.

MJ: I imagine you also probably have to kiss a fair number of frogs to get to some princes? How many companies would you estimate that you talk to in a given year, and how many deals do you generally end up doing?

SB: I probably meet with 100 companies in a year. It may not be a face-to-face meeting, but we have a long call with somebody or an in-person meeting.

I'm generally making one to two investments a year.

MJ: Have there been years where you've made no new investments?

SB: Yes. I'm not going to do a deal just to do a deal. Sometimes it's the cycle of the market. You come out of a recession, or you're in the middle of a recession, and people that don't need to raise capital are not going to raise capital when prices are low. If a company is cash-flow positive, there's no reason for them to go dilute themselves or sell part of their company when valuations are depressed. So they wait.

Interest-rate cycles don't always impact deals. Sometimes people are choosing debt over equity, but debt is always cheaper than equity. Whether debt is 2 percent or debt is 12 percent, it's always cheaper than equity. When interest rates are low, we tend to see higher growth rates.

MJ: I know competition for deals in private equity has been pretty stiff of late. How consistent are the terms of your investments?

SB: Deal terms are pretty consistent. There are times when we try to preemptively bid, but really you can no longer get a discount for trying to get ahead of an auction process. I'd say rather you probably pay top dollar if you're getting ahead of an auction process because today, people tend to be more sophisticated. They're not going to stop a process unless it's a strong offer.

Return Expectations

MJ: So if terms are similar, how do profits stack up? In venture capital, I know their bogey is a 10× return on average. What kind of return are you looking to get?

SB: That's a great question. I'd say it has changed over time, as the market has gotten a little bit more competitive. The easy answer is you want to make three to five times the money in three to five years. The reality in today's market and with today's competition is that you're probably looking for three times your money in five years.

I'd say if I made five times my money, that would be hitting it out of the ballpark for growth equity. Both Physicians Formula and Sparta both returned over five times.

MJ: When they say that something didn't work out in venture capital, that investment could have gone to zero...

SB: On average for us, if something doesn't work out in the growth equity world, you get back 80 percent to 120 percent of your money. In order to feel like an investment worked out, you want to say you made two times your investment. Below two times you're probably disappointed. You're not usually losing more than 10 percent to 20 percent on an investment. Something really went wrong if you're losing more than 10 percent to 20 percent of your equity.

MJ: So your "failure rate" is much more contained. Let's focus for a minute on the deals that do work out.

SB: I really do love my current portfolio. Bailey 44, Kendra Scott, My Alarm Center, and PCA Skin are current holdings.

MJ: What makes them so attractive to you? Take PCA Skin for example.

SB: Size. PCA is of a size where tripling that company is definitely feasible. It's a good size for further growth, and being able to be really impactful there. It's also in a growing market: consumer-driven health care and beauty and skin care. Those are areas where you see higher-than-GDP growth.

MJ: If my spending is any indication, I know that's true.

SB: The baby boomers help with all of that. And then it's also focused on not going direct to consumer via the retail channels. It's more of a clinical product. It has a little bit more caché from a brand perspective.

There are a lot of small companies in the States, but there are not a lot of skin care brands that reach $5 million of EBITDA and beyond in the space. It may be the largest independent clinical skin care brand that exists today. So there is some scarcity value when you're thinking about a strategic acquirer at some point in time. That adds strategic value to the asset.

MJ: As a board member for that company, what types of things are you encouraging them to do in order to maintain and accelerate their growth rates?

SB: In many of these cases, part of the reason we invest is because we look at their current growth rate, we look at all the low-hanging fruit, and we're, like, "Wow! There's still a lot more growth here." Or "Oh! They could be growing so much faster." That's what we're identifying in our diligence process.

Then, once we come in, we try to help them execute on those growth plans. In some cases, we might put together a 180-day plan where we're highlighting all of those opportunities and getting the teams to look at starting to execute that plan, really, in the first six months of that investment.

If, for example, PCA Skin did not have a field sales force and everyone else in the market has a field sales force, then we would encourage that. Maybe that's an investment the entrepreneur just didn't want to make. But our view is, "Well, we have a little bit more risk tolerance. We're willing to make that investment, and we think that this is going to increase growth."

Women in the C-Suite

MJ: One of the things I noticed about your portfolio is that you tend to have a lot of women founders and women CEOs, like in PCA. That's an issue that is getting a lot of attention in private equity and venture capital right now. Do you think the increased concentration of women in your portfolio has to do with the type of companies in which you're investing or is it something you actively seek out?

SB: In hindsight, after making a dozen investments, I do tend to have had a number of investments that were led at some point by women founders or women CEOs.

If we look down the list—Physicians Formula, Airborne Health, Sparta Systems, Bailey 44, PCA Skin, My Alarm Center, Kendra Scott Design—all have or had women CEOs or founders. At Physicians Formula, we promoted a woman who was the head of marketing to CEO, and she led the company through an IPO. At Airborne, the founder was a husband and wife team. They wanted to bring in professional management when we came in and invested, and we brought in a female CEO. Bailey 44 has a female founder and female CEO. Kendra Scott is the founder. She is still CEO. My Alarm Center has a female CEO. PCA Skin had a female founder. With Sparta Systems, we hired a woman CEO. She was fantastic, and she brought the company through the exit.

Again, in all of those cases I was never seeking a woman-founded company or a woman CEO. I'm out looking for the best candidate for those roles. They just happened to be women, and they've all been great. My two highest investing outcomes so far in my career both had female CEOs.

MJ: Many of the companies you just mentioned had fairly stable executive teams during your tenure. I think people have this view of private equity that you come in, take over, and then fire everybody.

SB: It's definitely not our plan when we go in necessarily, unless the founders want out. Someone may come to us and say, "Hey, I don't want to be CEO anymore. I want to move up to be chairman. Let's do this together." We're all for that. But if someone says, "Hey, I want to continue run this business," that's great.

We're fully supportive of them continuing in that role. But, if we come in and the company goes from growing 20 percent to having a down 20 percent year, we start to scratch our heads as to whether this person really can continue to scale at that growth rate. Or do we need to think about providing help and adding to the management team or, if we do own control, do we need to make a change?

From my perspective, it is performance based. If you're a great CEO and the company is performing, fantastic! But if you're not performing in the role, we have an issue. It is hard when the person in that role happens to be the founder and it's their baby. It's not an easy discussion.

I think that is the time when private equity gets a bad rap by founders, because it is the assumption that "They're booting me out. I was the founder of the company." They don't really talk about the fact that they weren't maintaining good performance at the company, but we signed up for a growth company.

MJ: How much rope do you give people before they hang themselves?

SB: In every case where we've waited too long to make a change, we look back and say, "we should have done that a year earlier." I think we give people plenty of rope and plenty of time because ultimately we want it to work. We don't want to have to go through a management change. It's not fun for the business, It's not fun for me. But sometimes it is necessary.

CHAPTER 10

Mrs. Fix-It: Distressed and Turnaround Private Equity Investing

Raquel Palmer, Partner, KPS Capital Partners LP

I'm not particularly proud of the fact that my first brush with distressed investing was in the movie *Pretty Woman*, in which Richard Gere plays corporate raider Edward Lewis. Lewis buys distressed companies, breaks them apart, and sells the pieces for profit. In the movie, hooker with a heart of gold Vivian (Julia Roberts) asks if his business ventures are like "stealing cars and selling them for the parts." Gere replies, "Sort of, but legal."

By the end of the movie, however, Gere's character has experienced a complete about-face. Rather than dismantle James Morse's fictitious underperforming shipyard, Gere makes an investment in the firm and plans to build ships. While most people think of distressed and turnaround investing as early Edward Lewis, Raquel Palmer and her partners at KPS Capital Partners make it clear they belong in the latter camp.

Palmer has spent her entire career helping companies in distress. After obtaining her degree in political science from Stanford, she followed her childhood passion for business to investment banking. With the demise of Kidder Peabody coming only three months into her two-year analyst program, Palmer transitioned to distressed and turnaround advisory work at Keilin and Bloom, working with labor unions and employee groups at companies like United Airlines. In 1997, she and her partners opted to put their money where their advice was, and formed their first private equity fund to invest in distressed, special situations, and turnaround companies. Since then, KPS has raised more than $6 billion to invest in manufacturing and industrial companies around the world.

Named to *Crain's* "40 Under 40" list in 2011, Palmer currently serves as Chairman of the Board for Electrical Components International, Expera Specialty Solutions, Heritage Home Group, and International Equipment Solutions. She is also the head of her firm's investment committee. And while she can't help all of the companies she encounters, Palmer painstakingly searches for value at every turn. As a result, her firms' track record for turnaround success is impressive, based in part on the following guiding principals for turnaround investing:

- Don't be a cyclical investor. Bad management exists in every economic environment, so there are always opportunities to invest.
- While bankruptcies may offer a cleaner opportunity to build value, a company doesn't have to be in that much distress to be attractive.
- Don't look for themes or trends or cycles to generate profit. Look for opportunities where you can remove cost and create profits from the outset.
- Maintain dry powder for additional investments so you can deal with inevitable surprises down the road.

From Theory to Practice

MJ: What prompted your early interest in investment banking?

RP: My family is not a business or finance family at all. My mom worked in codes administration for the city of San Antonio. When your lawn got too tall, for example, you heard from my mom. My dad was in middle management. However, I have always been interested in business. I grew up at the beginning of the technology boom, which was an exciting time for many companies. As I learned more about business, I began to feel investment banking was one of the few fields that allowed for a broad introduction to many industries and strategies. I also assumed it would give me exposure to senior professionals and executives.

MJ: After getting your undergraduate degree, you went to Kidder Peabody. How did that work out?

RP: I really wanted to start my career in investment banking in New York City. I felt that, being from San Antonio, Texas, cutting my teeth in New York at the heart of the business world would allow me to have street cred. After that I believed I could go anywhere I wanted in the country, having established myself as someone who worked extremely hard and could learn in a very fast-paced setting.

At Stanford, I interviewed with many different investment banks, including Kidder Peabody. My decision came down to people in the end. I met nice, interesting, and very smart people in that interview process, but I felt that Kidder Peabody was really the best choice for me. Little did I know that it was at a company that was experiencing its own financial problems.

The same year that I accepted my offer, the company was brought down by the trading scandal with Joseph Jett. It also had financial losses, so GE decided to sell Kidder to Paine Webber. About three months into a new investment banking program, and after moving everything I owned to New York City, I found myself without a job.

MJ: Not an ideal combination by any stretch of the imagination.

RP: At that point, my entire analyst class was out on The Street looking for our next company to work for. I was very turned off by big investment banks and the fact that they were able to take someone, make them a promise of a two-year commitment, and then let them go after three months. I decided that I would open my search to smaller, more niche investment banks. I believed that they might value my work more than I felt it was at Kidder.

Losing my job turned out to be a blessing in disguise. I soon met my now partners, Michael Psaros and David Shapiro, who were working at a boutique investment bank named Keilin and Bloom. Keilin and Bloom represented labor unions and employee groups in complex restructuring transactions. What really attracted me to what they were doing is that nothing about their work was theoretical. I had found in my three short months at Kidder that I spent most of my time sitting behind a computer coming up with theoretical values for businesses or editing pitch books on our firm's credentials. The work didn't really feel real or meaningful to me.

At Keilin and Bloom, we were working in real businesses and representing real people whose employers were experiencing a lot of financial and operational distress. We were representing the underdog in many situations—steel workers or paper workers, for example. When the United Airlines pilots ended up completing an employee buyout of United Airlines, Keilin and Bloom represented the airline pilots.

We worked with industries that were in turmoil and that needed some sort of change. Oftentimes the workforce was asked to make changes to their collective bargaining agreements to reduce employment costs or employee liabilities. The management team might go to their employee groups and say, "We need a big concession. We need you to walk away from pension plans or health care." The employees didn't understand if their contributions were enough to save the company. They didn't know what they should be asking for in return for those concessions. They really didn't know what everyone else was doing. Were the suppliers or customers coming to the table? Was everybody with a vested interest in seeing the company survive doing enough as well?

We worked closely with the companies to create a turnaround plan of the business that not only included employee concessions but the contribution of many stakeholders. We found that we were very good at creating significant value for companies by transforming their costs structures and refinancing their balance sheets to give them enough liquidity to thrive.

MJ: So was it about getting to rescue a company or helping a company rescue itself?

RP: It was about seeing value in a troubled or underperforming business, oftentimes when others could not. What I get excited about is the part of my job when I look at company that is completely in trouble—it has operating losses, doesn't have the right strategy, doesn't have the right team at the helm—and I am able to create a plan to build a healthy and thriving business.

Advisor to Investor

MJ: So did you and your partners spin out from Keilin and Bloom?

RP: What we noticed, back in the mid-'90s, was that there were a tremendous amount of opportunity to invest in manufacturing and industrial companies in the United States that could benefit from our operational focus. There were really no private equity firms at the time that were willing to take on a troubled manufacturing company. Most of the private equity investors at the time were looking for big growth in health care, technology, and biotech. We were providing a very different approach and strategy.

A lot of the work we were doing as advisors is the same type of work we're doing today, which is fixing troubled companies. We were just doing it without the benefit of a fund. In 1997, we went out to raise our first fund and exited the advisory business. However, our fundamental strategy has not changed.

MJ: And that was your first dip into the principal investing waters?

RP: Yes. It was really at an interesting time for me in my career. I had to make the decision either to go to business school, like most people do after a few years in investment banking, or take on the challenge of becoming an investor.

Investing capital is a much more challenging position than financial advisory work. Advising a business on what steps they should take to turn their business around and actually executing on that plan as its owner is very different.

MJ: How seamless was your transition from advisor to investor?

RP: I would say the biggest difference is that as a principal investor there are companies we do not want to own at any price, and therefore take a pass on. As an advisor you work with every business that you're retained to work with. As a principal, you have to walk away from certain opportunities that just won't provide the appropriate return for our investors.

MJ: Did your specialization in manufacturing continue because of your work at Keilin or because that was where there was opportunity at the time?

RP: Our firm has always been focused on investing in manufacturing and industrial businesses. Our experience in improving the operations of our companies is how we create value for our investors.

During the past few years "operational focus" has become a buzzword that is used by every private equity fund, but it's really been at the heart of our business since the beginning. We find there are many more opportunities to change the cost structure of a manufacturing business. They tend to be asset heavy. Investment and strategy can lead to improvements in throughput, efficiency, and quality, which can, in turn, lead to significant improvements in cash flow.

Also, I think it is important to draw a distinction in turnaround investing. There are the investors that are focused on finding good companies with bad balance sheets. They simply write a check and fix the company's debt problems. They aren't fundamentally focused on improving the company itself. Our approach is not just looking for the bad balance sheet, but really a company that has severe operational issues or issues where we feel we can make the business better. Maybe they're not losing money, but they could benefit from our operationally focused approach.

MJ: What are the primary types of operational issues that you tend to find in companies? Are they product related, management related, distribution related?

RP: I would say every business is unique, but more often than not you have bad management or bad decision-making by ownership. It doesn't mean that every time we buy a business there's a bad manager at the helm. Oftentimes we'll come in and there's a new manager who has actually been working to fix the company's issues, and we will continue to work with them.

You also see great management that has been held back by a lack of focus from its ownership. We see this a lot in corporate carve-out situations, where a larger company has decided to carve out a business unit that is no longer core and sell it. Well, they probably decided it was no longer a core business about two years ago. The past two years they've just been ignoring it or putting it at the bottom of their priority list. In those situations, we are able to invest capital that has a very quick payback. Or we may support the management teams with their plans to expand the business. These businesses just need the capital and the attention, quite frankly.

We also often see a lack of information. Broken companies often will not have the proper management information systems in place. They are running by gut feel on where they think they are making money and where they're not. This can lead to a lot of bad decisions.

MJ: Can you give me an example?

RP: I think a great example of a troubled company that we made work is North American Breweries. We created that business in 2009. It started with a troubled brewery in upstate New York that was losing money and only using about 50 percent of its capacity. It was easy to say, "How on earth would I ever fix this company?"

In our diligence we quickly realized that, while the brewery had been neglected for some time, its cost structure could be improved with some strategic capital investment. If we could fix it, we would own one of the largest independent breweries in the United States. We also believed that, given the consolidation of the beer industry, there would be several brands that would be available for purchase to fill some of that excess capacity. In fact, during our diligence phase, we began also pursuing the purchase of Labatt USA from Inbev. Inbev was being forced to divest Labatt by the Department of Justice due to market concentration concerns in order to complete its merger with Anheuser Busch.

But the real hidden gem was the brewery's nationwide distribution network. Despite being a small brewery, they had a national distribution network because they also distributed a Seagram product.

If we could fix the plant, bring in additional beverage volume so that they could run the plant full, and execute on the two pages (single spaced) of other initiatives we came up with, you really could have a beautiful business that would be a perfect acquisition target for a strategic investor looking to come into the US beer market, which is the most profitable beer market in the world.

MJ: How do you find deals like that?

RP: That particular deal came through a local businessman who knew about the brewery's troubles, but our deal flow comes from a lot of different sources. We get calls from the traditional investment banks that know our reputation for looking at the more "storied" companies. We also hear from restructuring advisors and from employee groups and labor unions.

Endless Opportunities

MJ: Were deals like North American Breweries more plentiful in 2009 because of the financial crisis?

RP: Our fund is not a cycle play. We will find deals in every market. My partner likes to say there's an inexhaustible supply of bad management.

We don't necessarily need to buy a company in bankruptcy or that is busting covenants. If you look across our portfolio, about 75 percent of our deals were not in bankruptcy when we purchased them. When you hear "turnaround" or "special situations," people tend to think that most of our deals were created in a bankruptcy environment; however, we have been able to buy companies that are not in financial distress and make improvements.

MJ: So it's creative ways to leverage and grow what they already have?

RP: Absolutely. Last year, we created the largest specialty paper company in the United States, Expera Specialty Solutions. We simultaneously completed two purchases of competing businesses. We went to two separate owners and purchased their respective specialty paper products businesses—Wausau Paper, which is a publicly traded company, and Packaging Dynamics, which is a private equity-owned business. There's a tremendous amount of industrial logic in combining the two units. In both situations, these were divisions of their respective companies that were not priorities.

I think this is very different from other private equity strategies. We are creating value by building businesses and not looking to extract value by tearing them apart.

MJ: How do you identify any low-hanging fruit? If it's often about the management, do you always replace them when you buy into a company?

RP: It is situation specific. We are only looking to replace the management that caused the train wreck, or those who cannot adapt to our philosophy of continuous improvement.

We're focused on finding the right companies, and usually those are the leaders in their respective industries. We're focused on finding companies that have operational issues that we can fix. We not looking for companies where you're betting on the top line coming back or betting on a cycle or saying, "We'll be fine as long as this projection happens." What we're really saying is, "Can we take cost out of this company so we can have a meaningful return on investment?"

In a lot of ways we're de-risking our transaction from day one. Before we even write a check we've developed a business plan based on status quo revenue—a plan that expects no sunshine and no growth. One thing you can never correct for is not buying right. You need to be able to buy this business for a reasonable price that will allow you to get that return if you can execute on the business plan you put together.

MJ: Do have a sweet spot for the size company that you like to look at?

RP: We started in 1997 with a $200 million fund. We're now investing out of a $3.5 billion fund. We obviously now are completing larger deals because we can't manage 40 small investments. We are very involved and active with our companies, so we really want to make three to four smart investments every year. With that, we need to invest $100 million to $250 million in each new deal. We reserve capital for follow-on investment in those portfolio companies as well.

MJ: How often do you interact with the management of those companies?

RP: We are very active owners and spend a great deal of time with our portfolio companies. If we're looking at additional acquisitions, we tend to spend a lot more time together. If nothing extraordinary is going on in the business, we're talking once a week, we're reviewing numbers once a month, and we're having a board meeting once a quarter. At the very least I'm speaking to my CEO or CFO is once a week, and it often feels like it's every other day.

MJ: And you always take a control position?

RP: We are control owners in every situation.

MJ: What are some of the risk factors that you think about when you're getting ready to write one of these larger checks?

RP: I think the number one thing we don't want to do is catch a falling knife. We don't want to invest in businesses that are just in a complete spiral. Hidden liabilities are another area where we are very careful. You never want to step into a situation where there's a surprise a year later with some off-balance-sheet-type liability.

Fun with Diapers

MJ: So you talked about making beer and paper. Are there other favorite deals that come to mind?

RP: I would say Attends Healthcare was probably one of my favorites. It's a company that makes adult diapers, and it was a pretty fun deal from start to finish.

Everyone thinks of Kimberly Clark's business Depends as being the premier and the first adult diaper brand. Actually, the first adult diaper company was created by Procter & Gamble. P&G, as a company, tends to go for institutional credibility when launching a product line. They go to markets like hospitals and nursing homes to get a stamp of approval before going to the consumer. While P&G went to institutions, Kimberly Clark went to the consumer first. Retailers did not see a need for two brands of a new product line. So Attends ended up being this institutional brand that P&G eventually exited, given its lack of retail exposure. It then was passed through a couple of private equity funds.

When we were approached with the opportunity to buy the company, the business was suffering because it had missed the innovation bandwagon: it didn't have a pull-up version of an adult diaper in the United States. Its current ownership had decided to focus on the more profitable European unit and had neglected investing in new lines in the United States.

The owners wanted a short sale process and had stated they wanted to complete the transaction in two months. The company wanted to pick one buyer to move ahead with. At the time I was seven months pregnant. I said, "Look, I, more than anyone else, will get this deal done on in 60 days because if I don't, I will be in the hospital trying to get it done." They chose us to move forward with.

Management had such great ideas and really had spent a lot of time thinking about what they would do if they had capital. That's a question that we ask every time we go into a situation, and often times you're pleasantly surprised with a list of "This is how I would spend money. Here's how we would fix this business." Sometimes you go into a situation, and there are just crickets. But this time the team had a ton of great ideas.

Out of the box these guys were just killing it. It was one of those businesses that every month they made more cash flow than the month before. The management believed in the company so much that they actually bought 10 percent of it as well. Ultimately, we ended up making 15 times our invested equity capital on that deal.

MJ: That may be the first time that anyone has described adult diapers as "fun." I don't know if you remember the faux commercials from *Saturday Night Live* for "Oops! I Crapped My Pants"?

RP: I might have seen those a time or two during the investment. There is not one potty humor joke that we did not hear during our ownership. We got the last laugh, though, as we took Attends from losing $5.4 million of EBITDA per year to generating almost $35.4 million. Anyone could get excited about that.

MJ: What about deals that didn't make 15 times your investment?

RP: I think "controllable" is the key word here. It's controllable cost and controllable factors that make our business plans work. We've had very, very few problem portfolio companies. If you think about the $6 billion in capital that we've raised, we've only had about $100 million that has not generated a return.

A few of our smaller investments had problems over our 17-year history. One of them that sticks out in my mind is Republic Engineered Products. The business plan that we put together was completely sound. The issue was, we were pouring heated steel during the blackout in 2003. We lost a very key part of our manufacturing facility because of the loss of power. It was a mini explosion. Nobody was injured and nobody was hurt, which is the first thing you worry about. But unfortunately, we didn't have any additional capital to put into that business because we had invested our entire fund.

It was a lesson for us to keep a lot of dry powder because stuff happens. The lesson learned on all of our troubled companies is that there's always going to be factors that you can't control and, law of averages, you will have some of these problems.

MJ: So very few losses and at least one 15 times cash return. Is 15 times invested capital your target?

RP: That was an outstanding deal. Not all of them return that much. Our focus has always been cash return on cash invested. Can I turn a dollar into seven? How do I create the most value for our investors on a dollar-for-dollar basis?

Finding Values

MJ: You work with three partners in your firm. Do you feel like you bring different things to the table?

RP: I think the four of us are all very different. We complement each other well. I would say what makes me a little bit different is, I will spend time looking at anything. Even if it looks like there's no hope in sight, I will still take the meeting. I will still go and show up to the business to see if there's anything I can find that we can use and create value. I don't mind spending time with the hairier businesses. It doesn't mean that we ended up doing those hairier deals, it just means I don't like giving up on something. I'm pretty stubborn.

MJ: The word is tenacious, not stubborn, by the way.

RP: You're right. I'm tenacious.

MJ: You mentioned being pregnant at the time of the adult diaper deal.

RP: I have three children, and that was my last. I have a ten-year-old, an eleven-year-old and my seven-year-old.

MJ: How does that work?

RP: I have great role models in my own mother and grand-mother, who is 93 and still with us. Quite frankly, I never even doubted that having a career and being a mom was something I could do. I always say, "How can I complain? My grandmother was a maid. She had nine children. She made it work. I live in New York City, I have a tremendous amount of resources, including a very supportive husband, I shouldn't complain."

My partners and the family values of our firm also help me balance work and family life. The environment we have created here is very family oriented. Work-life balance is seen as a necessary quality for being a good investor. My partners also understand how difficult it can be when you're getting pulled in multiple directions. They are also very active fathers in their children's lives, and that makes all the difference.

MJ: Do you think that's unusual within a private equity firm? Having a smaller, family-oriented firm?

RP: When you start to get into the bigger size funds, the multiple-billion-dollar funds, I do think it's unusual to have the people on the door, the K, the P, the S, in meetings. I think it offers a lot of comfort to a seller to know that they aren't going to go through some large, opaque organization with layers of investment committees. I am the chairman of our investment committee. I talk with my partners every day. If I tell you we are interested in a deal, it's because we are genuinely interested.

MJ: So it's still a high-touch, very people-oriented type of business for all four of the partners there?

RP: Absolutely. We have a budget review in Westchester, New York, every year where we bring all of our CEOs and CFOs in, and we go through their budgets. One of those nights we'll have a dinner party at Mike Psaros' house, and everybody comes. We all sit and have a big dinner with all of our teams. It usually involves people drinking a lot of wine and then playing basketball at Mike's house for the remainder of the evening.

MJ: Why basketball?

RP: Because he has a basketball court, and I think boys can't see a basketball court without picking up a ball and shooting it.

MJ: That is true. Aside from beer and adult diapers, have there been any other transactions that you would consider more off the beaten path?

RP: We've had a wide range of investments in many industries. From adult diapers to beer to Waterford-Wedgwood to businesses that are less sexy, like Waupaca Foundry and Global Brass and Copper, which is the largest brass manufacturer in the United States.

Maintaining Manufacturing

MJ: Do you ever see yourself transitioning into other areas of private equity or moving away from industrials and manufacturing?

RP: Every single business we own has to make something. That's our focus and it's that simple. Waterford Wedgewood is a prime example of a consumer products business with a manufacturing problem. What we saw in the company was a broken manufacturing platform and duplicative organizational structure. We knew we could fix those issues. We're very opportunistic. We will look at any business as long as it makes something.

MJ: Would you say that's how you stick to your knitting?

RP: That's right. It's manufacturing. I would say the only move we've made beyond our original strategy is to be more global.

We now will invest in companies outside of the United States. Almost all of our portfolio companies have divisions or joint ventures in many different parts of the world. We have learned about investing in countries all over the world.

MJ: Because you're doing turnarounds, do you usually get a warm or a chilly reception from employees at your portfolio companies?

RP: We get a warm reception from people who are excited to see change in a company. I would say that there are oftentimes managers who know they aren't performing, and who aren't going to be so psyched to see us coming. They probably feel like their days are numbered. They're usually right.

MJ: So if people are happy to see you and you've already figured out your low-hanging fruit and business plan before going in, what are your biggest post-transaction challenges?

RP: You're not able to execute on your business plan before you buy a company. If there is any consolidation that needs to happen or any change of managers that needs to happen, it has to happen on day two or three. It can't happen on day one. Execution is the biggest challenge. You have to have a laser focus on achieving the goals and plans we set forth in our investment thesis. This is a daily grind, and we depend heavily on getting the right management teams in place to make sure it happens.

MJ: And how do you balance your short-term execution with your long-term goals?

RP: There absolutely is private equity out there that is focused on the short term. However, when you're dealing with restructurings and operational turnarounds, you have to look to the long term. You can't simply put lipstick on a pig and expect somebody to come in and not see right through that.

Private equity gets beaten up for taking value out of these companies and stripping them. That is the antithesis of what we do. It is painful to hear and to read those stories. Every business that we buy, we put so much of our time, effort, and sweat into turning it around and finding the right people to run it. We painstakingly study the cost structures of our companies, make capital decisions, develop strategic plans to turn uncompetitive businesses into successful enterprises for the long term. You have to understand that many of the businesses we invest in would have liquidated had we not acquired them.

MJ: The other thing I guess you can hold onto is that you didn't put the company in a bad position.

RP: That's true. A lot of times in bankruptcy, you're able to draw that distinction because you simply buy the parts of the business that you need down the road instead of buying everything. You don't have to wind down the parts that aren't interesting.

Avoiding Labor Pains

MJ: So does that make bankruptcies easier to deal with?

RP: I love bankruptcies. You're able to buy a business free and clear of a lot of legacy liabilities. You're able to start fresh and buy the assets that are going to make a successful business going forward. I would do bankruptcies every day of the week. There are just not a lot of companies of scale being forced into that type of situation. HHG, our furniture platform, we created by purchasing assets out of bankruptcy. The only other large-scale bankruptcy that we saw over the past couple of years besides Heritage was Hostess.

MJ: Cupcakes? The Ho Ho company?

RP: Twinkies, yes. But that was a difficult turnaround for us because it really did involve literally just buying the brands and certain manufacturing assets. You were basically walking away from all of the union contracts. Our history, as I said, started with our relationship with organized labor. We still continue, to this day, to have a fantastic relationship with all the major unions in North America. We would never do anything that would jeopardize that relationship that we have.

MJ: That was a deal that you passed on, then?

RP: We ended up passing because the only solution involved was taking steps that we just would not do.

MJ: Are there other things that make you walk away from a potential transaction?

RP: Fraud. We've seen it a few times, where we started to do our financial due diligence and there was fraud involved. We walked away. We just said, "If they are lying about their numbers, there has to be more wrong here." That's a nonstarter.

MJ: Is that something that you see a lot, or is it something that is pretty rare?

RP: It's rare. I think I've seen it twice in all of the due diligence I've done on businesses. If there's even a hint that the numbers don't smell right, we bring in forensic accountants. We can get to the bottom of that pretty quickly if we think something fishy is going on.

MJ: So you can separate bad management from felon management, but it's still ultimately a people business?

RP: It's always people. I think that's true for the CEOs you hire. It's true for the investment professionals you hire. We always say, "In the NBA you can't coach height. In the NFL, you can't coach size. In private equity, you can't coach judgment." We have to find people who not only are smart (because there's a ton of smart people out there that want to work hard) but who also have a passion for business, manufacturing businesses in particular, and good judgment. That's really difficult to find.

CHAPTER 11

Billion-Dollar Listings: Investing in Real Estate

Deborah Harmon, Co-Founder and
CEO, Artemis Real Estate Partners

Roughly two-thirds of Americans own their home,[1] making real estate a significantly more popular investment than the stock market. In fact, for many investors, owning property is seen as part and parcel of the American dream, and the tangible nature of the investment is almost universally appealing. It's not for nothing that Franklin D. Roosevelt once said, "Real estate cannot be lost or stolen, nor can it be carried away. Purchased with common sense, paid for in full, and managed with reasonable care, it is about the safest investment in the world."[2]

And while the theory of following Roosevelt's three real estate investment tenets may seem simple, the reality often proves more difficult. In fact, the global recession coupled with investor overleveraging and a lack of liquidity caused broad measures of commercial real estate prices in the United States to drop by more than 40 percent in 2008 and 2009.[3] Property owners, developers, direct investors, and those exposed to mortgage-backed securities and other real-estate-linked instruments were all swept up in the carnage.

But where others saw crisis, Deborah Harmon saw opportunity. A veteran of several real estate booms and busts, Harmon left retirement in 2009 to co-found Artemis Real Estate Partners with her partner Penny Pritzker, now US Secretary of Commerce. Her real estate investing motto? "As you move in real estate through this inevitable cycle from crisis to stabilization and then to recovery, chance favors the prepared mind."

And Harmon was nothing if not prepared. After obtaining her degree in political science from Johns Hopkins University, Harmon made the leap to corporate finance at Bankers Trust. While there, she was recruited to join the real estate team, and, despite early reservations about the asset class, began to pursue real estate investing and a Wharton MBA. She later became the youngest female Managing Director at Bankers Trust before joining the J.E. Robert Companies [JER] and becoming President and Chief Investment Officer.

Indeed, Harmon is the antithesis of many real estate investors. She finds putting capital to work when others are running for the exits exciting, and looking for deals when the markets are stable scary. But like most real estate professionals, she lives by the rule "Location, location, location." Her other rules for real estate success include the following:

- The best time to invest in real estate is when there is still a significant amount of uncertainty coupled with the first hints of optimism.
- Protect the downside, and the upside will take care of itself.
- Look for capacity for current cash flow.
- Find a good operating partner with deep knowledge and connections either in a specific product type or region. Good partners can make a deal, and bad partners can break a deal.
- Global financial and industry-specific cycles can create distressed real estate investment opportunities, but not all distress is created equal. Pay attention to what makes a particular crisis unique and invest accordingly.
- Don't rush to make investments just to deploy your cash. If the opportunities aren't there, wait.

Moving into Real Estate

MJ: How did you make the leap from political science to real estate?

DH: I graduated from Johns Hopkins with a degree in political science and international relations. I took one business course at the end of my senior year, and I loved it. I had not taken any other business courses in college, which I'm not sure I'd recommend for people today, but I knew that I wanted to run my own business at some point.

My objective coming out of college was to obtain a set of broad business skills. I had no formal exposure to real estate through university coursework, and therefore did not view it as a viable career option. Until that point, my main experience with real estate had been that my grandfather, who was a lawyer during the Great Depression, received a building in lieu of cash as payment for legal services rendered.

In my senior year in college, I was accepted into the training program at Bankers Trust. It had the shortest credit-training program, but was the most intensive—precisely what I was looking for. When I came out of the Bankers Trust program, I went into corporate finance with a group that did leveraged buyouts for middle-market companies.

One of my early team experiences, believe it or not, was all women. I participated on multiple, diverse, high-performing teams. It was trial by fire at 22 years of age. The responsibility that was given to me significantly outweighed my experience, which proved to be a tremendous training environment.

MJ: Wasn't that pretty unusual for the time? Having an all-female team in corporate finance?

DH: I was really gender blind in my twenties. I had no idea that it was unusual. The training program was 50/50 gender balanced, and I just assumed this was the case more broadly.

In retrospect, it was actually far easier to enter the investment business when I did, because there were so many more banks and investments banks with training programs. I think that avenue has been significantly reduced with all the consolidation in banks and the 2008 financial crisis.

MJ: And did you like the work?

DH: I loved everything about my experience at Bankers Trust. After three years, in 1985, management came to me and said, "We'd like you to move to real estate." I have to be honest: I was devastated. In 1985, commercial real estate was an industry where women were rarely seen, and I didn't have a burning passion to enter it.

Then they sweetened the offer. I always knew I was going to go back to business school, and the bank offered to pay for my MBA at Wharton while I kept working. I had a choice: take two years off the job market and be dependent on loans, or keep working and making money, have no social life, but end up with a Wharton degree and five years of work experience. In the end, I gave up vacation for two years, worked full-time, went to Wharton, and postponed my wedding.

MJ: Why did they want you to go into real estate so badly?

DH: In 1985, if you were a corporate finance analyst or associate coming out of the training program, very few people went into real estate. Real estate hadn't become a traditional part of the investment banking suite of services. Bankers Trust was trying to institutionalize real estate, and I was among the early crop of credit-trained analysts transferred to real estate. They felt that there was significant opportunity.

I knew it was definitely a growth area. They had put in a new head of real estate, Richard Gunthel, who also came from corporate finance. He ended up being a fabulous mentor. I used my leveraged buyout skills right away. I felt I was a legitimate contributor at 25 years old.

I started in California supporting the corporate KKR team. We financed the leveraged buyout of Motel 6 and M&T Ranch, which was an avocado farm and ranch in Oakland, California. I financed deals across the country, developing relationships with real estate owners, operators, and developers from California to New York. This experience gave me a tremendous introduction to real estate. I fell in love with the entrepreneurial nature of the industry and the larger-than-life clients and partners. I was exposed to transactions across product type and geography. I was able to work from the peak to the trough of an entire market cycle from '85 to '90, spanning a tax-driven oversupply of real estate fueled by the savings-and-loan crisis to the crash of 1989 and 1990.

In retrospect, I think I learned more from the crisis periods. I always say failures are the tuition you pay for success. Being able to see failure and success early on in my career...

MJ: You had seen enough bad things to be prepared for them in the future?

DH: Exactly right. Otherwise, you don't know what you don't know. My last act at Bankers Trust set me up for the next stage of my career. I had moved from working on transactions to the managerial responsibilities of running a team—the first real estate team dedicated to running the Northeast. I learned how to be an entrepreneur by first being an intrapreneur within the Bankers Trust infrastructure. I hired the people. Our team developed new client relationships. We worked on the first real estate equity investments, and introduced investment banking services. And, because commercial real estate was so new, I was doing all of this at the age of 27.

My first joint venture partner was Stephen Ross of The Related Companies, and our first equity investment was 625 Madison Avenue. Steve brought Bankers Trust in as a 20 percent equity partner. We had a terrific partnership until the New York banking laws abruptly changed and we were required to exit our position immediately and prematurely. I went to Steve and said, "You have to help Bankers Trust sell our minority interest in this building quickly, while generating the same projected returns we underwrote, despite the much shorter hold period."

Steve found the only Japanese buyer who would purchase a minority interest in the building, partly because of a trendy nightclub, Au Bar, we'd put in the basement. That was when I learned the value of relationships with an extraordinary operating partner. Good operating partners are far more important than the physical asset. You can do good deals with good operating partners. You can do a bad deal with a good operating partner and still have a good result. A good deal with a bad operating partner can have a terrible result.

In 1988, I was promoted to run the New York team and then became Managing Director. At the time, I also inherited a $100 million unsecured loan to Donald Trump. As the market turned in late 1989, I experienced my first genuine real estate crisis. That was an extraordinary education, to observe how each New York City developer, many of whom were overleveraged, responded to the crisis.

If Trump went bankrupt, approximately 14,000 jobs in the Northeast would have been lost because he employed people at casinos, airlines, retail, and office buildings. He was the first "too big to fail." Nobody fully appreciated the impact his potential bankruptcy could have on the local economy. I worked for a year straight locked in a conference room in Manhattan trying to claw our way back from a 100 percent write off to a healthy percentage of par.

That period of time taught me everything about what can go wrong, and I learned a valuable lesson: I'd much rather spend my professional life buying debt at a discount during distressed economic times.

Working with The Donald

MJ: Do you remember how well you did with The Donald?

DH: Normally you collect 10 percent to 15 percent on the unsecured dollar. We did significantly better. We completed the restructuring, saved the jobs, and Trump lived to fight and prosper on other days...

MJ: ...and to fire people on TV...

DH: Donald's brand, even in his darkest hours, remained tremendously resilient. I remember we flew to Atlantic City so I could underwrite a casino. The casinos were filled with the deafening sound of slot machines. As Donald walked through the casino, I was trying to keep up with him, and the sea of people parted and as arms reached out to touch Donald for good luck, I remember thinking, "if they only knew the precarious state of affairs in New York." It was a lesson that perception is not always the reality.

Of course, he went on to be extremely successful, and the complicated multi-business transaction prepared me with a once-in-a-lifetime "PhD" in restructuring. It was probably the highlight of that time period for me.

MJ: So what came next?

DH: I was 29 years old, and it was my husband's turn to move for his fellowship, and he chose the National Institutes of Health in Washington, DC. I wasn't thrilled about leaving New York City. I took what I thought was an extraordinary risk leaving a large, secure, lucrative position as the youngest and only woman Managing Director in real estate at Bankers Trust.

In my final year at Bankers Trust, we began bidding on assets sold by the RTC, the Resolution Trust Corporation, which was born out of the US savings-and-loan crisis. The RTC had collected about $90 billion of bad assets, mostly real estate nonperforming loans and bank-owned properties due to foreclosures.

As I was looking to relocate from New York to Washington, DC, Stephen Ross introduced me to Joe Robert, the founder of the J.E Robert Companies. JER at the time was known as an RTC contractor, working on behalf of the US government to manage and dispose of the RTC assets. In the world that I came from, few people had ever heard of JER. But Joe and I shared a vision that the RTC could provide the greatest transfer of wealth from the public to the private sector in our careers. I joined to create a separate principal investment group to buy the RTC assets at a significant discount.

JER had the basic skills to manage assets, but they had no access to institutional or Wall Street capital. JER was an opportunity to take my skill set and knowledge, and help create a new business that would become a best-in-class operating partner for institutional capital.

Crisis Opportunities

MJ: You really wanted it to be a meaningful step, then? Not just a lateral move?

DH: Yes. It also was an opportunity to be a bigger fish in a smaller pond. And, from a personal perspective, I hoped I could add sufficient value before starting a family. I hoped to earn, in advance, the flexibility I would need to have children. It was also an opportunity to round out my skills and experience, so I could take on roles like capital raising, management, and business development—serving as Chief Investment Officer and ultimately President over my 17-year tenure.

I was pregnant within one month of joining JER. It really did matter that I'd found an environment where I had the opportunity to make an immediate and meaningful contribution. My son Dan was born one month after I negotiated one of the greatest joint ventures from my early days at JER. We signed the documents during the last week I could travel before giving birth. It made JER the exclusive operating partner to Goldman Sachs in a joint venture that would invest $2 billion in equity and purchase $7 billion of assets from 1991 to 1996. The deal definitely earned me flexibility.

MJ: You left JER in 2007?

DH: It was really tough in 2006 to find things you wanted to buy, especially if you were a buyer of value and distress. I left JER at the peak of the cycle. I guess the lesson there is timing is everything, and sometimes it's better to be lucky than smart. I thought I was going to retire and transition from the professional to the philanthropic chapter of my life. However, my retirement was short lived.

It turned into a sabbatical of about a year. In 2008, with the collapse of Lehman and Bear Stearns, I saw the FDIC [Federal Deposit Insurance Corporation] increasingly becoming a holder of nonperforming loans and real estate. I thought, "Wow. It's exactly what I experienced when I was 29. It's going to happen again. I've been to this movie before." This time around I wanted to be the decision-maker—in control of the capital—and create a company that would perform and make a difference in the industry.

MJ: It was an opportunity too good to refuse?

DH: Absolutely. I am passionate about distress. Whenever markets are characterized by fear and uncertainty, it has typically created investment opportunities too good to pass up. At the same time, prior partners of mine at JER approached me to say, there are no real estate private equity firms with a woman owner or founder. Why don't we become the first?

I had the great fortune to be able to bring with me trusted colleagues with whom I had worked, in many cases for ten years or more, including Artemis President Alex Gilbert. Having the opportunity to build a new firm—its people, its culture— from the ground up was a huge advantage. I had the chance to assemble a team that shared my approach to risk management and that valued diverse perspectives. I felt that was a winning combination—one that could generate superior performance, while widening the circle of opportunity for others in the industry, doing well and doing good. The next step was obvious: I reached out to my friend and industry colleague Penny Pritzker.

MJ: How long did it take you to raise your first fund?

DH: We went out in the market in March of 2010, and we had to achieve $150 million minimum for the first close. We had $150 million five months later. I deliberately didn't close at that time because I knew that you rarely, even in good times, more than double the size of your first close in the final close. We had a final close in January of 2012 of $436 million.

MJ: That was a very quick and large close, particularly for the environment.

DH: We were told that was the fastest and largest first-time fundraise for a first-time firm. We had the track record, the skill set, and the timing was ripe to invest. This was a cyclical buying opportunity. There was an abundance of distressed assets combined with a weakened banking system—a perfect storm for what we call situation distress.

MJ: So it was an attractive, cyclical opportunity. How did you think about investing at that time?

DH: Real estate is cyclical. The 2005 to 2007 cycle was a period of peak exuberance. Investors underpriced risk. There was significant overleveraging. Then we moved quickly from exuberance to fear and into a market ripe for distressed investing because it was characterized by uncertainty. US real estate saw the greatest amount of distress from 2008 to 2010.

What does that mean? That means that investor sentiment was characterized by fear and inaction. When that happens, risk becomes overpriced. People are scared to make a decision and fearful to make an investment. You want to begin investing when the overall market still has a significant amount of uncertainty, but you see the first green shoots of optimism. The smart money was buying real estate debt at a discount.

When we started investing after the crisis, we focused on smaller transitional assets, under the radar screen of the larger funds, where there was little, if any, bank financing available. For example, we didn't invest in downtown New York City, but maybe in Brooklyn. We didn't invest $100 million of equity. We did $10 million to $30 million equity deals. History has taught me that there is significantly greater mispricing in secondary markets, smaller-size transactions, and transitional assets.

Sometimes you can invest ahead of a particular market's improving. For example, we could anticipate the rebounding of San Francisco, but there was not a lot of capital going into the ring markets around it and other major cities. We were very strategic in focusing on assets in those surrounding markets. Today the capital is searching for yield in these markets. You know the saying about location, location, location? The key is to find locations ahead of where the capital is going, so when it ultimately arrives, you have highly attractive exit options.

MJ: So geography matters. What about type of property?

DH: We have a top-down and bottom-up approach to real estate investing. From the macro perspective, we evaluated how each real estate product type would be expected to recover from this current crisis, and tried to invest at the bottom of the cycle in advance of the recovery. This was a different crisis than in the '90s, so we expected that the recovery would be different as well. We anticipated that the recovery would be slower and that it would not be led by the consumer. For example, in multifamily properties, my experience taught me that the only time you can get opportunistic returns is to invest at the bottom of the cycle—postcrisis. So we began investing in multifamily properties early in our fund.

Because corporations were the first to recover, amassing growing profits and reducing expenses, we chose to focus next on investing in the industrial sector. We felt retail was going to be the last product type to improve. Basically, we tried to get into each opportunity right before it turned the corner to recovery.

Many people in my business generate investment success through real estate development. Artemis may do that on occasion, maybe 10 percent of the time. But we prefer to buy existing assets below their intrinsic value. That means, for example, when the seller is distressed and we are able to buy the asset below replacement cost. The asset itself may be just fine. Those are the best deals, and they are found during periods of economic distress and illiquidity.

MJ: Were the opportunities plentiful because so many people were overleveraged?

DH: Yes. Overleveraging creates distress, and it comes in many forms. For example, a distressed bank selling nonperforming loans, a nonstrategic holder of real estate who sells real estate to generate liquidity for its core business, an individual or, in the case of Artemis, special servicers that took over delinquent CMBS loans [commercial mortgage-backed securities]. Between 2010 and 2012, the most active sellers to Artemis Fund I were special servicers.

Buying below market value is the most dependable route to profit. It's a key element in limiting risk and producing consistent attractive risk-adjusted returns. If you look at Artemis Fund I, 75 percent was invested in some form of distressed opportunity. It's harder to find distressed opportunities today because so much capital has come into the real estate market. But you can still selectively buy below replacement costs.

MJ: Obviously there were great opportunities in both the '90s and in 2009 and 2010. Because one crisis was demand driven and one was supply driven, were the buying environments any different?

DH: The largest distressed seller in the '90s was the RTC on behalf of the US government. Given the large amounts of real estate oversupply in the early days, we often bought vacancy and poorer quality assets at 30 cents on the dollar. While we could buy assets more cheaply, the quality was significantly worse than what we bought in 2010. In the '90s it was difficult to judge how much product could be dumped on the market. You didn't want to become the highest-priced buyer of distressed real estate assets.

The very first portfolio we bought at JER was called Savers Savings, mostly multifamily properties and nonperforming loans in Arkansas and Texas. We bought $260 million of debt for $80.5 million. Not only did we buy the assets at a discount to the original debt, but we got a further 25 percent discount because we paid all cash at closing instead of taking government financing. We ended up generating a 60 percent return on our equity.

An Appetite for Apartments

MJ: Sixty percent? Is that unusual?

DH: I will tell you that the multifamily investments that Artemis bought from distressed sellers in 2011 and 2012 had better-quality assets and geographic locations. In fact, our total multifamily portfolio has a realized return of 63 percent IRR [internal rate of return] and a 2.5-times multiple. The largest investment in Fund I was purchased from a seller that had broad liquidity problems, and this asset was burdened by an above-market CMBS loan. While he was focused on selling his entire portfolio, we only purchased a subset of the portfolio.

The investment was a Class A-, four-property multifamily portfolio consisting of nearly 1,400 units in Dallas, Houston, Nashville, and Kansas City. The portfolio saw less competition due to its unattractive CMBS debt. The purchase price of nearly $118 million ($84k per unit) represented a 15 percent discount to market value for similar assets. This was far less of a discount than JER got in the early '90s.

The portfolio was acquired with $93 million of in-place CMBS debt, or 70 percent loan to value. The units were 94 percent occupied. The joint venture invested approximately $7 million to renovate the properties, including exterior improvements to the clubhouse and other amenities, as well as interior improvements, such as new appliances, countertops, light fixtures, and flooring. This investment's base case at acquisition was projected to generate an 18.5 percent IRR return, with a 1.7-times equity multiple. This four property portfolio was sold in September 2014 and achieved returns of a 56 percent IRR and 2.4-times equity multiple.

It was a great investment. But honestly those kinds of returns, particularly for multifamily, don't happen often in real estate.

MJ: So you went in and made improvements and then resold. Is that your typical deal structure and exit?

DH: We typically buy below replacement cost. We fix a temporary flaw in the asset: reposition, release, or redevelop. What usually happens following a distressed environment is the seller's lack of liquidity results in underfunding of the asset. They don't invest in upgrading the units in multifamily properties or fund tenant improvements/leasing commissions in office properties. We purchase the assets with specific capital improvement plans, then we sell when we can generate a two times profit multiple.

Because the market was so attractive for our investment approach in 2011, we actually bought and sold ahead of projections in our first fund. We will return the capital to investors ahead of schedule and exceed our projected life-of-fund returns. Honestly, I didn't think this was going to happen. I thought this recovery was going to take longer. I told all the investors that my average investment life when I did this before was two years, but they should expect three to four. Ultimately, though, I expect the return of capital to be consistent with other distressed cycles—about two to three years for return of capital.

MJ: How do you control risk in the portfolio?

DH: In 2002, post the 9/11 crisis, while working together at JER, Artemis' current CFO and I created a risk and portfolio management function as part of the investment committee. That's commonplace today, but it wasn't a decade ago in real estate. Our goal was to measure and manage risk and to ensure diversification. I do not believe you achieve diversification just by having 20 percent multifamily, 20 percent this and 20 percent that. A common misconception is that diversification is simply holding many different things. I think diversification is only effective if different investments are thoughtfully pieced together into a strategic portfolio.

For each investment, we assess the primary risks to achieving our target return, and then we strive to assemble a diversified portfolio by equity size, product type, and geography, and also by business strategy risk. That means we don't have any one investment that can seriously tank the returns of the fund.

There are other funds that will be equally, if not more, successful in boom markets because they decided to load up on one product type. That's not what we do. Our philosophy is to protect the downside, and the upside will take care of itself. In my view, you achieve sustainable, attractive risk-adjusted returns if you are committed to understanding, measuring, and mitigating risks at both the investment and the portfolio level.

The Tenets of Tenants

MJ: Those are examples of deals that have gone well. Can you think of ones where maybe things didn't turn out exactly as you'd hoped?

DH: In 1999, 2000, and 2001, many in real estate discovered if you changed your name to so-and-so dot-com, you'd trade at a higher multiple. Many were investing in data centers and tech this and tech that. From our perspective, many tech tenants didn't have current cash flow, and we are all about cash flow. That's how you protect yourself. In fact, investing in the tech sector generally made us uncomfortable. Yet, if you believe in diversification, it is reasonable to include some tech exposure in a portfolio of that vintage.

I couldn't get comfortable with data centers because they were single purpose. The lack of current cash flow in start-up technology companies was equally worrisome. I did manage to get comfortable doing a deal that was called Midpoint Technology. It was a technology business park in Silicon Valley. Its major tenant was Excite@Home, a subsidiary of AT&T.

I still wasn't comfortable with the value the operating partner wanted us to come in at, so we structured the investment as mezzanine debt. For discussion sake, let's pretend the acquisition was $150 million, and we were comfortable at a $125 million valuation. There was first mortgage financing of $100 million, and that left a $50 million gap. We created a $25 million mezzanine piece to bridge that gap that was senior to $25 million of equity. Our mezzanine debt was structured with a high current-pay interest rate of 12 percent and 50 percent of the cash flow, but from a risk management perspective, I was happy to give up some of the upside to protect my downside. The business plan was to lease any vacancy in the office park, with the expectation that new tenancy would continue to benefit from the massive tech surge. We would get our portfolio tech exposure through this structured investment.

What we didn't anticipate was that AT&T, which had a controlling stake in Excite@Home, which occupied nearly 80 percent of our space, would allow Excite to file for bankruptcy. I learned a valuable lesson about tenant concentration. In addition, we took false comfort that the lease was signed by AT&T's US subsidiary and not the well-funded parent. As a result, we didn't have as much negotiating leverage as we thought. What saved us from a total write-off was the fact that we had structured the investment as mezzanine debt and therefore collected two-thirds of our basis through current interest. Had we been equity owners, it could have been a 100 percent write-off.

This transaction taught me the risk of single tenant credit exposure and how important it is to have multiple exit strategies. I never do deals where the outcome is binary. I look at every deal and say, "My downside risk needs to be that I can return my capital." If that's the downside, then we will continue our due diligence and spend time evaluating the probability of generating our target return.

MJ: Are there other ways to mitigate risk?

DH: Of course. On the multifamily investment we discussed that generated a 56 percent IRR, both Artemis and our operating partner did a tremendous amount of due diligence prior to acquisition. Our operating partner was local and was solely focused on multifamily. Collectively, the team walked through every unit in the portfolio. We also walked other competitive units and evaluated recent trades for comparable vintage properties. We evaluated the competitive size of the units. Will they compete effectively with nearby apartments? Were they located at intersections with desirable transportation and strong demographics? This is a small component of what we look at when evaluating a multifamily property.

MJ: I know the focus of your risk management is to limit single tenant risk, to structure deals well, and to diversify. I'm not

sure that any of that worked well for many investors in 2008. How do you guard against a total market meltdown? Is that something you worry about?

DH: The only way you could have guarded against what happened in 2008 in real estate was to have been minimally leveraged and to have basically stopped investing between 2005 and 2007. The reason why the commercial mortgage securities and everything else declined in 2008 was that it was not just a real estate recession. We experienced a global economic recession. Everybody got hurt. Unless you had stepped out of the business before 2008, you couldn't avoid being negatively affected.

I think you protect yourself by looking at risk and opportunity, and determining where across the spectrum of product type, geography, and/or capital structure you can generate the best risk-adjusted returns, and sometimes the answer is turning off the capital spigot. Those that survived 2008 shared two primary characteristics: modest-to-no leverage and significant liquidity.

We have tended to outperform in down market cycles because our leverage was lower than our competitors, typically 60 percent or 65 percent loan to cost when our competitors' leverage was 75 percent to 80 percent loan to value. When valuations declined by 30 percent to 50 percent, equity was wiped out. If you didn't have liquidity to re-cap and fight another day, you lost your property.

You have to appreciate that risk exists in whatever you buy. Each investment we make, we evaluated on its individual merits and its impact on the fund portfolio. We try to be very thoughtful in measuring, managing, and minimizing risk.

But ultimately, crisis creates opportunity, and I have enjoyed investing through five crisis opportunities: Savings and Loan/ RTC, the tech wreck, health-care reform, 9/11, and the great global recession of 2008. In my investment experience, each of these crises was a tremendous catalyst for opportunity.

The New Cycle

MJ: If you don't worry as much about correlation as you do about the individual opportunities, what does give you the heebie-jeebies?

DH: Today [2014] is a challenging time to invest as there is a tremendous amount of capital flowing into real estate. It feels at times to me like 2006, not in terms of new construction/supply, but in terms of pricing and valuation. It's a risk-on environment in real estate—meaning investors are willing to take on significant risk, often in the form of higher prices to purchase assets. Thus, the reason we have been so quick to sell our Artemis Fund I assets. But on the buy side, it keeps me up at night. We will continue to maintain our discipline. We have been very slow and deliberate to deploy capital, and we only invest when the transaction meets our standards.

Discipline and selectivity define our work today. We have looked at $24.5 billion of transactions in the last 12 months, and we've only done 1 percent of them. Am I going to, two years from now, feel that I was too conservative? That I missed an opportunity to deploy capital? That I should have had more confidence that the economic recovery was going to happen quickly? Every night I worry that I'm being too risk averse right now. But that is consistent with our focus on protecting the downside.

MJ: Is that really risk aversion, or is it sticking with your experience and discipline?

DH: I'm definitely thinking about what's worked for me over the last 25 years—thoughtful diversification. But I am averse to the kind of risk I see in the market right now because it is difficult to buy below replacement cost. It's very hard to be a value buyer at this point in the cycle. Realistically, instead of having 30 percent to 40 percent of our capital deployed in the first year as was the case in Artemis Fund I, I expect we'll have 20 percent of our capital deployed for the same time period in Fund II.

We will shoot at our target returns, and we may underperform in a bull market like this because we aren't momentum buyers. I worry that our investors might forget about the downside protection and look at funds with higher short-term returns.

MJ: Investor short-term memory loss.

DH: I'd like to believe that those investing with Artemis right now, for all the right reasons, appreciate our discipline and pursuit of long-term, risk-adjusted returns. This is a significant component of our investment proposition.

MJ: If that is short-term thinking, what does it take to be a successful long-term real estate investor?

DH: You have to have a healthy respect for risk. You have to be defensively opportunistic. Dispassionate. Don't ever fall in love with your real estate. You have to have deep industry relationships and the ability to assess and select the best operating partners that are going to perform in good times and bad, because they are critical to your success. I describe our investment approach as a constant creative tension: pushing in one direction—a passion for profit—while pulling in the other—due to my intense fear of loss.

Funds of Funds Investing

CHAPTER 12

The Sleuths: Fund of Funds Investing

Connie Teska and Kelly Chesney, Founders,
Pluscios Capital Management

R esearching hedge funds is an exercise in finding clues and
connecting dots. Because you are ultimately evaluating
people, not products, there are no spreadsheets with defini-
tive answers, and no price to earnings (P/E) ratios or valuations to
guide you. For that reason, many investors turn to professional fund
evaluators for assistance. These investment professionals, usually con-
sultants or hedge fund of funds managers, provide the experience and
analytical skills to solve the mystery of manager selection.

However, not all professional investors are created equal. Funds
of hedge funds hemorrhaged assets after 2008, due at least in part to
some funds of funds' failure to identify illiquid assets, protect against
losses, and avoid at least one professional shyster, Bernie Madoff.
Some investors found that the clues their professional fund pickers
had been hired to find had somehow been overlooked. Many of the
funds of funds that remained scrambled to fill newly discovered holes
in the due diligence process. At Pluscios Capital Management, however, it was business as usual.

Connie Teska and Kelly Chesney have been hedge fund gumshoes
since the mid-1990s. Equally willing to pour over trading screens
and partnership agreements as they are to stake out office bathrooms
and parking lots, their motto could be lifted straight from Sir Arthur
Conan Doyle: "You know my method. It is founded upon the obser-
vation of trifles."[1]

Perhaps it is Teska's background in investigative journalism or Chesney's conservative legal proclivities that have refined their sleuthing skills. Teska graduated from Medill School of Journalism at Northwestern University before going on to pursue an MBA at Kellogg and a career in finance. Chesney pursued a JD at ITT Chicago-Kent College of Law before earning her MBA, also at Kellogg. Each logged a number of years at First Chicago/Bank One/ J.P. Morgan before founding their own fund of funds firm in 2006, Pluscios Capital Management.

Their road has not always been smooth. Losses in 2008 (–17.3%) and 2011 (–4.9%) were manageable, but not escapable. From July 1997 to December 2013, however, they have generated a compound annual return of 8.8 percent, nearly double that of the Hedge Fund Research Funds of Funds index, which returned 4.7 percent over the same period. To put that into cumulative terms, the Pluscios team has gained 299.6 percent since inception, while the index has climbed only 114.1 percent.

You won't find a straightforward set of rules when you talk to Teska and Chesney about their portfolio management style. There is no Pluscios Due Diligence Checklist for sale. Instead, they rely on extensive research on managers, partnerships with portfolio managers, and their 17 years of fund of funds experience to ferret out market trends and poor investments. However, they will tell you some of the keys to their long-term success.

- Create a partnership with the managers in whom you invest. Make sure they will call you when there are problems, and that they understand how you invest as well.
- Don't chase returns. If you are chasing, you are, by definition, already behind.
- Use all of the information you can gather. The smallest clues can help you discover problems before they spiral.
- Don't be hot money. If a manager is still doing what you hired them to do, and is still hitting your return hurdles, stay with them.
- Look for managers who are dissimilar, including women and minorities. If you allocate to underlying funds that all look the same and think the same, you're not diversified. You've got ten slight variations on the same theme.

Raise Your Hand

MJ: Connie, I know that you were in journalism and then became interested in finance. That seems like a pretty non-linear path.

CT: I graduated from Medill School of Journalism at Northwestern University with a journalism degree and an education degree – a double major. I was able to teach journalism in high school for a year. Then I realized I wasn't making a whole lot of money. I decided to look into some PR [public relations] jobs. I worked for GTE Automatic Electric, which is no longer around, as the editor of their four-color scientific research journal for about two years. Then I decided to start going door to door trying to look for a new job and ended up at First Chicago, where they offered me a job in their media relations area. I took that job and started to get interested in finance after I had done a number of different stints in the bank. I was given the opportunity to transfer into the corporate investing area, which is where I really learned about different securities and investing. At that time, banks weren't really making a lot of money from lending. They were trying to put their proprietary capital to work.

I worked for a great guy who really became a mentor. He was interested in learning himself, as well as teaching people under him. We started to realize that, whatever we did internally, it made a lot of sense for us to invest some cash externally in order to start a dialogue with the smartest minds out there.

KC: I just want to point out here that First Chicago didn't have a job posting for this job. Connie literally walked in off the street. She thought, "This would be a good place to work." The folks from back then will tell you that part of it was chutzpah that got her in the door.

CT: I think my training in journalism really is what trained me to be able to connect the dots. We were just realizing that we needed to be investing externally. We had to find people who were going to be as good at their investing jobs as we were, if not better. We had to try to bridge that learning gap so that we could figure out what we were going to do to make money for the bank, and also protect the investments that we were making externally. That was in the mid-'90s, and that's really when we began to look at hedge funds.

MJ: Which were relatively unknown at the time. I think the first major magazine article about hedge funds came out in '94 or '95.

CT: Clearly, it was not yet institutional. But we were intrigued, and we started interviewing folks and realizing that what we had was a version of a hedge fund, but on a much smaller scale. Internally we were trying to make money from mispricings of securities. We started talking to managers and realized that, maybe if we outsourced, gave them a little bit of money, and started a dialogue, we would be able to increase our capacity and knowledge, and figure out how to continually make money so that we could increase the multiple of the bank's stock.

It was very, very successful. We decided it was time to think about creating a business out of what we were doing. That's when I put my hand up and said, "Well, I've done all the research. I've done all the work. If we're going to allocate capital to a business like this, where we allocate money to outside managers, I would like to run it."

MJ: And there's that chutzpah that Kelly mentioned again.

KC: I was just going to say it again. When she put up her hand and asked for it, she was the right hand of this EVP. He said, "Okay. That's great but who's going to do your job?" When we started the hedge fund portfolio, she was literally doing two jobs in order to get the opportunity to run this portfolio.

CT: The reason was, I loved it. You were talking with really, really smart people. You were learning something at every interview. They were explaining what their trade was. You were asking them questions about risk management. You were able to roll up your sleeves and dig into what they were doing. At that point, hedge funds were skill based. We would go from place to place and decide who was good and who wasn't. Then we started to develop our whole due diligence process.

All along, you were constantly learning. That's what I liked about the position. When you were talking to a convertible arb manager or a long short equity manager, every multi-hour interview was about learning something new. This was very successful on an individual basis, fund by fund, but it was more successful as a portfolio effect. If you overlaid this portfolio of hedge fund investments over whatever else we were doing, you took the volatility out, and it created a portfolio effect. It reduced the risk for the overall portfolio and created an opportunity for us to make money.

A Watershed Year

MJ: I started in hedge funds right at the beginning of 1998. I still remember when Long Term Capital blew up in August of that year, and thinking, "Oh, my God. What have I gotten myself into? This industry isn't going to be around for long." That was right around the time you took over this business at the bank. Did Long Term Capital Management have an impact on your thinking or your business?

CT: Long Term Capital had a huge effect on us. The whole industry changed after that. Prior to 1998, it was much more acceptable for managers to provide very little transparency into a fund's strategy or organization. At least once, we went to visit a well-known manager in his office, and we were ushered into an elevator up to a conference room. The manager came in and he said, "Okay. Here you are. How much money are you going to give me?" We said, "Well, what do you do?" "What do you mean what do I do?" he asked. "Look at all the trading. Didn't you see all the screens out there? We make money. How much money are you going to give us? I have a long-standing relationship with the bank, etc." It was about a ten-minute meeting. We walked out.

We walked downstairs, and my boss said to me, "What are we going to do now?" I said, "Well, I still don't know what he does." He said, "Yeah. That was kind of hard to get." I said, "We can't give him any money because he doesn't follow any of the things we set out to do, any of the parameters we're looking for." He looked at me and said, "Great. You get to write the memo to the other side of the bank explaining why we can't give him any money."

MJ: I imagine that wasn't a very fun memo to write.

CT: That memo led to another memo, which led to another, which basically forced us to continue to articulate what our purpose was with this investment portfolio. What parameters we were looking for. Many of those parameters we still use today as part of our due diligence process. We needed to understand the risk that each of the securities and investment areas represented. We had to lay that all out, particularly for the trading floor, so that they would understand that just because someone was a client, it didn't mean that we were necessarily going to invest in them.

MJ: Did you feel pressure to override your process?

KC: There was no pressure because traders aren't aggressive or anything

MJ: I can smell the sarcasm here all the way from Chicago on that. Just FYI.

KC: The fact of the matter was, we worked for an organization that was very conscious of conflict. My first job with the bank was to be the conflict attorney on corporate deals. While there might have been pressure, and Connie might have gotten stares in the cafeteria after that, they knew that after that memo got written, that was the way it was going to be. We were a bank. A bank is conservative.

MJ: Well, a bank is supposed to be conservative. Certainly, we saw in 2008 that there were some banks that maybe lost some of that conservatism.

CT: We were a top ten bank. We were extremely conservative. We had policies and procedures. We were buttoned up. Yes, there was pressure, but the pressure was more for us to make sure we knew why we were not going to invest. He only gave us ten minutes. We couldn't know what he did in ten minutes.

KC: We have never gone in with the concept of "We want to invest with the rock stars." We want to look for the managers with skills that earn the fee structure and that can take advantage of different opportunities.

On-the-Job Training

MJ: So you had no blowback from the bank?

CT: The default of Russia happened around the same time. They were almost simultaneous. We're talking about August of 1998 to October 11. That period is ingrained in my memory. I lost a lot of sleep.

We thought we were pretty good in emerging markets. We had a direct hedge fund in emerging markets. We certainly had been through the peso devaluation in 1994. We understood emerging markets, and had our own trading desk. We also went out and invested in emerging market managers. We had assessed the risks up and down, and felt we were pretty smart. It turns out that we never anticipated a country defaulting.

We assessed that this was a three-standard-deviation event. Therefore, it was not foreseeable. You plan for everything. It's what you don't plan for that comes up and bites you. Our risk management principles for the portfolio were born out of the Long Term Capital Management and emerging markets crises. What we realized is all risks aren't the same. We need to put more risk capital against higher, riskier assets, such as emerging markets. We created a risk policy that ultimately said we needed 50 percent more capital against our investments in emerging markets. That meant they had to be 50 percent better to even allow us to put in any capital.

So emerging markets became opportunistic for us, even though we had a direct trading desk, as opposed to an equal bucket like long short equity or relative value arbitrage trading strategies.

Today, with Pluscios, we still keep that approach. When we look at it, we say we have our core investments, which includes our absolute value (which is our long short equity), our relative value (which are our arbitrage strategies), and our catalyst (which is our event driven). Then we opportunistically invest in emerging markets and global macro because their volatility can be significant. Their effect on the portfolio is significant. We need to make sure when we're creating a core diversified product and putting all those strategies together that we actually have anticipated something like a Russian default and its impact on the overall diversified portfolio.

MJ: It sounds like that was an incredibly transformative period for you and had a lasting impact on your strategy.

CT: Not only on our strategy but also on how we looked at risk and the importance of risk management. When everybody said after 2008, "Look at everything we learned and what we're doing and how we're changing," we didn't feel the need to change because we had already done it in 1998.

The other thing that was interesting was that was also around the time the Art Institute [of Chicago] had a hedge fund blowup.

MJ: I remember that. Integral Capital Management.

CT: Our EVPs were on the board at the Art Institute. We were called in that morning when it was in the *Wall Street Journal*, and it was major headline. Immediately, I got called and asked, "Is that in our portfolio?" The answer was no. Then the question was, "Why not?" That's when I was called to the Board of Directors. They were like, "Jesus! If this can happen to the Art Institute, it can happen to us." It turns out that unless you really understand the underlying securities, the risk you're taking with them, the headline risk is oftentimes what kills this business.

Because management was on the board of these not-for-profit organizations, we saw what others were doing and how they were doing it. We had to show that our process was so much more in-depth, so much better, so much more buttoned up. When we started Pluscios, we got to say that the training we had and the experiences that we had really are what have led us to be able to build a Class A organization.

KC: One of the things we learned in 1998 was the margin call/ liquidity risk. In 2007 and 2008, we started talking to our underlying managers about, "What's your setup with your prime brokers? What do you have? Where do you have it?"

We were still using a lot of our A-team core managers that we had at the bank. Many of them, most of them, had gone through 1998. They had already started deleveraging and diversifying prime brokers, and moving cash to custodian banks. That was one of the reasons that we could outperform in 2008, because our managers were able to see that coming. There is a benefit to being old.

Birth of a Fund of Funds

MJ: Experienced, not old. Speaking of longevity, Kelly, you and Connie have been a team for quite some time.

KC: I met Connie when I moved over to the bank from private practice and was hired by the lawyer that was the head of the corporate investments and capital markets group. I had, on one side, capital markets, which was derivatives, foreign exchange, and repos as clients. Then, on the other side, I was one of only a couple of lawyers that had the corporate investments group.

I was going through the legal documents and looking at legal risks and the different risks involved and what we needed. We had special requirements for investment terms, side letters, and things like that. That's where Connie and I actually started working together.

Then, First Chicago became part of Bank One, and they really scaled back the capital market business. Bank One was much more of a retail bank and had bad experiences in the past in derivative trades. A big part of my job was going to go away. I was really concerned about what I was going to do. Connie said, "Well, stay and why don't you pursue an Executive MBA?" She and my boss agreed that they would sponsor me within the bank for the Executive MBA program. So I went to Kellogg and got my MBA. To me that was pretty eye opening.

My view to that point was purely legal. What were our risks? How do I protect us? You go to business school, and it's, like, "Wow. There is this whole amazing world out there." A world I found interesting and I enjoyed very much. That was the point where I said, "Just being a lawyer is great, but there are other things I want to do." That's when I moved over away from being a lawyer, just a lawyer if you will. That's also when I left the bank. They had hired Jamie Dimon. He was making changes. I wasn't sure what jobs would be available. I did strategy consulting for several years. Then I went back to the bank as the COO of the fund of funds business that Connie ran.

MJ: So you both are at the bank. You're running a successful fund of funds business. It sounds like you have a fair amount

of autonomy and structure. What led you to decide to launch your own fund of funds?

KC: We did have a ton of autonomy. We were even in a different building. Quite frankly, once the J.P. Morgan merger was completed, it took some time before they decided that they wanted to combine our group with the New York group. They offered Connie and me positions. They wanted us to move to New York and take jobs there. It just wasn't the right time for us in our lives for that. That was the point where we had to make a decision. Do we want to be bankers for the rest of our lives? Do we want to do whatever the bank wants us to do, where they want us to do it? Or do we want to be funds of funds managers? Do we want to try to pursue what we actually love? That is why we both left the bank in 2006.

MJ: Did you want to be entrepreneurs?

CT: If we could have stayed doing what we were doing, in a large organization, I'm not sure we would have started Pluscios. But the bank always has the right to put you in any job they want. They'd say to me, "You're a great manager. You can go do this, this, this, or this." What we realized was, we wanted to have a career in hedge fund investing, not a career in banking.

KC: The best opportunity to do that was to be entrepreneurs. Connie is clearly more entrepreneurial than I am. I didn't go to law school because I'm a risk taker by nature. It was really our best opportunity to continue doing what we were doing.

MJ: You say you're not an entrepreneur. Didn't you mention that you did strategy consulting for a few years?

KC: Everything that I did, and I do joke that I have a very checkered past, got me to the point where I could add value in an entrepreneurial organization. It hasn't been a straight line, but it has prepared me for what we do today.

As we mentor folks I tell them is that it's about gaining skills. Skills that you can use in other pursuits. It may not be your ideal job, but if it's building skills that might lead you to your ideal job, then it's an awesome place to spend some time.

MJ: **When funds of funds first became popular, it seemed like a lot of them were what I'll call "access funds." What they were offering was access to large, closed funds. It seems to me that one of the hallmarks of your approach is that you take a top-down filter and stress asset allocation over access.**

CT: I think the difference is, we didn't start out as asset gatherers. We were investors of bank capital. For a long time we had three rules. Don't lose money, don't lose money, don't lose money. The other rule was that if you wanted to make money, if you wanted a good bonus, you had to make money for the bank. Really, our framework was built with that in mind, preserving capital but also generating strong performance. We have the luxury that our first investor, the bank, was a very sophisticated investor. They knew what we knew in terms of asset classes.

KC: So the original corporate investments group, one of the things that they did was to move capital opportunistically. If they had a high yield bond portfolio and it wasn't a good time in high yield bonds, they would move the money to another group, another desk that had many more opportunities. That's how we grew up. That's how we understood that you really should be investing. It was never "set it and forget it."

That was really our focus from the start, looking at what the opportunities were top down, then going back and building the portfolio one manager at a time to ensure that we captured those opportunities.

MJ: **So how did your asset allocation change during various points in time?**

CT: We'll start with 2006–2007 time frame. There was a large allocation to absolute value, which were your bottom-up stock pickers. Equity markets were rising, and we wanted to take advantage of that. We were searching out managers that provided alpha. Then we started to see that there was an opportunity that there would be a risk change. That, of course, started in August 2007. We dramatically moved the portfolio out of absolute value into relative value. When we hit 2008, we had really swapped the two major strategies in that portfolio. Now, we had much more emphasis on relative value. That's the type of thing you see us do.

In catalyst, it's cyclical. There's always something that's working. When you come out of distressed debt, you get into mergers and acquisition. There's credit opportunities. There's capital structure arb. It's a constant flow as you go through different economic cycles.

The other thing that we did in 2008 was realize that we wanted to increase our exposure to global macro. One of the reasons for that is we thought it would be a hedge against increased volatility and what was happening in the markets. We actually took our global macro to its full allocation in the core diversified product through 2008. It had positive performance, if I recall correctly, of about 15 percent. That was an overall hedge to the rest of the portfolio, which ended up losing money, but was slightly better than the benchmark.

Ultimately, at the end of 2008, we determined that that trade was over, and we took global macro way down, to 1 percent or 2 percent of the portfolio. In hindsight, that was the right decision because global macro has not been great since then.

KC: I think another example of the way we invest was in the 2002–2003 time frame. We brought up our allocation to our catalyst managers in 2002. We took a little bit of a hit. We were a little bit early. But in 2003, we did really well. One of the things that we believe is that you can't be the last one to that kind of party. We wanted to be positioned. We're willing to be a little contrarian and take a little bit of timing risk. Then we get positioned with the best managers out there. We have our choice. We get to participate in the cycles from the beginning.

MJ: Are there any strategies that you won't invest in?

CT: We don't invest in what we don't understand. We won't invest in cosmetic receivables. Or art. Or wine.

KC: The eccentric things.

MJ: I guess the trailer park hedge fund would have been out of the equation for you then. But what about things like asset-backed lending [ABL] or structured credit?

KC: Understand that the structured credit, ABL, all of those things – I came from a bank where I was a bankruptcy attorney. I did a lot of structured credit in terms of the law side. Those are things that we understand very well. There are a lot of things out there now where folks have created very complex structures with multiple levels and layers of SPVs, special purpose vehicles, for these niche and esoteric investments that have generated significant returns. But if I look at it, and I can't follow the cash flows, or understand where there's any leakage or payments out, then it's not a strategy that we need to be in.

MJ: So the movie financing that some hedge funds have gotten into? Those types of things that are off the beaten path would not be your style?

KC: I think what happened in 2005 and 2006, even in 2007, was there were a lot of folks out there that were searching for returns. They went into things that perhaps didn't meet the same liquidity profile of the other asset classes. We are responsible for managing liquidity at the portfolio level. Something might generate a great return, but if we are locked up longer, that's a risk.

MJ: So you're trying to take calculated risks? If you can generate the returns and still stay in something straightforward, with good liquidity, you would prefer that route?

CT: Exactly.

Active Capital

MJ: You mentioned liquidity. How do you deal with fund level liquidity in the context of being more active on the asset allocation side?

KC: Clearly, we don't day trade. It's just not possible. When we are growing, we're able to adjust allocations by putting new money to work. And we do have quite a seasoned portfolio at this point. We're out of the lockup on many of our investments.

Mostly when we invest with a manager, we look for someone to partner with us. There are a couple of things that we expect. We expect them to call us and let us know things before we read about them on the front page of the *Wall Street Journal*.

The other thing is for them to understand that we **are** active managers. Really, if an underlying fund is a good businessperson, they're not going to want to sit on cash if they don't have opportunities for it. Those are the kinds of business people we look for. We've had managers give money back when they don't have opportunities. We also have managers that we tell, we're going to bring the allocation down and redeploy it to where we think it will generate more value for our fund at this point in time. But we tell them if they see opportunities coming down the road, give us a call and we will then reallocate it back to you.

MJ: That's the second time you've mentioned the longevity of some of your investments. How long do you tend to stay with managers?

KC: Some we've been in for 15 years, since the beginning of our fund, and some of our investments were made just last month. Some of the managers have been in business since the early '90s or the mid-'90s. Some have been in business since the beginning of 2013.

It's really quite a range. For us, that's really part of the asset allocation. We believe you can get different things from different types of managers. You'll find a core, but you'll also find a quite robust satellite piece of our portfolio as well.

CT: We try to be long-term investors. As long as they can continue to deliver the risk-adjusted return that we signed up for, we will stay with them.

MJ: There have been studies about mean reversion of returns that question the concept of long-term hedge fund investing. It sounds like y'all would disagree with the premise that all managers' returns revert to the mean?

CT: As long as their opportunity is not going away and they are still meeting their hurdle, we will stay with them.

KC: The managers that we have and that we've had for a long time, I think we can classify for the most part as niche managers. They do what they love, and they're happy doing what they love. They don't want to necessarily rule the entire universe or have the biggest fund in the world.

Have there been managers that we started out with that did great and then got too big and there was mean reversion? Sure. But they're not in the portfolio anymore. If their focus is aligned with ours, which is delivering returns, then they're not going to grow to $100 billion.

MJ: Those really large managers might be difficult to be partners with as well, because when someone gets that big, you can become more of an account number and not necessarily an investor.

KC: When we were at the bank, we were probably a much more significant investor in managers that were new at the time. But that's how we developed the relationships we have. I guess Connie and I never got the memo that we're not big, important investors anymore. We still really expect and demand that kind of partnership and treatment. After 2008, a lot of really good managers got burned by funds of funds because they pulled all their money. They didn't really want to take in funds of funds any more.

After doing reference checks on Pluscios, and on Connie in particular, they learned that we are long-term investors, as long as we're treated like a partner.

MJ: So you like more niche managers in general. What's your size range and sweet AUM sweet spot?

KC: Our sweet spot is generally between $200 million and a $1 billion. We have managers that are much smaller than $200 million and bigger than $1 billion at this point, however.

MJ: You also mentioned the concept of the core and satellite portfolios. How many funds are in each? How do you think about the two working together?

CT: I think there's a couple of ways to define that. For us, the core portfolio are those funds that we have the longer-term relationship with. Those that have grown to be a significant portion of our portfolio.

MJ: And how much would that be?

CT: We look at those to be in the 4 percent to 6 percent range. In a few cases, maybe it's slightly higher. Then there are the

2 percent to 3 percent allocations, and the 1 percent to 2 percent positions. We dip our toe into funds with the idea of graduating to bigger allocations. I think our top ten positions are 50 percent of the portfolio.

MJ: Relatively concentrated, but not hugely concentrated.

KC: I think we're nicely diversified without getting to the point of dilution. Generally, we will have between 24 and 30 managers. We may go up and down from that a little bit, depending on where the markets are and what the opportunities are. From our perspective, that's a great number to get the diversification we're looking for without having managers that are duplicative.

Betting on Integrity

MJ: So you have chosen 24 to 30 fund managers. Do you think choosing people is harder than choosing stocks or other investments?

KC: We do all of the quantitative analysis. In fact, everything we do has both a quantitative and qualitative aspect. But I would say the qualitative side is a big differentiator for us. We believe that we have a lot of experience and are really good at doing the qualitative work. It's a more difficult aspect to judge because you can't just quantify it. You can't just put it in a spreadsheet, run some analysis, and find out if this is a good person.

That's why Connie and I both meet with and have met with every manager that's in our portfolio. Those are things that I think you judge in person. I don't care how many background or reference checks you run on people. If Connie and I are going to invest in someone, we want to sit down and look eye-to-eye with them. We want to understand how they invest. How they react to markets. What gets them excited about the market. What gets them fearful about the markets. But we also need to know what kind of person they are. After 2008, after Bernie Madoff, the whole world came out and talked about integrity. They said that you have to do due diligence, and your due diligence has to include integrity. Well, I can show you presentations on that going back to the bank. In the 1990s and 2000s, integrity was on the list of things that we evaluated and judged.

MJ: I think sometimes it is incredibly difficult to judge people's integrity, which is why a con man like Bernie Madoff is able to bilk people out of billions of dollars. How do you make that judgment? Are there any clues that you are looking for in particular? Is it inconsistencies? Is it attitude?

KC: I think it's everything. Bernie Madoff was a great example. Very few people actually met with him directly, and even fewer yet went into the office and really saw where everything was done. Those are things that we ask for. You look for the inconsistencies. We see the manager at different times, then we compare notes and if we get different stories.... I usually go for the operational due diligence. Connie goes in for the investment side. If what they say doesn't match up, why not? Those are all things where it's all about connecting the dots.

CT: And it's about listening. What did we hear and what is important? If we go to the ladies room and we see an employee, how did they seem? You start a conversation with them. There are just all sorts of ways to judge integrity, but it's also a gut feel for the atmosphere and what's happening in the office when you're there.

KC: I think it's also important to take the qualitative information that we have and opinions that we have, and then compare it to the quantitative information. Do they match up? He says he doesn't take risks, but the numbers show a completely different picture. It's really about putting all of those pieces together.

CT: It's about knowing the underlying strategy. When you're looking at it and you compare it to its peers and they are doing X, and this manager, he's doing Y. When you question him as to how he can do Y, sometimes it doesn't quite make sense. Is it just leverage? Is it something else? Is it a long guy who's going short? Is it a short seller who has been long the couple of years? You have to be able to thin slice and connect those dots.

KC: Due diligence is getting an intimate understanding of the manager. Even after the due diligence package is done and we've invested, something like September 2008 comes around and you want to have a deep enough understanding of that manager and each of those managers to understand what they will do. Which ones are moving to the sidelines and going to cash? Which ones are moving to be trading around? What do we think the risks are in the portfolio?

MJ: What about operational risk evaluation? That has really taken on more importance over the last five years or so. I would assume since Kelly has been operationally focused from the get-go, it's always been an area of focus for you?

KC: It gets back to the bank, right? What were the parameters and what framework did we set up for investing in hedge funds at the bank. And we've maintained those parameters through today. Part of it was, we understood operationally what we needed. We built it into the internal hedge funds. We knew what the infrastructure should be. So, yes, that has always been a big focus for us. And it's come a long way from the early days when Connie would go in and visit a long/short manager at his home office or whatever strange place he or she might be, and say, "Okay, what do you do for custody/security?" And he would say, "Well, that's a fireproof desk you're sitting at and the stock certificates are right in the drawer."

Those were the days when we started investing in hedge funds. It was actually harder to find more institutional quality funds. Now all of that has become table stakes, and it's interesting that once it became table stakes, that's when everybody says you've got to start looking at it.

MJ: Are there any red flags that stand out for you in your operational reviews?

KC: I think everything can potentially be a red flag. My favorite example is, I went to look up an accounting firm I hadn't heard of, and they had no website, but they did have a Facebook page that had pictures and talked about all the parties they had. There are a lot of managers out there. We don't need to do that.

If they don't have quality service providers. If they haven't taken the time to think about the operations, the trade flow, and control and disaster recovery, and all of those things. Or if they gloss over it. If I ask about limits on who can execute trades or who can move money, and then you find out that those limits or permissions haven't been enforced, for us that's the red flag of a weak operational side. If they won't let you sit down at a screen and show you the entire book while you're in the office, and they won't explain to you what they are doing.

MJ: Trust but verify? Nothing like Ronald Reagan to inform the due diligence process. What about red flags within strategy evaluation?

KC: Eighty percent of our client base is institutional, and we consider ourselves an institutional investor and a fiduciary. I think concentration is one of those things that we have a hard time getting past. There are a lot of hedge funds out there, and there may be smaller ones that tend to attract high net worth clients and do really well over time. But then you go and look under the covers, and you find out they run three stock positions and a basket short as a hedge. To us that's not really adding value or providing diversification. The blow-up risk there is huge.

Style drift is interesting because it's something that we have always looked for, and it is something that has caused us to redeem from managers. And yet we look for managers who are nimble and can take their base set of skills and find new opportunities to which to apply those skills. Style drift is the topic of the day in hedge funds.

And it is something to look out for. We do look for that. We've had high-yield managers that wanted to do capital structure arbitrage or things like that. Usually what happens is that they anticipate that their investors will say, "You've never had experience doing that." So they run out and they hire someone to do that part of the strategy. Well, we don't know who that person is and, more importantly, we don't know how well they will work together.

MJ: It seems like style drift is a bit of a dichotomy in the hedge fund industry. On the one hand, you want someone that's nimble, and on the other, you want to know what your manager is doing.

KC: From our perspective that's why you never hire or invest in just one hedge fund. That's what you need a portfolio. We really believe that at any one time, not every manager in the portfolio is likely to be making money. There are certain years, like 2009, where they might, but you generally expect that some managers aren't going to do as well at all times. The whole point of having a diversified portfolio is to capture a variety of opportunities.

MJ: How do you resist the urge to go with the herd on those investments?

KC: We're not really looking at what our peers are doing. We're spending our day trying to build the best portfolio that we can. Our goal is to find those managers with the skill set and talents and a trading style and strategy that we believe is sustainable and valuable for the long term, rather than be the last one to the party after a fund has shown up in a *Barron's* article.

Portfolio Diversity

MJ: We've talked a little about your investments with niche managers. What about other types of emerging managers? I know you have had investments with women and minority managers in the past.

KC: Clearly we are diverse ourselves. We actually co-underwrote a study with the National Council for Research on Women roughly five years ago that showed that women invest differently than men. They view risk differently. They take risk differently.

That's not just a diverse manager, that's diversification of the portfolio and it builds a stronger and better portfolio. We believe that if you have all the same type of folks, if it's the Stepford-hedge-fund managers, even if they are doing different things, they are going to end up doing them the same way. And so you're not really getting diversity, you're getting ten different flavors of vanilla.

That's true in terms of minorities as well. We think that folks who view things differently and process things differently are a benefit to the portfolio. Also, we want folks to give us a chance to sit at the table and make a pitch for business, and so we want to give diverse managers that same opportunity. There's no guarantee that we're going to hire them, right? We don't expect to get hired just because we're women. We expect to get hired because we're the best person or the best investor. But maybe we got in the room because we're women, and maybe that's why we got included in the search.

MJ: What percentage of your underlying funds tend to be diversity managers?

CT: It varies over time, because if they are investing in a strategy that we don't believe is opportunistic at this point, we may reduce their allocation. And, of course, if they are struggling and can't run their business, we may have to withdraw. But I would say we generally have diversity allocations in the 15 percent to 30 percent range.

MJ: So we've talked a lot about the problem funds you've avoided. What about the ones you haven't missed?

KC: I think where we've been the least successful is when we find a fund that we think is great, but the rest of the investor world doesn't view the fund in the same way. Then there's a sustainability issue with the fund in terms of them being able to raise other capital and maintain capital.

MJ: I think the perception, particularly in the hedge fund industry, is that there's this huge risk of fraud or blowup. Have you have any blowups or significant problems in the portfolio since it started?

KC: Here's my analogy: in travel, people generally consider flying to be more risky and to have a greater chance of death. And yet more people are killed in car accidents every year. It's just that you see those one at a time, here and there. It is very much the same in the hedge fund industry. If there are 10,000 hedge funds, and they had 40 or 50, let's say even 500 blowups, is that really any different in other investing areas? We've had hedge funds that have had some bad drawdowns from managers, but we haven't had any blowups.

MJ: What did you do during those drawdowns?

KC: We pride ourselves on the fact that we don't panic. We had a manager from a particular time period in 2008 that lost around 50 percent.

CT: But we didn't get out of it.

MJ: So would you say that you are very adept at maintaining your conviction?

CT: We'll go out and sit down with that manager and ask, "All right, what's going on? What's in your book? What are you seeing? Where do you think the opportunities are? What is causing this issue now?" And we can make a decision from there.

We are much more patient investors. I'm not going to tell you that we don't have drawdowns. But when we look at managers that are struggling, we also look at their percentage of the portfolio and whether there is there asymmetric risk. If they are underwater by 25 percent, that is 25 percent that we won't pay incentive fees on, right? There is a value to a high water mark. If they continue to go down, we try to figure out how much can they hurt the portfolio and what else we think is going on.

Pulling the Trigger

MJ: So that kind of problem happened in 2008, obviously. Walk me through what you did with the portfolio. Did you make adjustments or redeem from or fire managers (aside from your macro play)? I know the fund performed extremely well in 2009...

KC: I guess 2008 actually started in 2007. The issues in mortgages became obvious. And so what do we do? We got out, and we went and we visited our managers.

A huge problem in 2008 was managers had assets, especially in the mortgage-backed space, that they couldn't get dealer quotes on. Because if the dealers quoted them the price they really wanted to pay managers, and then that dealer's book would have to get marked down to those prices.

So it became a question of valuation and how they were handling valuation. How were they handling margin calls, liquidity, and things like that? It was really understanding what was going on with the portfolio and talking to people in the marketplace. By October 2008, we were actually beginning to get comfortable that our managers had found their sea legs, that they had a strategy going forward, and that they were very excited. A lot of them had sold and liquidated positions to provide the dry powder to go into 2009 and pursue those opportunities.

We didn't fire a single manager in 2008. Part of it was going into the funds' offices and seeing whether the analysts are on their computers doing the resumes. Were they crying in the bathroom because they're so depressed? We did that to get comfortable saying, "We don't have to fire anybody at this point in time."

That was probably one of the toughest things we did: holding pat. We saw our peers just redeeming like crazy, and everybody was heading for the exits. You're standing there and it's like, "Oh, is this the right decision?" We knew in our gut it was.

And that's really why we performed so well in 2009. We had our convictions, we understood the risks that we were taking in the portfolio, and we knew that there was so much embedded in these portfolios that once that market cleared and things start to turn, we would realize a lot of those opportunities.

MJ: You know that's actually the third time you mentioned doing due diligence in the bathroom.

KC: If you go into a hedge fund, a lot of times the only person you see is the investor relations person. If you go in and you're an institutional investor, maybe you see the investor relations [IR] person and the portfolio manager. And we actually judge people, right? We need to get as many data points as possible.

Some of the early traders were very successful, but on the other hand some were so difficult to work with that they couldn't keep any staff around them. For us that wasn't a sustainable business. So we learned early on that you talk to the other folks in the office. You try to get a feel for what those people say and how they feel. Does their body language jive with the IR person, who is getting paid to say wonderful things?

We go to parking lots and check out cars, too. It's not just bathrooms where you can find interesting information.

CT: You can find out how many Ferraris are down there.

MJ: I assume you're not kidding.

CT: I think that there are anecdotal clues all around us. It's just opening your eyes to those things and putting them together.

MJ: So if market turmoil doesn't make you redeem, what does trigger you to pull money from a fund?

CT: If they stop making the money that we anticipated or expected them to be able to make. If they just have lost their edge.

KC: When we've gone in and we've talked to them, and they have hard limits and stop losses and things like that. And they hit them and blow through them. They don't do what the policy said they were going to do in those situations.

CT: Or when somebody says, "You know I'm not making money in my strategy right now, so I'm suddenly going to go short the market. I've hired this short seller guy because I just don't think that I can continue to make enough money for these assets." To which we say, "We didn't hire for you for that, thank you very much."

MJ: I assume if you see somebody crying in the bathroom, that triggers redemptions as well?

KC: Well, it will definitely make us look twice. And don't forget, not calling Connie when you're going to be on the front page of the *Wall Street Journal*. That gets you up on the top of that list, too.

PART III

Investing As and Like a "Girl"

CHAPTER 13

Lessons from the "Broad Market"

Gender and investing is a sensitive subject. I have a lot of conversations with industry participants about why diversity is good for the financial industry and why diverse managers, particularly women, exhibit strong outperformance. These conversations invariably start off positively ("tell me more"), but often end up someplace altogether different.

One of the most common ways these conversations fall off a cliff is when I hear something like the following:

> "Don't you think that the reason women generate better returns is because it's been so hard for them to get to be money managers and that, as a result, only the best and the brightest have made it? When there as many mediocre women in the industry as there are men, performance will normalize."

I have actually heard this last sentence verbatim, so indulge me for a moment while I set the record straight.

It has historically been difficult for women to climb up the ranks of finance and investing to open their own hedge, private equity, venture capital, and long-only funds. And, yes, there is a relatively small sample of those professional money managers to study, which may explain why this research was necessary in the first place. Perhaps the day will come when a mediocre woman will have the same opportunities in investing as an average man. I will hula-hoop on the front steps of the New York Stock Exchange if and when it does.

The fact is, however, professional investors are not the only pool of women on whom behavioral investment research has been done. Many of the largest and most statistically relevant studies that demonstrate gender outperformance have been done on large pools of retail investors.

The Barber and Odean study referenced in Chapter 1 was based on data from 35,000 household accounts at a discount broker. And while I'm sure some of the women represented therein may have been "the best and the brightest," it seems unimaginable that only the top-performing women were represented in this study, while the male sample included both the cream of the crop and the cream of the crap. The same goes for Vanguard's research on 2.7 million IRA accounts and other large-scale studies.

The truth is, diversity investment research challenges the way things have "always been done." Discussions like this are disruptive, and while we've clearly gotten used to disruptive innovation when talking about ride shares and Airbnbs, it isn't as comfortable when we're talking about the cognitive and behavioral characteristics of human capital.

As a result, I don't think we should create a new category of gender-specific statistical bias: the best and brightest bias. The cognitive and behavioral alpha created by women is real, and it merits discussion, investigation, emulation, and investment. The returns alone deserve attention. When you consider the additional diversification benefits of investing with diverse managers, the inclusion of women becomes critical.

Homogeneous groups tend to think alike. They also tend to overestimate their problem-solving skills and consider a narrower range of information. They may also be less open to new ideas. And there are fewer areas in business more homogenized than in investment management.

So I'd like to suggest that we expand our definition of diversification. Maybe it's not all about the asset allocation mix of stocks, bonds, futures, real estate, and other asset classes. Perhaps it's not even the number of funds you invest in or the mix of strategies you have. Maybe, just maybe, diversification includes the way in which the money managers collect, interpret, and evaluate market data, and the cognitive alpha they create for you.

And, for the record, I am not advocating that investors choose only women money managers. Investing solely with any singular group is the very antithesis of diversification. I am suggesting that you look for a variety of sources of cognitive and behavioral alpha within your portfolio of managers or attempt to cultivate some of those skills within yourself.

How do you begin to look for and create your own cognitive alpha? Try following the following "broad guidelines" for investing:

1. **Get away from the crowd**—Many of the women in this book avoid the herd when investing. From Leah Zell, who looked to international small caps because "there were no skis behind her," to Fran Tuite who chooses uniform and fertilizer companies over the lure of technology and new economy stocks, many of the managers profiled in *Women of The Street* have chosen an investment road less traveled. Think of Thyra Zerhusen, who insists that if you do what other investors do, you can't make money. Or of Marjorie Hogan, who is purposely keeping her fund size smaller so she can access and exploit niche deals that fall off of larger funds' radar. In a 2005 study by Barber and Odean, the researchers showed that "individual investors are net buyers of attention-grabbing stocks, e.g. stocks in the news, stocks experiencing high abnormal trading volumes, and stocks with extreme one day returns."[1] Avoiding this herd can be part of maximizing returns and minimizing volatility.

2. **Be willing to be the first**—Theresia Gouw talked about how critical it is in venture capital to be one of the first, if not only, calls from a founder, as well as how important it is to invest in the early successes in a sector. Olga Chernova discussed being early in credit arbitrage plays and how that enhances her returns as later convergence in a trade narrows spreads and maximizes returns. Debbie Harmon invests in the first shoots of optimism, while uncertainty remains strong. Connie Teska and Kelly Chesney discussed finding talent for the fund of funds portfolio early to get access to niche talent, as well as being active in asset allocation to get in front of trends.

3. **Be a long-term investor**—One thing that is particularly interesting about the interviews in *Women of The Street* is the longevity of these managers' underlying investments. From Connie Teska and Kelly Chesney, who have maintained hedge fund investments for up to 15 years, to Fariba Ghodsian, Tuite, and Zerhusen, who have had investments in their funds for 10 years or more, the women in these chapters are not "churn and burn" investors by any stretch of the imagination. By limiting unnecessary trades, by refusing to chase gains or fads, and by minimizing tax consequences, female investors boost their returns to investors.

4. **Maintain high conviction**—The women interviewed for this book tend to run what is known in investing as "high-conviction" portfolios. This means that a portfolio may be diversified into a number of positions, but will not choose so many investments that the portfolio returns become diluted by picking second-, third-, and fourth-tier ideas. There has been a growing body of research that shows high-conviction portfolios outperform diversified funds, and Warren Buffett even once quipped, "Wide diversification is only required when investors do not understand what they are doing."[2] In fact, a 2015 study from portfolio platform SigFig looked at 750,000 accounts at AOL, DailyFinance, CNNMoney, USA Today and Forbes found that women generated a median net annual return of 4.7 percent in 2014, versus 4.1 percent for men.[3] Further, the male-managed portfolios were more likely to have negative returns, 25.8 percent, than the female-run portfolios, at 20.4 percent.[4]

5. **Remain confident**—When a stock or other investment is going against you, it can be difficult to maintain your positions. None of the women in this book have been net sellers into a drawdown or market crash if the fundamentals of an investment remain strong. As we saw in the Vanguard financial crisis research in Chapter 1, this can spell higher long-term returns for investors. Obviously, capturing the full upside run for either a market cycle or position is optimal. Riding a position down, selling, and then missing gains is a poor recipe for the rebound.

6. **Continuously evaluate your investment thesis**—Of course, blindly following your convictions or "falling in love" with your investments can be just as bad as selling too soon. One of the ways in which managers like Olga Chernova and others protect against unrequited investment love is to constantly re-evaluate their investment theses. A frequent refrain in these pages has been "would I buy the same stock (bond, CDS, company) again now?" If the answer to that question is, yes, then selling may not make sense. Even within the private markets, investors like Theresia Gouw try to separate market noise from investment or business failure so they can determine whether to ride out a bad market or cut their losses.

7. **Regularly take a step back**—Whether it is through the use of stop losses (like the 2% stop-loss used by Olga Chernova) or

through periodic investment breaks like those used by Marjorie Hogan, clearing your head can improve your market judgment. A pause in trading activity helps reset your emotions and makes you test your investment thesis.

8. **Be disciplined**—One of the recurring themes in *Women of The Street* is rule-based investing. Concentration limits are widespread among the public market participants, along with market capitalization restrictions and hard or soft stop losses. Sonya Brown looks for strictly at companies with 20 percent growth and 20 percent earnings before interest, taxes, depreciation, and amortization (EBITDA). Anything less isn't considered for investment. Discipline can assist with both the long-term successful execution of a strategy and with controlling regret when investing.

9. **Stick to your knitting while maintaining an open mind**— There is little doubt that having expertise in a particular investment arena or style can help you maximize your return. Whether it's the connections and know-how you need to help founders or management teams with growth or capital raising plans, or whether it's knowing your sector and its participants cold like biotech investor Fariba Ghodsian, knowledge about investments is a powerful thing. Perhaps it allows you to see market emerging cycles like Olga Chernova or Marjorie Hogan, so you can be proactively positioned. Perhaps it helps you develop a "gut feeling" about a company that later turns out to be a fraud. Maybe it's "seeing the movie again" like Deborah Harmon, or insisting that portfolio companies "make something" like Raquel Palmer. Regardless of how your experience manifests, doing what you do best is a smart way to manage money. With that being said, however, it is also important to look for new opportunities and new markets. The managers highlighted in this book are adept at finding related or similar investments in which they can leverage their existing expertise. This combination of innovation and "meat and potatoes" has proven to be a powerful generator of profits.

10. **Invest in people, not just fundamentals**—As much as we want to reduce investing to quantitative factors, the interviews in this book showcase how critical the people factor can be. Theresia Gouw and Sonya Brown are charged with evaluating

the skills of founders and management teams for their private market investments. Thyra Zerhusen, Fran Tuite, Leah Zell, and Fariba Ghodisan all meet with management teams before buying a company's stock. Marjorie Hogan relies on human error and miscalculations in legal documents for a portion of her profits. Connie Teska and Kelly Chesney must judge the integrity and trading skill in others, and Deborah Harmon looks for strong operating partners. In all cases, knowing the people behind the investment is crucial to returns.

Girls Just Want to Have Funds

If investors take the advice in *Women of The Street* and begin to seek out female money managers, they will find that there is still a critical shortage of women in investing. There are probably fewer than 125 female hedge fund managers today, and a smaller number of female private equity, venture capital, and long-only fund managers. Even in wealth management, which has historically been more female friendly, women comprise only 30 percent of wealth advisors and 23 percent of all certified financial planners.[5]

I hope this book has shown that women can successfully manage money, but I also hope it provides the next generation of female money managers with virtual mentors. And, the manager who looked to Hetty Green as a mentor, which I mentioned at the beginning of this book, none of these role models died before refrigerators became common. In that vein, it seems clear that women who want to manage money professionally should consider the following:

1. **Find a mentor**—Most of the women profiled for *Women of The Street* noted the influence of a strong mentor or mentors. Whether it was learning about concentration, liquidity, strategy execution, or even just providing the initial spark of investment interest, mentors mattered. And, remember, mentoring can be formal or informal and mentors can be female or male. Women like Deborah Harmon are developing formal mentoring programs and encouraging others to do the same, but many of the women profiled have informal mentor relationships that have lasted decades.

2. **Juggling is possible**—All but two of the women interviewed for this book have children. Almost half of the interviewees had three or more kids. Motherhood and money management can work. The secret to "having it all" seems to be having both

a supportive workplace and spouse. Control over your schedule and time was also a recurring theme, something that self-
employed fund managers have in spades. Simply put, if everyone
wants it to work, it can work.

3. **There's more than one path to success**—One of the more interesting things to note is that the *Women of The Street* aren't
cookie-cutter images of one another. Degrees in nonfinancial
fields are fairly common. You don't have to go to a certain school
or earn a particular undergraduate degree to succeed in investments. Engineering, media, journalism, math, and other fields
can also get you where you want to go.

4. **Gender matters, but less than you think**—Most of the women
I interviewed knew they didn't look like their (mostly male)
colleagues. The majority said they either didn't notice or didn't
care. Refusing to be intimidated or to "play the game" meant
these women could focus on what mattered: mastering their
markets and maximizing returns. At the end of the day, they
believe their performance speaks for itself.

5. **Network!**—Networking can help with finding new companies
(Sonya Brown, Theresia Gouw, Raquel Palmer). Networking
can help with finding seed investors or partners (Olga Chernova,
Marjorie Hogan, Fran Tuite). Networking helps uncover
new investments (Thyra Zerhusen, Connie Teska and Kelly
Chesney). There is no aspect of investment strategy and business that cannot be enhanced by networking. Undergraduate,
graduate, professional, community, founder, and investor networks can all contribute to investment success.

The financial industry needs more women investors (or investors
who think like women) for a number of reasons. Returns are key.
Both individual and institutional investors need strong performance
and cognitive and behavioral alpha to meet future financial obligations. Diversification is also crucial, both to individual investors and
the markets. Without diversity of thought and investment approach,
investors end up with an Eskimo portfolio—one that has 50 different
names or managers, all of which translate into a single word ("snow").
A lack of cognitive diversity in the overall market enhances systemic
financial risks as the herd stampedes toward bubbles and busts.

Luckily, investors need not choose between cognitive diversification
and behavioral profits. You get both when you invest "like a girl."

Notes

Introduction: "The Women"

1. Karl Moore. "Neuroscience Explains Why Wall Street Needs More Women." *Forbes* December 21, 2012. Blog post retrieved from http://www.forbes.com/sites/karlmoore/2012/12/21/neuroscience-explains-why-wall-street-needs-more-women/.
2. "Want to Be the Richest Person in America? Follow Hettie Green's Example." *Forbes* August 22, 2013. Advisor Intelligence blog post. Retrieved from http://www.forbes.com/sites/advisor/2013/08/22/want-to-be-the-richest-person-in-america-follow-hetty-greens-example/.
3. Acton Institute for the Study of Religion and Liberty, Volume 17, Number 1. "Lord Ralph Harris of Highcross." Retrieved from http://www.acton.org/pub/religion-liberty/volume-17-number-1/lord-ralph-harris-highcross.

1   The Feminine Investing Mystique

1. National Center for Education Statistics "Fast Facts/Teacher Trends." Retrieved from http://nces.ed.gov/fastfacts/display.asp?id=28.
2. National Center for Education Statistics "Fast Facts/Teacher Trends." Retrieved from http://nces.ed.gov/fastfacts/display.asp?id=55.
3. Hemington Wealth Management 2011, "Women of Wealth: Why Does the Financial Services Industry Still Not Hear Them?" Family Wealth Advisors Council. Retrieved from http://hemingtonwm.com/wp-content/uploads/2013/11/FWAC_WomenOfWealth.pdf.
4. Judith E. Nichols. "Understanding the Increasing Affluence of Women." Supporting Advancement.com. Retrieved from http://www.supportingadvancement.com/vendors/canadian_fundraiser/articles/womens_affluence.htm.
5. Hemington Wealth Management 2011. "Women of Wealth: Why Does the Financial Services Industry Still Not Hear Them?" Family Wealth

Advisors Council. Retrieved from http://hemingtonwm.com/wp-content /uploads/2013/11/FWAC_WomenOfWealth.pdf.

6. Andrew Barber. "Wealth Management Firms Continue to Lag Recruiting Women Advisors." Institutional Investor. March 10, 2014. Retrieved from http://www.institutionalinvestor.com/Article/3317767 /Wealth-Management-Firms-Continue-to-Lag-in-Recruiting.html# .VCS1bUsyH1q.

7. Neesha Hathi. Investment News. June 4, 2014. "Three Steps to Greater Gender Diversity in the RIA Industry." Retrieved from http://www .investmentnews.com/article/20140604/BLOG09/140609982/three -steps-to-greater-gender-diversity-in-the-ria-industry.

8. Investment Company Institute September 27, 2002. "Half of American Households Own Equities, Equity Ownership Increases amid Bear Market, Study Finds." Retrieved from http://www.ici.org/pressroom/news /ci.02_NEWS_EQUITY_OWNERSHIP.print.

9. Investment Company Institute. *2013 Investment Company Fact Book*. 53rd edition. Retrieved from http://www.ici.org/pdf/2013_factbook.pdf.

10. Ibid.

11. Kevin Olsen. Pensions & Investments. November 21, 2013. "Loop Capital: State, Local Pension Plan Funding Drops in 2012." Retrieved from http://www.pionline.com/article/20131121/ONLINE/131129951 /loop-capital-state-local-pension-plan-funding-drops-in-2012.

12. Rebecca A. Sielman. Milliman. November 2013. "Milliman 2013 Public Pension Funding Study." Retrieved from http://www.milliman.com /uploadedFiles/Solutions/Products/public-pension-funding-study-2013 .pdf.

13. Wells Fargo October 23, 2013. "Middle Class Americans Face a Retirement Shutdown; 37% Say 'I'll Never Retire, but Work Until I'm Too Sick or Die,' a Wells Fargo Study Finds." Retrieved from https:// www.wellsfargo.com/about/press/2013/20131023_middleclasssurvey/

14. University of California Berkeley, Haas School of Business. "Boys Will Be Boys: Gender, Overconfidence and Common Stock Investment" Brad M. Barber and Terrance Odean. Retrieved from http://faculty.haas .berkeley.edu/odean/papers/gender/BoysWillBeBoys.pdf.

15. Vanguard. "Are Women Better Investors Than Men?" Retrieved from https://retirementplansp.vanguard.com/VGApp/pe/pubnews/Women BetterInvestors.jsf.

16. Ibid.

17. New York Society of Securities Analysts (NYSSA) April 10, 2010. "Outsiders and Outperformers: Women in Fund Management." Retrieved from http://post.nyssa.org/nyssa-news/2010/04/outsiders-and -outperformers-women-in-fund-management.html.

18. Ibid.
19. Rania Ahmed Azmi. "Mutual Funds Performance: Does Gender Matter in an Emerging Market." 2008. Retrieved from https://editorialexpress.com/cgi-bin/conference/download.cgi?db_name=IAFFE2008&paper_id=30.
20. No adjustments were made for survivor bias (funds that later went out of business and/or quit reporting performance) due to the difficulty in ascertaining when a fund is no longer reporting to a commercial data source and when it is no longer in business, as well as the difficulty in obtaining performance during a fund's wind-down period.
21. Rothstein Kass (now KPMG) January 2013. "Women in Alternative Investments Study: A Marathon, Not a Sprint." Retrived from www.KPMG.com.
22. Ibid.
23. Ibid.
24. Dipali Pathak. Baylor College of Medicine. "Physician Confidence Not Always Aligned with Accuracy in Diagnosis." August 26, 2013. Retrieved from https://www.bcm.edu/news/school-of-medicine/confidence-not-aligned-with-diagnosis.
25. Ibid.
26. Tadeusz Tyszka and Piotr Zielonka. "Expert Judgments: Financial Analysts vs. Weather Forecasters." Retrieved from http://studiapody plomowe.pl/uploads/import/kozminski/pl/default_opisy_2/206/14/1/working_paper_no_2.pdf.
27. *Journal of Economic Psychology* Volume 41, April 2014, Pages 31–44. "On Confident Men and Rational Women: It's All in Your Mindset" Sabine Hugelschafer and Anja Achziger. Retrieved from http://www.sciencedirect.com/science/article/pii/S0167487013000445.
28. "Financial Experience and Behaviors among Women" 2012–2013. Retrieved from https://www.cgsnet.org/ckfinder/userfiles/files/Pru_Women_Study.pdf
29. University of California Berkeley, Haas School of Business. "Boys Will Be Boys: Gender, Overconfidence and Common Stock Investment" Brad M. Barber and Terrance Odean. Retrieved from http://faculty.haas.berkeley.edu/odean/papers/gender/BoysWillBeBoys.pdf.
30. Wired.com July 13, 2012. "Testosterone Is to Blame for the Financial Crisis, Says Neuroscientist" Olivia Solon. Retrieved from http://www.wired.co.uk/news/archive/2012-07/13/testosterone-financial-crisis
31. National Academy of Sciences of the USA July 1, 2009. "Gender Differences in Risk Aversion and Career Choices Are Affected by Testosterone" Paola Sapienza, Luigi Zingales & Dario Maestripieri. Retrieved from http://www.pnas.org/content/106/36/15268.full.

32. *Journal of Psychology and Financial Markets* Volume 2, Issue 1, 2001. "The Influence of Gender on the Perception and Response to Investment Risk: The Case of Professional Investors" Robert A. Olsen & Constance M. Cox. Retrieved from http://www.tandfonline.com/doi/abs/10.1207 /S15327760JPFM0201_3#preview.

33. WIF Institute of Economic Research May 2004. "Gender, Financial Risks and Probability Weights" Helga Fehr-Duda, Manuele de Gennaro & Renate Schubert. Retrieved from http://www.cer.ethz.ch/research/wp _04_31.pdf.

34. http://www.investmentnews.com/article/20150218/FREE/150219928 /could-more-women-traders-cut-volatility.

35. Ibid.

36. University of California Berkeley, Haas School of Business. "Boys Will Be Boys: Gender, Overconfidence and Common Stock Investment" Brad M. Barber and Terrance Odean. Retrieved from http://faculty.haas .berkeley.edu/odean/papers/gender/BoysWillBeBoys.pdf.

37. *New York Times* October 19, 2011. "Don't Blink! The Hazards of Overconfidence" Daniel Kahneman. Retrieved from http://www.nytimes .com/2011/10/23/magazine/dont-blink-the-hazards-of-confidence.html? pagewanted=all&_r=0.

38. John Coates. *The Hour between Dog and Wolf: Risk Taking, Gut Feelings and the Biology of Boom and Bust.* June 14, 2012. Penguin Press.

39. eFinancialCareers.com. "New Figures Show Women Make Better Traders Than Men on Every Metric Imaginable" January 26, 2015. Retrieved from http://news.efinancialcareers.com/uk-en/197066/exclusive-figures -show-women-make-far-better-traders-men/

40. National Academy of Sciences of the USA February 18, 2014. "Cortisol Shifts Financial Risk Preferences" Narayanan Kandasamy, Ben Hardy, Lionel Page, Markus Schaffner, Johann Graggaber, Andrew S. Powlson, Paul C. Fletcher, Mark Gurnell & John Coates. Retrieved from http:// www.ncbi.nlm.nih.gov/pmc/articles/PMC3948282/.

41. Ibid.

42. National Academy of Sciences of the USA February 2012. "Both Risk and Reward Are Processed Differently in Decisions Made under Stress" Mara Mather and Nichole R. Lighthall. Retrieved from http://www .ncbi.nlm.nih.gov/pmc/articles/PMC3312579/

43. Ibid.

44. "Sex Differences in the Responses of the Human Amygdala" 2005. Stephan Hamann, Department of Psychology, Emory University. Retrieved from http://languagelog.ldc.upenn.edu/myl/ldc/llog /Brizendine/Hamann2005.pdf.

45. National Academy of Sciences of the USA July 1, 2009. "Gender Differences in Risk Aversion and Career Choices Are Affected by

Testosterone" Paola Sapienza, Luigi Zingales & Dario Maestripieri. Retrieved from http://www.pnas.org/content/106/36/15268.full.

46. *Science Magazine* April 7, 2006, "A 'His' or 'Hers' Brain Structure?" Retrieved from http://news.sciencemag.org/2006/04/his-or-hers-brain-structure.

47. Ibid.

48. *New York Magazine* March 30, 2010. "Women Were Better at Trading Stocks During the Financial Crisis than Men" Zeke Turner. Retrieved from http://nymag.com/daily/intelligencer/2010/03/women_were_better_at_trading_s.html

49. Brain and Behavior Research Foundation December 12, 2013. "Chicken or Egg? New Research Shows Men and Women's Brains Are Wired Differently." Retrieved from http://bbrfoundation.org/brain-matters-discoveries/chicken-or-egg-new-research-shows-men-and-women's-brains-are-wired.

50. Ibid.

51. Ibid.

52. CNBC October 10, 2007 "Details Emerge in SAC Sex Harassment Case" Charles Gasparino. Retrieved from http://www.cnbc.com/id/21224443.

53. Federal Reserve Bank of Minneapolis October 3, 2013. "Interview with Richard Thaler" Douglas Clement. Retrieved from https://www.minneapolisfed.org/publications_papers/pub_display.cfm?id=5184.

54. *Forbes* June 5, 2014. "15 Hedge Fund Titans All Hold This Stock" Joel Kornblau. Retrieved from http://www.forbes.com/sites/joelkornblau/2014/06/05/fifteen-hedge-fund-titans-all-hold-this-stock/.

55. *Forbes* August 14, 2014. "Hedge Funds Feasting on Apple Again" Nathan Vardi. Retrieved from http://www.forbes.com/sites/nathanvardi/2014/08/14/hedge-funds-feasting-on-apple-again/.

56. Vanguard December 2009. "Equity Abandonment in 2008–2009: Lower among Balanced Fund Investors" John Ameriks, Jill Marshall and Liqian Ren. Retrived from https://pressroom.vanguard.com/content/nonindexed/Equity_abandonment_in_2008_to_2009.

2   Aim Small, Miss Small: Targeting International Small-Cap Stocks

1. Morgan Brennan. *Forbes* September 18, 2013. "The Investment Zen of Sam Zell: Inside the Grave Dancer's $4 Billion Business Empire." Retrieved from http://www.forbes.com/sites/morganbrennan/2013/09/18/the-zen-of-sam-zell-inside-the-grave-dancers-4-billion-business-empire/.

2. John H. Christy. *Forbes* October 30, 2000. "Queen of Small Caps." Retrieved from http://www.forbes.com/global/2000/1030/0322110a.html.

3. Hedge Fund Research. HFRX Global Hedge Fund Index. www.hfr.com

4. Loosely translated, "Central European."

3 Quite Contrary: Going Long in Mid-Cap Stocks

1. Massachusetts Institute of Technology. "The Tragedy of Coriolanus" Act 2, Scene 3. William Shakespeare. Retrieved from http://shakespeare.mit.edu/coriolanus/coriolanus.2.3.html.

4 Getting Extra from Ordinary: Investing Long and Short in Micro- and Small Caps

1. Goodreads.com. Bill Moyers quote. http://www.goodreads.com/quotes/176299-creativity-is-piercing-the-mundane-to-find-the-marvelous.

5 She Blinded Me with Science: Investing in Biotech

1. Odyssey's Virtual Museum. H.T. Helmbold's Genuine Fluid Extract Bottle. Retrieved from http://odysseysvirtualmuseum.com/products/H.T.-Helmbold's-Genuine-Fluid-Extracts-Bottle.html.
2. Odyssey Marine Exploration. "Medical Cures for the 19th-Century Sufferer." Retrieved from http://www.shipwreck.net/oid/quackmeds.php.
3. "Industry Overview: Pharmaceuticals and Biotech." Wetfeet.com December 3, 2012. Retrieved from http://www.wetfeet.com/articles/industry-overview-pharmaceuticals-and-biotech.

6 Puzzling It Out: Distressed Credit Investing

1. Montgomery Investment Technology Tools, Inc. Excerpts from the Berkshire Hathaway Annual Report for 2002. Retrieved from http://www.fintools.com/docs/Warren%20Buffet%20on%20Derivatives.pdf.

8 In the Beginning: Seed and Series A Venture Capital Investing

1. Napoleon Hill. *Think and Grow Rich*. Cleveland: The Ralston Society, 1937.

9 The Pragmatist: Growth Equity Investing

1. Dictionary.com. Definition of Pragmatic. http://dictionary.reference.com/browse/pragmatic.
2. Rimin Dutt. "Airborne Isn't Immune to the Charms of PE." *Wall Street Journal*. Private Equity Beat October 12, 2009. http://blogs.wsj.com/privateequity/2009/10/12/airborne-isnt-immune-to-the-charms-of-pe/.

10 Mrs. Fix-It: Distressed and Turnaround Private Equity Investing

1. Dennis Jacobe. "U.S. Homeownership Hits Decade Low." Gallup April 26, 2012. Retrieved from http://www.gallup.com/poll/154124/u.s.-homeownership-hits-decade-low.aspx.
2. St. James & Canter Luxury Real Estate. "Famous Real Estate Quotes: A Collection of Famous Quotations from Some of the Leaders in Investing, Business and Finance." Retrieved from http://www.stjamescanter.com/famous-real-estate-quotes-a-collection-of-famous-quotations-from-some-of-the-leaders-in-investing-business-and-finance/.
3. James Corl and Siguler Guff. "A Historic Opportunity in Distressed Real Estate." Bank of New York Mellon November 2013. https://www.bnymellon.com/us/en/our-thinking/foresight/a-historic-opportunity-in-distressed-real-estate.jsp.

12 The Sleuths: Fund of Funds Investing

1. Goodreads.com. Sir Arthur Conan Doyle, "The Boscombe Valley Mystery." http://www.goodreads.com/quotes/tag/sherlock-holmes?page=2.

13 Lessons from the "Broad Market"

1. Brad M. Barber and Terrance Odean. "All That Glitters: The Effect of Attention and News on the Buying Behavior of Individual and Institutional Investors." California Technical Institute (CalTech) January 2005. Retrieved from http://www.hss.caltech.edu/~camerer/NYU/10-BarberOdean.pdf.
2. Brian Routledge and Anthony Forcione. "When Less Is More: The Value of Concentration." State Street Global Advisors. Retrieved from https://www.ssga.com/library/povw/696328_When_Less_is_More_The_Value_of_Concentration_1_CCRI1394100556.pdf.
3. CBSNews.com "Who Makes Better Investors: Men or Women?" Erik Sherman February 12, 2015. Retrieved from http://www.cbsnews.com/news/whos-the-better-investor-men-or-women/.
4. Ibid.
5. Neesha Hathi. "Three Steps to Greater Gender Diversity in the RIA Industry." Investment News June 4, 2014. Retrieved from http://www.investmentnews.com/article/20140604/BLOG09/140609982/three-steps-to-greater-gender-diversity-in-the-ria-industry.

Past performance is not necessarily indicative of future results.

About the Author

Meredith A. Jones is an internationally recognized researcher, writer, speaker, and expert in the alternative investment industry. Over the past 16 years, she has presented her original research and insights to industry participants around the world. She is a frequent speaker on the international conference circuit and has had her findings published in books and major media outlets, including *The Economist*, *The New York Times*, CNBC, *The Wall Street Journal*, *Financial Times*, *The Journal of Investing*, and others.

She began her alternative investment career at Van Hedge Fund Advisors International where she was Director of Research. She continued her research at PerTrac Financial Solutions and Barclays Capital, Inc., producing groundbreaking reports on emerging managers and diversity investing, before becoming Director of the Rothstein Kass Institute, an alternative investment think tank. As founder of MJ Alternative Investment Research, Meredith continues to provide timely research, education, and actionable insights to the alternative investment community.

Index